**Return Date**

ON
WE
LO

# HERITAGE SITES: STRATEGIES FOR MARKETING AND DEVELOPMENT

# Heritage Sites: Strategies for Marketing and Development

Edited by
*DAVID T HERBERT, RICHARD C PRENTICE*
*and COLIN J THOMAS*
*Department of Geography*
*University College of Swansea*

# Avebury

Aldershot · Brookfield USA · Hong Kong · Singapore · Sydney

Published by

Avebury

Gower Publishing Company Limited,
Gower House, Croft Road, Aldershot,
Hants, GU11 3HR, England

Gower Publishing Company,
Old Post Road, Brookfield, Vermont 05036
USA

Printed and Bound in Great Britain by
Athenaeum Press Ltd., Newcastle upon Tyne.

ISBN  0 566 07099 5

# Contents

# List of tables

# List of figures

# Editors' foreword

As more leisure time becomes available to a wider range of people, there is ample evidence for a growing demand for recreational facilities which may enable that leisure time to be fully used. The advent of more and more leisure centres and more specialised centres for sporting activities is one side of this coin and is also indicative of the greater priority which health and fitness is assuming in many people's lives. On the other hand, much leisure time is spent at home and the significance of the media, especially television, has grown enormously in the past few decades. For a nation of urban dwellers the significance of days-out or trips to the countryside has assumed importance and it is largely in this context that heritage sites, as places which people are able to visit in their leisure time, have roles to play. From being the fragments of relict evidence of life in former times attracting the attention of the dedicated few, many of our historic monuments have assumed major significance as foci for tourists and leisure-seekers. Both in the public sector in whose care many monuments are placed and in the private sector, where individual owners have seen the 'visitor' as a means of generating income to maintain old properties - and also of making sizeable fortunes - there have been positive responses. There is now a 'heritage industry', very diverse in its content and practices, for which guidelines and rules for good practice are still being formed and in which the issues of promotion versus preservation remain.

This book addresses the key features of the emergence of heritage sites as visitor attractions. It is based upon a major research project in Wales but also draws heavily upon a much wider range of experience available in the extant literature. As a book it has several roles. It is a guidebook for practitioners, the managers of the heritage industry, with practical suggestions on how to manage heritage sites; it contains in-depth research on the characteristics of visitors and sites and the interaction between them and as such serves the interests of academics, planners and policy-makers in the broader fields of tourism, recreation and field-study; it also has a more general interest for the many people in a wider public who have more than a passing interest in heritage sites. The heritage industry is already with us, it is essential that there is sufficient responsible and careful research to allow us to understand the phenomenon and its many implications; the central aim of this book is to contribute to that understanding.

David Herbert
Richard Prentice
Colin Thomas

University College of Swansea,
February, 1989.

# List of contributors

The Seren Team


**Arwel Edwards** lectures in geography at University College of Swansea and is Director of the Social Science Research Institute at the College. He has teaching and research interests in economic geography, regional economic planning and developments and the U.S.A. Dr. Edwards has recently completed research contracts in marinas and small businesses.


**David Herbert** is Head of the Department of Geography, University College of Swansea, and is Vice Principal of the College. Professor Herbert's interests include urban studies, social problems in cities and aspects of leisure and recreational study. Professor Herbert recently concluded a project on work and leisure in South Wales. He is currently a member of the Sports Council for Wales and acted as Chairman of the working party which produced a National Strategy for Sports in Wales titled 'Changing Times, Changing Needs'. Recently appointed to the Pembrokeshire Coast National Park Committee, he is now closely involved in countryside planning and related issues.

Merle Prentice was research assistant on the Cadw projects and is currently working on projects for the Manx Museum and National Trust and the Isle of Man Department of Agriculture, Fisheries and Forestry. Her particular interests include social, developmental and educational psychology.

Richard Prentice lectures in geography at University College of Swansea, and is Chairman of the Board of Planning Studies. His particular interests and publications are in leisure and tourism policies, social planning and quantitative methods. As well as research for Cadw, Dr Prentice has undertaken research on the Isle of Man into leisure and heritage tourism developments, in particular for the Isle of Man Department of Agriculture, Fisheries and Forestry and for the Manx Museum and National Trust.

Colin Thomas lectures in geography at University College of Swansea. His main interests are in urban geography, census and health statistics and quantitative methods. His principal research interest is retail geography and the associated field of consumer behaviour, on which topics he has published widely in both academic journals and consultative reports.

Graham Humphrys, who lectures in Geography at University College of Swansea, was a member of the Seren team, but not a contributor to this book.

Cadw: Welsh Historic Monuments

John Carr is Director of Cadw and took up this post in January 1985. The bulk of his career was previously in newspapers, both as a journalist and as a manager. From 1961 to 1965 he worked on the Western Mail and from 1967 to 1980 for Times Newspapers Ltd. From 1981 to 1984 he was Business Development Director of the Neath Development Partnership. He is a graduate of Cambridge University where he read English, Archaeology and Anthropology.

# Acknowledgements

In particular, we would like to acknowledge the help of Cadw, who financed much of the research from which this book has been prepared, and the Jane Hodge Foundation, who assisted us with a grant towards the cost of word processing this book. We would like also to thank the officers and librarians of the following organisations who helped us with the preparation of this book by providing examples, documents and statistics:

An Foras Forbartha, Dublin
Bord Failte, Dublin
Cadw, Cardiff
Countryside Commission, Cheltenham and Newtown
Countryside Commission for Scotland, Perth
Department of Agriculture, Fisheries and Forestry, St. Johns, Isle of Man
Economic and Social Research Institute, Dublin
English Heritage, London
English Tourist Board, London
Irish Museums Trust, Dublin
Manx Museum and National Trust, Douglas, Isle of Man
Mid-Wales Development, Newtown
National Trust for Scotland, Edinburgh
Oifig na n Oibreacha Poibli, Dublin
Scottish Development Department Historic Buildings and Monuments Directorate, Edinburgh

Scottish Tourist Board, Edinburgh
Shannon Free Airport Development, County Clare
Shannonside Tourism, Limerick
Wales Tourist Board, Cardiff

We wish to thank the following for permission to reproduce
copyright material: The National Trust for Scotland
(Appendix to Chapter 5); English Heritage (Figure 8.1);
Professor P. E. Murphy of the University of Victoria (Figure
8.2); and The National Museum of Wales Welsh Folk Museum
(Figure 8.3).

We wish also, to thank Mrs Merle Prentice for her research
assistance on the several Seren projects and Mr. Guy Lewis
of the Department of Geography, University College of
Swansea, for drawing the diagrams for this book.

DTH
RCP
CJT

# 1  Leisure trends and the heritage market

DAVID T HERBERT

## Introduction

Heritage has the distinction of being widely discussed but rarely defined. Noting the absence of definition in any of the Acts of Parliament dealing with heritage, the first annual report of the National Heritage Memorial Fund concluded that:

> We could no more define the national heritage than we could define, say, beauty or art ... The national heritage of this country is remarkably broad and rich. It is simultaneously a representation of the development of aesthetic expression and a testimony to the role played by the nation in world history. The national heritage also includes the natural riches of Britain.
> (Jones, 1985, p. 206-7).

The book in which this quotation appears (Hewison, 1987) is a critique of the British "heritage industry"; a critique which grew in the author's words 'out of hearing it regularly asserted that every week or so somewhere in Britain, a new museum opens'. This to Hewison seems appalling. A symptom of a nation immersed in nostalgia and living in its past; concerned with manufacturing heritage rather than with manufacturing goods. Whatever one thinks of such a critique, and our view is that it is grossly overstated, there is without doubt a large and growing 'heritage industry'. This industry covers a very wide range of activities - the question of definition and the content

1

of this range is one to which we shall return - and is permeated by a number of common strands not the least of which is the conflict between the need to conserve what is truly our inheritance and the need to provide access and understanding of these same phenomena to all the people who wish to experience them. This book is concerned with this issue. Its bias is towards widening access to heritage, towards issues of marketing, policies for interpretation and towards the place of heritage sites in the context of a progressively more mobile and recreation-seeking society. At the same time it will seek to reflect the central values of conservation and preservation which are of key significance in the heritage industry. The very large majority of the "custodians" of heritage, whether they be the private owners of country houses, the government agencies responsible for historic sites and monuments, or the national organisations which hold and manage properties and tracts of land, all seek to show due and proper respect to history and the natural state of the heritage in their care. That respect is evidenced in the ways in which sites are managed, properties are maintained and interpretative activities are promoted.

This book, although cast as a general review of the development and marketing of heritage sites, has arisen from a particular experience of studying historic sites in Wales. Cadw is the Welsh verb 'to keep' and is the name given to the government agency, Welsh Historic Monuments, charged with the maintenance of many castles, monasteries, and similar historic sites in Wales. Data gathered in a series of surveys of visitor patterns, attitudes towards pricing and interpretation, and other issues will be used in the chapters which follow.

This research experience in Wales forms the main set of case studies in this book but there is of course a wider literature, available in published texts and journals, in which other examples and case studies are documented and this will also form part of our discussions. Whatever the merits of the 'heritage industry' it clearly has a significant presence in the second half of the twentieth century. Heritage has its own special meanings but the 'heritage industry' is in many ways a subset of the 'leisure industry'. Heritage sites are being developed in various ways because it is evident that they can contribute to the demand for places of recreation, places at which people can spend some of the time which for them is designated as leisure. It is therefore with the concept of leisure and with changing patterns of leisure activity that we must begin. People have more leisure time, personal mobility is higher, there is a latent demand for places of interest to visit; it is against this background that the marketing of heritage can be reviewed.


The idea of leisure

The concept of leisure is in many ways of relatively modern origin. It is true that leisure time must always have been part of people's lives but it need not have been categorised as such, there is no obvious division of time labelled as 'leisure'. As Patmore (1983) points out, for long periods of history the separation of work and leisure was less a separation of an individual's uses of time than of the separation of 'working' and 'leisured' classes. For the great mass of working classes leisure was embedded in life rather than a separate part of it. Especially during the twentieth century there have been significant changes in the organisation of society which have the effect of throwing the idea of leisure into sharper focus. Organized labour has campaigned hard to free people from the 'tyranny of work', notions of more leisure time, more leisure activities, flow from that campaign. Defining leisure is not easy. Stockdale (1985) talked of evaluating the conceptual structure of leisure on the one hand and individual's perceptions of leisure on the other. In empirical research it has often been convenient to acknowledge the conceptual haze which surrounds the notion of leisure but to adopt some pragmatic working definition such as time left over when work and chores are completed or time over which the individual exercises choice and undertakes activities in a free voluntary way. Patmore (1983) adopted a convention that leisure relates to time and to non-work time in particular; recreation on the other hand referred to specific activities pursued in leisure time. Stockdale (1985) also has a triad of perspectives on the meaning of leisure. In the first of these she regards leisure as a period of time, an activity or state of mind in which choice is the dominant feature; leisure time is time free for chosen activities. In the second, leisure is regarded as the antithesis of work and commitments and is residual; in the third, people define leisure in terms of its meaning for themselves and it can occur at any time and in any setting.

A basic problem with defining leisure is that neither time-based nor activity-based definitions can be more than approximations. A period of time or an activity perceived as leisure by one individual may not be so viewed by another. To some gardening or childcare is a pleasure, to others it is a chore. These are issues which blur attempts to record and measure ways in which people use what we may loosely term 'leisure time'. Before looking at broad trends in the use of leisure time and attempts to 'record and measure', some other theoretical positions can be briefly noted.

Several recent writers have been concerned to theorise leisure and to give it some proper place in the methodology of the social sciences. Both Parker (1976) and Roberts (1978) have offered substantial texts which offer significant insights. Parker has been particularly interested in the work - leisure relationship (see also: Herbert, 1987, 1988), whilst Roberts has argued that age, sex and marital or household status help us to understand how people use their leisure-time. Certainly in the evidence which will be presented from surveys in Wales, socio-demographic variables of this kind and also social

3

class are of considerable significance. More recently, both Parker and Roberts have been criticised on the grounds of eclecticism and loosely theorised work:

> It is remarkable now how little these two primary sociologists of leisure in Britain engaged in any attempt to construct a systematic theoretical orientation for the sociology of leisure.
> (Horne, Jay and Tomlinson, 1987, p. 2).

One view of leisure in the 1970s (Dumazedier, 1974) was of 'ideal type', leisure had an autonomous character, research was concerned with distinct issues such as concern for the impact on environment and the provision of facilities. Another view (Smith, 1987) sees leisure as central to all processes of 'social bonding'. It provides relaxation which gives recovery from fatigue, entertainment which provides deliverance from boredom and personal development which serves to liberate the individual from the daily automation of thought and action. Featherstone (1987) argues that leisure pursuits can be mapped onto social space in a more general form; leisure is one indicator of class, gender and generation which is reflected by a particular life style. Dunning (1983) expressed this as ways in which general life-style tastes are structured by relation to particular class fractions and groups. Again, Patmore (1983) used leisure life-styles. Individuals do not so much engage in ad hoc miscellanies of activities as develop broad systems of leisure behaviour consisting of a number of inter-dependent elements. Leisure is closely interwoven with other aspects of life style and in aggregate these become typical of groups and individuals.

From this position it is possible to typify various groups in society by leisure life-styles as it is possible to classify them by place in the housing market or in the spectrum of political opinion. Evidence from successive General Household Surveys is that age, gender, social class, income, car ownership and education are the main determinants of participation in different forms of leisure. Smith (1987) picked out gender and stage-in-life-cycle as key indicators, Kelly (1981) argued that family life cycle, especially the stage of becoming a parent, was the major variable to analyse. Bourdieu's (1978) class-based interpretation of leisure saw leisure tastes as part of the whole range of human activities affected by possession of material and cultural capital. For the working class, sport after youth means watching popular sports, for middle classes the preference is for sports which can be pursued well into retirement. Leisure in the ageing process is mediated by differences along class dimensions. These current forms of thinking on leisure provide some context, more is contained in the changing work-leisure relationship and the quantities of time which become available for leisure.

# Leisure trends

The annual government publication Social Trends now provides
a regular and accurate source of information on trends in
leisure along with a range of other social indicators. The
most persistent message is that time spent at work is
decreasing, time available for leisure is increasing, and
there are significant related changes in family life and the
role of women. This is amplified in the detailed diary
studies of Gershuny and Jones (1987) which show a gradual
reduction in the working week, a rise in unemployment and
'involuntary' leisure time, more early retirement and
significant changes in women's access to leisure time.
Taking leisure time as residual time once work and personal
care is removed, all the groups in the diary survey showed
gains in leisure time between 1961 and 1984. For men in
full-time employment the gain was 36 minutes per week, for
women in part-time employment it was 47 minutes, for women
in full-time work it was 50 minutes and for non-employed
women it was 70 minutes. With a tighter definition of
leisure which excludes time spent with children, gains in
leisure time still ranged between 30 and 60 minutes per
week. Social Trends 1988 showed that retired men with 95
'free hours' per week are the group with most leisure time
and women in full-time employment with 38 hours have the
least. Interestingly, Social Trends shows that full-time
housewives had 54 hours of leisure time per week, only
marginally more than men in full-time employment. A survey
reported in 1985 Social Trends showed the distribution of
leisure time throughout the day for various categories of
people and although, as might be expected, leisure
activities were generally concentrated in weekday evenings
and week-ends, there were some interesting variations. A
general increase in paid holidays was another significant
increase in the source of leisure time. In 1980, 88% of
workers had 4 weeks holiday or more per year compared to
only 20% in 1970. Much of this was taken abroad and in
1983, 63% of adults had been on holiday abroad compared with
36% in 1971. Despite this trend to travel abroad, a large
amount of holiday time remains available for leisure
activities within Britain. As Patmore (1983, p. 234)
suggests:

> Leisure movements to distant places give deep enjoyment
> and lasting stimulation, yet most leisure is spent in
> familiar places, with the constraints as well as the
> challenges that implies.

Most commentators on changing leisure patterns recognize
the significant changes affecting women. Gershuny and Jones
(1987) found that more women have jobs, more work part-time,
and increasing amounts of time are devoted to children but
that some reduction in routine domestic work has accompanied
improved technologies of the home. Despite this latter
trend, which was most evident in the 1960s, there remains an
inequitable dual burden of paid work and unpaid housework on
employed women. Women do between two and three times as

much routine domestic work as men. Social Trends 1988
portrays a similar situation, female employees had less
leisure time than male employees, spent more time on
essential activities such as domestic work, essential
shopping and associated travel, but spent less time than men
on work and associated travel. Against this is the evidence
from diary surveys of the period 1961 to 1984 (Gershuny and
Jones, 1987) that men were undertaking more domestic work in
the later 1970s and 1980s, but by no means enough to redress
the balance:

> The irregularity in the change in domestic work over the
> period 1961 to 1984 results from the balancing of the
> technologically generated reduction in women's routine
> domestic work, against increases in child care, shopping
> time and men's domestic work.
> (Gershuny and Jones, 1987, p. 33).

This evident increase in time devoted to child care may well
have recreational implications and points up the issue of
defining leisure which has already been discussed.

Against this background of significant changes affecting
the availability of leisure time, the next question is
concerned with what people do with such 'free' time. Most
leisure time is home-based and the single most popular
leisure activity is watching television. In the winter of
1987, men watched on average 25.5 hours of television per
week whilst the figure for women was 30.75 hours. There
were other sources of variation with, for example, the
elderly watching well above the average number of television
hours. Although television is the dominant single home-
based activity, there is a range of others such as do-it-
yourself, reading, gardening and listening to music which
absorb significant amounts of leisure time. Outdoor
recreation reflects personal mobility and is often closely
related to car-ownership; leisure travel has increased in
the last two decades but the number of group excursions has
declined. Between July and September 1982 it is estimated
that there were 600 million leisure day trips; in the summer
of 1984, some 60% of people interviewed had been on at least
one drive to the countryside during the preceding four week
period. This percentage did fall to 54% in a similar 1986
survey and this was attributed to adverse weather
conditions. Walking was by far the most popular outdoor
activity with about 18% having been on a walk of at least
two miles in the previous four weeks. The Countryside
Commission (1985) found that almost 50% of the population
make a trip to the countryside at least once a fortnight on
average throughout the year, rising to 70% in the summer.
The number of people taking part in formal and informal
sport in the countryside during the summer has increased
from 7% in 1977 to 25% in 1984; by comparison the number of
drives or outings remained static at 41%. These trips into
the countryside are dominated by urban dwellers looking
towards rural settings for recreational purposes, much of
that recreation is informal and has the general character of
a 'day-out' or a 'trip' or an 'outing'. Some visits to the

6

countryside, however, have more specific aims and more particualar destinations. The trip is aimed at some specific place and it is from the promotion, development and creation of such places that the heritage industry has grown.


## Historic sites and leisure activities

The English Tourist Board (1985) showed that 2741 studied tourist attractions in 1984 were visited by 194 million people. These attractions covered a wide range from stately homes and safari parks to pleasure grounds. 54.2 million of these visits however were to historic buildings and a further 54.1 million were to museums and art galleries. This type of site which in some form or other displays heritage holds a significant place in the provision of attractions for people seeking to make use of their leisure time. Social Trends 1988 showed that large numbers of people included a visit to a historic building, stately home or museum in their recreational activity. 40% of those interviewed in 1986 had made such a visit in the previous four weeks. As with most kinds of recorded leisure activities, there were significant variations by social class. DE households (semi-skilled, unskilled, etc.) were least likely to have made a visit to the countryside or to have been to a historic site. Social Trends (1985) showed that 13% of AB groups (managerial, professional) had visited a historic building compared with 5% of DE. Between 1983 and 1984 there was a 5% increase in visits to historic buildings and 4% to museums and art galleries. The kind of increase which had been evident over a number of preceding years was attributed to better marketing, extra facilities, more special events, longer opening hours and a greater public awareness.

The number and range of historic sites is imprecise. There were, for example, 338,079 listed buildings on the Department of Environment record for 1985 and 29,222 of these had been added in the previous year. Only just over 5,000 of these were Grade 1 listed buildings. Again of this vast number of historic sites, only a fraction is open to the public and attracts visitors in significant numbers. From the AA and RAC guides and the regional tourist board literature, there were 1,664 historic buildings open to the public in England. In addition there were 2,675 Anglican churches which are officially listed as Grade 1 buildings for which records are kept, there are many millions of visits to historic towns and villages which it is not possible to monitor. During the period May to September, 1983, an English Tourist Board survey of Chester, recorded 245,000 staying and 865,000 day visitors. The notion of visitor attractions is new. Of the 2,741 surveyed by the English Tourist Board, only 10% had been open before 1900 and 66% had opened since 1960. Since 1970, 1,240 additional properties in England had opened their gates to the public for the first time including 293 historic buildings. Many of these have an instant impact. The Jorvik Viking Centre at York opened in 1984 with 692,000 visitors in that year; by 1986 this had increased to 900,000. The Tower of London remains the most attractive historic site with over 2 million visitors. Major tourist attractions such as the Tower of London and Edinburgh Castle attract large numbers of overseas visitors and these, particularly North American, figure prominently in a wide range of historic sites. Although many visitors to historic sites are on holiday away from home, day-trippers form significant numbers of visitors. In 1985, for example, 10% of all day trips included a historic house in the day's itinerary and 11% included castles. What might be termed 'developed resources', such as stately homes, country houses and historic monuments, formed the main stop for more than one in six of all countryside visitors. This notion of developed resources involves a conscious decision to invest in a property and to develop it in ways intended to attract visitors. The National Trust which owns 13% of the historic buildings regularly open to the public in England, has a policy to present historic houses as 'homes' rather than as empty museums.

## Trends in visiting State-managed historic sites

An encouraging trend in the 1960s and the 1970s was one of large increases in the memberships of leisure interest organizations including some which are directly concerned with historical monuments. The National Trust showed a membership increase of 700 per cent over the period 1960 to 1970 and its membership stood at just under one million in 1979. An English Tourist Board survey (1981) suggested that there were 56 conservation or heritage groups with a membership of one and a quarter million. Of interest here is both the considerable overall size of the commitment and the diversity of special interests within this broad category. A number of organizations which take people out into the countryside for short or medium term trips also showed significant increases in this period. These included the camping and caravan clubs as well as organizations such as the Youth Hostels Association and the Rambling Association.

Despite the general rises in the available tourist population within Britain together with the growth of membership of leisure organizations, the recorded numbers of visitors to historic sites within Wales which are now administered by Cadw showed a general decrease in the period 1974 to 1984. The decline was very general with Castell Coch as the only real exception. The larger monuments, defined by 1974 visitor totals, suffered very similar orders of loss irrespective of location. These observed trends for visitor numbers in what are now Cadw's sites (Figure 1.1) can be compared with the experience of Irish and Scottish monuments. Although most of the Irish monuments began to experience falling numbers of visitors in the later 1970s, there had been a less sharp decline and indeed a good deal of evidence since to suggest that some sites have recovered

# Figure 1.1.
## Cadw monuments

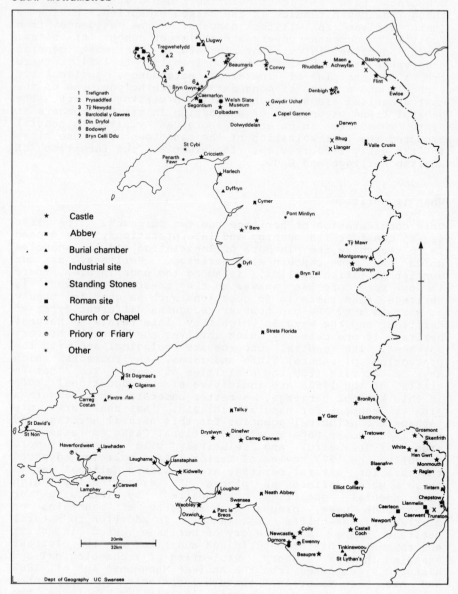

1 Trefignath
2 Prysaddfed
3 Tŷ Newydd
4 Barclodial y Gawres
5 Din Dryfol
6 Bodowyr
7 Bryn Celli Ddu

★ Castle
ℵ Abbey
▲ Burial chamber
✻ Industrial site
• Standing Stones
■ Roman site
X Church or Chapel
⊕ Priory or Friary
✳ Other

20mls
32km

Dept of Geography UC Swansea

and begun to increase once again. Clonmacnoise, for
example, is particularly successful and shows a doubling of
its 1978 visitor numbers by 1984. Most of the Irish
monuments have at least held their own over this period
though the Dowth Tumulus is the marked exception, having a
sharp decline in visitor numbers. The evidence from
Scottish monuments covers a much larger number of sites.
Again, decline in visitor numbers is the most general
observable trend over the period from 1980 to 1984. There
are a few examples of increased attendance, particularly
Inchcolm and a group of monuments in Strathclyde, one of the
most urbanised areas, have maintained visitor numbers. The
general trend of decline or stagnation in visitor numbers at
State monuments in an era of increased visitor potential
prompted the reorganisation of the management of these sites
in the early 1980s; with, for example, the formation of
English Heritage and Cadw.


## What is heritage?

This consideration of heritage has two purposes. The first
is to consider its meaning and interpretations, the second
is to recognize the plethora of legislation and of agencies
which has some concern with heritage. Heritage, as our
earlier quotation implies, is among the undefinables, there
is no more precise answer to the question of what is
heritage than there is to questions such as what is beauty
or what is art? We can however recognize different types of
heritage and the ways in which they interrelate. Natural
heritage is one category which involves the natural history
movement, its central concerns are ecological and with the
protection of natural flora and fauna, environments which
may be at risk from the activities of man. The 'nature
trails' of the 1960s are indicative of the educational role
in this kind of heritage, a better understanding leads to a
greater respect for natural habitats. National Parks are
perhaps the principal agencies for this natural heritage and
the 1945 Dower Report defined National Parks as extensive
areas of beautiful and relatively wild country. More
recently, the 1973 review of National Park policies advanced
the case for 'natural heritage areas' within National Parks.
These were defined as places of exceptionally high
environmental qualities, unimpaired by intrusive or
incongruous uses, places such as parts of mountains or
moorlands, sea-cliffs or islands. In addition to natural
heritage there is a category of heritage vested in built
environments; historic buildings and sites are the clearest
examples in this category. Protection of archaeological and
historic sites dates from the Ancient Monuments Act of 1882
and has been maintained through legislation and appointed
agencies since. More recent legislation includes the
Historic Buildings and Ancient Monuments Act of 1958, the
Ancient Monuments and Archaeological Areas Act of 1979 and
the National Heritage Acts of 1980 and 1983. Legislation of
this kind recognizes heritage in buildings and sites which
have some special historical significance or architectural

merit, they form part of our heritage which should be preserved. English Heritage was established in 1984 under the terms of the 1983 National Heritage Act, its main statutory duties are:

1. to secure the preservation of ancient monuments and historic buildings;
2. to promote, preserve and enhance the character and appearance of conservation areas;
3. to promote public enjoyment and to advance knowledge of ancient monuments and historic buildings and their preservation.

English Heritage has these roles in England, Cadw has them in Wales. There is a host of voluntary societies concerned with heritage and whereas the Civic Trust for example has a key in some forms of protection, the Nature Conservancy fullfils a similar function in others.

The third form of heritage which can be identified is best summarised by the term 'cultural'. In its broadest interpretation this covers a very wide and almost intangible set of conditions. A nation's art treasures, its musical traditions, its minority languages and dialects, its customs and ways of life all form components of this kind of heritage. This cultural heritage can however be found in buildings and in places. Historic buildings, for example, are often linked with people and come to life when that link is revelaed. To paraphrase Chesterton, 'the soul of a historic building is a story and the soul of a story is a personality'. Some heritage sites contain no fabric, no visible remains of buildings, their significance rests solely on the association with people and activities. The field at Waterloo where a great battle was engaged, the spot at Gettysburg where Lincoln stood, these and others form part of heritage. In broader terms, the French geographer, De la Blache, saw landscape as part of cultural heritage 'a medal cast in the image of its people' and the National Parks review similarly talked of the dry-stoned walled fields of the Derbyshire limestone plateau as part of our cultural heritage. The historic buildings which survive were the homes of the rich and famous, they were built to endure. More recently the growth of heritage centres such as York's Jorvik Centre and the Welsh Folk Museum have sought to broaden the range by recreating homes of artisans, workplaces and crafts. The mean worker's cottage is as much part of our heritage as is the mine owner's mansion or ornamental garden.

Heritage takes many forms. The thrust of this book is concerned with historic sites and buildings but it is wise to acknowledge this wider context within which their consideration must be set.


Conclusions

A concern for our heritage springs from genuine altruistic motives. It is reflected in the many Acts of Parliament which are designed to grant powers of protection and preservation, it is reflected in the many voluntary organisations and statutory agencies which have emerged to focus on some specific aspect of heritage. From the National Trust to the Civic Trust, from the National Parks to the local heritage or conservation groups, from Friends of the Earth to English Heritage and Cadw, there is a considerable force of people who are devoting their energies to the best interests of our heritage. Generally it is true to say that these agencies and organisations enjoy a broad base of support among the public at large. This concern for heritage exists and will continue but it is also true to say that there has emerged in recent years a considerable 'heritage industry'. This heritage industry is the product of many things. The new boom in leisure time or the 'fourth wave' as Dower termed it some years ago, the need for the private owners of stately homes to generate sufficient income to maintain their properties and to become businessmen and entrepreneurs in the process, the need for even some Government agencies to generate income and to have the ability to restore as well as to maintain, the felt need to educate, entertain and provide enjoyment for the millions of people who look to the countryside and its places of interest for part of their recreational needs.

This book will reflect the need for conservation but is mainly concerned with the 'heritage industry' and the roles which historic sites have in the servicing of recreational needs. It is organised to profile the kinds of people who visit historic sites, their reasons for making those visits and the expectations that they have of 'heritage' sites. The book is also centrally concerned with issues of marketing. It raises and considers the ways in which promotional activities can attract visitors and examines the roles of the media, the informal social networks and the educational system. Interpretation has become an increasingly prominent aspect of site development. It varies from simple signs and wall plaques to elaborate audio-visual displays and staged events and reconstructions. Interpretation does throw into sharp focus the need to find a balance between preserving the intrinsic qualities of the site and providing sufficient information to enhance the meaning and understanding of individual sites.

The notion of a heritage industry does move the management of sites into questions of pricing policy. Many historic sites are simply made available to the public with minimal provision of access and facilities and at minimal costs. They carry no admission charges mainly one suspects because the costs of administering such a charging scheme would outweigh the returns of income. There is also a strong feeling against charging for admission to heritage, cultural and educational places: charges have long been resisted in many museums and art galleries, for example, despite the fact that the flows of visitors are often substantial. Once a decision is made to charge visitors for admission to a site, the level of the charge becomes crucial. Entrance charges can be a deterrent, they could re-inforce the lack of representation of lower income groups which already is

revealed in visitor profiles.  Pricing policy in this  area
is increasingly practised but is not fully understood,  this
book  makes  a substantive contribution in this  area.   Any
place  or facility which attracts visitors in large  numbers
has  an  impact  upon the local community  in  which  it  is
placed.  These  impacts are variable.  There are  positive
impacts which may generate local employment or income, there
are negative impacts which may lead to increases in noise or
congestion  and  lead  to  some  deterioration  of  natural
environments.  These impacts are identified and discussed in
Chapter 7.

As has been stated, much of the empirical data included in
this text has been drawn from surveys of Cadw sites in Wales
as  part  of  commissioned  research.   It  is  therefore
particularly  appropriate  that  we  should  include  a
contribution from John Carr,  Director of Cadw,  in which he
traces  something  of  the  history  of  the  organisation,
outlines  its structures and responsibilities and  discusses
the  ways  in which Cadw has developed  its  management  and
marketing  strategies.   With 127 historic sites in its care
and  a  full-time staff in excess of 200,  Cadw is  a  major
heritage  agency  and  its experiences are  well  worthy  of
scrutiny.

This  book adds to the growing literature on the field  of
leisure activities.   It is focussed on one kind of facility
for leisure,  the heritage site.  This facility has special
qualities  no more evident than in its need to maintain  the
critical balance between conservation and  access.   Through
the  detailed  surveys  which  are reported  and  the  close
scrutinies  of literature we aim for insights into  the  key
issues  of management,  marketing,  priorities and policies.
The heritage industry is now part of our leisure scene,  the
better  its  needs  are understood then the  safer  are  the
qualities  it seeks to protect and the more  attractive  are
the services which it purports to offer.

References

Bourdieu,  P. (1984).  Distinction: a social critique of the
    judgement of taste.  London: Routledge and Kegan Paul.
Central  Statistical  Office (1985).  Social  Trends,  15.
    London: Her Majesty's Stationery Office.
Central  Statistical  Office (1988).  Social  Trends,  18.
    London: Her Majesty's Stationery Office.
Countryside  Commission  (1985).  National  countryside
    recreation  survey:  1984.  Cheltenham: Countryside
    Commission.
Dumazedier,  J.  (1974).  Sociology of leisure.  Amsterdam:
    Elsevier.
Dunning,  E. (1983).  'Notes on some recent contributions to
    the sociology of sport'.  Theory,  Culture and Society, 2,
    135-142.
English  Tourist  Board,  Planning  and  Research  Services
    Branch,  Socio Economic Research Unit (1981).  Aspects of
    leisure  and  holiday  tourism.  London: English  Tourist
    Board.

English Tourist Board (1985). *Sightseeing in 1984*  London: British Tourist Authority: English Tourist Board.

Featherstone, M. (1987). 'Leisure, symbolic power and the life course'. In Horne, J., Jary, D. and Tomlinson, A. (Eds.). *Sport, leisure and social relations*. pp. 113-138. London: Routledge and Kegan Paul.

Gershuny, J. and Jones, S. (1987). 'The changing work/leisure balance in Britain: 1961-1984'. In Horne, J., Jary, D. and Tomlinson, A. (Eds.). *Sport, leisure and social relations*. pp. 9-50. London: Routledge and Kegan Paul.

Herbert, D. T. (1987). 'Exploring the work-leisure relationship: an empirical study in South Wales'. *Leisure Studies*, 6, 147-165.

Herbert, D. T. (1988). 'Work and leisure: exploring a relationship'. *Area*, 1-12.

Hewison, R. (1987). *The heritage industry*. London: Methuen.

Horne, J., Jary, D. and Tomlinson, A. (Eds.), (1987). *Sport, leisure and social relations*. London: Routledge and Kegan Paul.

Jones, A. (1985). *Britain's heritage: the creation of the National Heritage Memorial Fund*. London: Weidenfeld.

Parker, S. (1976). *The sociology of leisure*. London: Allen and Unwin.

Patmore, J. A. (1983). *Recreation and resources: leisure patterns and leisure places*. Oxford: Blackwell.

Roberts, K. (1978). *Contemporary society and the growth of leisure*. London: Longmans.

Smith, J. (1987). 'Men and women at play: gender, life-cycle and leisure'. In Holme, J., Jary. D. and Tomlinson, A. (Eds.). *Sport, leisure and social relations*. pp. 51-85. London: Routledge and Kegan Paul.

Stockdale, J. E. (1985). *What is leisure? an empirical analysis of the concept of leisure and the role of leisure in people's lives*. London: Sports Council and Economic and Social Research Council.

# 2 Visitors to heritage sites: a market segmentation by visitor characteristics

RICHARD C PRENTICE

## Introduction

Markets may be divided up, or segmented, in various ways, ranging from the social or economic characteristics of visitors to the benefits they gain by visiting (e.g. Frain, 1986). The present discussion looks at one aspect of segmentation: the social characteristics of visitors. Segmentations of this kind should be regarded as basic to analyses of the effectiveness of promotional, pricing and interpretative strategies, for it is likely that visitors may react differently to strategies. If it is possible to group visitors in terms of their reactions to such strategies and identify pertinent differences in the social characteristics between groups, targeting can be more easily effected using the social characteristics as the means of targeting. However, social segmentation of visitors should only be regarded as part of any market segmentation, and not as the complete analysis. Ultimately, we need really to know the benefits visitors derive from their visits, if we are fully to develop heritage products. Much work in market segmentation for historic sites stops short of this fuller segmentation; instead, diverse visitor surveys abound providing information on social characteristics but often little else from which general conclusions may be made as to pertinent segmentations. The present discussion seeks to find a coherence from a selection of these studies as a background to understanding the market for heritage sites.

2 Visitors to heritage sites:
a market segmentation
by visitor characteristics

RICHARD G PRENTICE

Table 2.1.
Social class of visitors to heritage sites

| Site: | Caernarfon Castle | Chepstow Castle | Irish National Monuments | National Trust | Ragley Hall | Castle Howard | Tatton Park | St. Fagans Welsh Folk Museum |
|---|---|---|---|---|---|---|---|---|
| Author(s): | Owen and Mears (1974a) | Mears (1976) | Bord Failte (1974) | Mass Observation (UK) Ltd (1978) | B.T.A. and Countryside Commission (1968) | B.T.A. and Countryside Commission (1968) | B.T.A. and Countryside Commission (1968) | Owen and Mears (1974b) |
| | % | % | % | % | % | % | % | % |
| Professional ) Intermediate ) | 15 | 40 | 40 | 45 | 30 | 24 | 20 | 32 |
| Skilled non-manual | 38 | 30 | 40 | 33 | 34 | 33 | 34 | 30 |
| Skilled-manual | 33 | 21 | 13 | 16 | 27 | 32 | 36 | 29 |
| Partly skilled/ unskilled | 14 | 9 | 7 | 6 | 9 | 11 | 10 | 8 |

Cont ....

16

Table 2.1 cont .....

| Site: | Ulster American Folk Park | Bunratty Folk Park | Museums and galleries | Historic gardens | Giant's Causeway | National Trust for Scotland membership | National Trust membership | National Trust visiting sites | Welsh population 1986 | |
|---|---|---|---|---|---|---|---|---|---|---|
| Author(s): | N.I.T.B. (1982) | Shannon Free Airport Development Department (1984) | E.T.B. Market Research Department (1982) | Gallagher (1983) | N.I.T.B. (1982) | McGrath (1982) | Mass Observation Inter-tion (UK) Ltd (1978) | | Welsh Office Inter-censal survey | |
| | % | % | % | % | % | % | % | | males % | females % |
| Professional | } 28 | } 38 | } 37 | 18 | } 36 | 36 | } 51 | | } 21 | } 8 |
| Intermediate | | | | 45 | | 50 | | | | |
| Skilled non-manual | 43 | 38 | 38 | 16 | 40 | 11 | 35 | | } 14 | } 47 |
| Skilled-manual | 16 | 31 | 17 | 10 | 19 | } 3 | 10 | | 39 | 7 |
| Partly skilled/unskilled | 13 | 31 | 7 | 11 | 5 | | 4 | | 26 | 38 |

Source: As authors.

17

## Social class of visitors to heritage sites

Comparisons of the social class of visitors to heritage sites are hindered by the varying definitions of social class used in these studies. In Table 2.1 a range of studies are summarised in as comparable a form as possible. These studies include a range of heritage sites, including surveys at monuments, historic houses, museums, folk parks and gardens. A general predominance of white collar workers and their families as visitors to heritage sites is apparent, with one exception, Bunratty Folk Park. However, the extent of the predominance of white collar workers at the sites tabulated varies. Membership of the National Trusts is almost exclusively white collar; indeed, membership of the National Trust for Scotland was almost wholly made up of professional or intermediate white collar workers. Upwards of three quarters of surveyed visitors to the Irish National Monuments in 1974, to the National Trust properties in 1978, to museums and galleries in England in 1982, to historic gardens in England in 1983 and to the Giant's Causeway in 1982 were white collar workers or their families. Compared to their extent in the general population, partly skilled and unskilled workers were universally under-represented amongst visitors to the heritage sites set out in Table 2.1, the exception being Bunratty Folk Park. Skilled manual workers and their families in particular varied in comparative extent among sites, comprising a third of the visitors to Tatton Park, Castle Howard and Caernarfon Castle in the late 1960s and early 1970s, but only half of this proportion at English historic gardens, National Trust properties and the Ulster American Folk Park in the late 1970s and early 1980s. Some caution needs, however, to be exercised to avoid any perspective of inevitability in the social class profile of visitors to heritage sites. Although in a study of visitors to three major British museums social class was not explicitly measured, a proxy measure of age at which full time education was completed was included (Heady, 1984). If we take the proportion of visitors who had completed their full time education at sixteen years of age or younger as a proxy measure for manual worker and skilled non manual visitors, visitors to the National Railway Museum were notably different in social profile to those at the Victoria and Albert Museum and at the Science Museum. At the National Railway Museum in York more than six out of ten visitors who had completed their full time education had done so at sixteen years of age or younger, compared to a quarter and a third at the two London museums respectively. These findings suggest the importance of the type of contents displayed by museums, and possibly of regional location, in determining the social class mix of visitors. The sites included in Table 2.1 are, of course, also major sites. The social class pattern of visitors to other sites is generally unknown. Surveys on the Isle of Man of visits made to the National Glens confirm some social class bias in the direction found for the major sites set out in Table 2.1, but not such an extensive bias (Prentice, 1986;

18

Table 2.2.
Social class of visitors to Cadw's sites

| | Easter 1986 survey Inside site | Summer 1986 general survey inside site | Summer 1986 pricing survey in-side | out-side | Summer 1986 interpretation survey inside site | ALL surveys inside site | Heritage in Wales members who joined in 1985 |
|---|---|---|---|---|---|---|---|
| N = | 2,074 % | 1,811 % | 961 % | 369 % | 858 % | 5,704 % | 984 % |
| I Professional | 27 | 18 | 16 | 13 | 17 | 21 | 19 |
| II Intermediate | 33 | 36 | 34 | 36 | 37 | 35 | 30 |
| III NM Skilled non-manual | 15 | 12 | 13 | 15 | 11 | 13 | 29 |
| III M Skilled manual | 14 | 20 | 25 | 22 | 23 | 19 | 11 |
| IV, V Partly skilled/ unskilled | 6 | 7 | 7 | 6 | 7 | 7 | }10 |
| Other | 4 | 7 | 5 | 8 | 4 | 5 | } |

Sources: Seren (1986a); Seren (1986b); Seren (1986c); Seren (1986d); Seren (1986e).

Table 2.3.
Social class of visitors to individual sites managed by Cadw, 1986

| | Tintern Abbey | | Castell Coch | | Caerphilly Castle | | Kidwelly Castle | Caerleon Fort and Amphi- theatre | Raglan Castle |
|---|---|---|---|---|---|---|---|---|---|
| N = | 273 E | 237 S % | 290 E % | 259 S % | 349 E % | 202 S % | 120 E % | 181 E % | 243 S % |
| I Professional | 32 | 25 | 21 | 14 | 29 | 20 | 36 | 24 | 22 |
| II Intermediate | 36 | 45 | 31 | 34 | 37 | 36 | 34 | 45 | 36 |
| III NM Skilled non-manual | 11 | 10 | 14 | 14 | 14 | 11 | 11 | 13 | 13 |
| III M Skilled manual | 11 | 11 | 24 | 23 | 10 | 17 | 11 | 9 | 16 |
| IV, V Partly skilled/ unskilled | 5 | 3 | 8 | 9 | 4 | 6 | 4 | 8 | 5 |
| Others | 5 | 6 | 2 | 6 | 5 | 10 | 4 | 1 | 8 |

Cont ...

Table 2.3 cont ....

| | Conwy Castle | | | Harlech Castle | | | Caernarfon Castle | | | Criccieth Castle | | Valle Crucis Abbey | | Beaumaris Castle | |
|---|---|---|---|---|---|---|---|---|---|---|---|---|---|---|---|
| N = | 357 | 186 | | 205 | 227 | | 211 | 236 | | 166 | | 111 | | 221 | |
| | E | S | % | E | S | % | E | S | % | E | % | E | % | S | % |
| I Professional | 23 | 10 | | 24 | 23 | | 33 | 15 | | 33 | | 29 | | 14 | |
| II Intermediate | 28 | 26 | | 28 | 32 | | 33 | 31 | | 37 | | 29 | | 43 | |
| III NM Skilled non-manual | 19 | 13 | | 22 | 10 | | 11 | 13 | | 13 | | 12 | | 15 | |
| III M Skilled manual | 18 | 27 | | 14 | 25 | | 12 | 23 | | 9 | | 16 | | 18 | |
| IV, V Partly skilled/ unskilled | 8 | 11 | | 3 | 5 | | 8 | 8 | | 4 | | 6 | | 6 | |
| Others | 4 | 13 | | 9 | 5 | | 3 | 10 | | 4 | | 8 | | 4 | |

Note: E = Easter; S = Summer.

Source: Seren (1986a); Seren (1986b).

21

Table 2.4.
Social class of holidaymakers and day-trippers in Wales

| | Staying visitors: | | | | Day-trippers: | | | |
| --- | --- | --- | --- | --- | --- | --- | --- | --- |
| N = | North Wales 1,405 % | Mid Wales 812 % | South Wales 1,004 % | TOTAL 3,221 % | North Wales 352 % | Mid Wales 306 % | South Wales 416 % | TOTAL 1,074 % |
| Social class: | | | | | | | | |
| Professional/Intermediate (AB) | 25 | 26 | 23 | 25 | 21 | 19 | 18 | 20 |
| Skilled non-manual (C1) | 23 | 28 | 36 | 28 | 23 | 18 | 27 | 23 |
| Skilled manual (C2) | 33 | 35 | 25 | 31 | 30 | 36 | 26 | 30 |
| Partly skilled/unskilled (DE) | 18 | 11 | 16 | 16 | 26 | 26 | 28 | 27 |

Source: Marplan Ltd. (1984).

Table 2.5.
Age groups of visitors to heritage sites

| Site: | Caer- narfon Castle | Chepstow Castle | Irish National Monuments | Ragley Hall | Castle Howard | Tatton Park | St Fagans Welsh Folk Museum | Ulster American Folk Park | Museums and gall- eries | Giant's Cause- way |
|---|---|---|---|---|---|---|---|---|---|---|
| Author: | Owen and Mears (1974a) | Owen and Mears (1976) | Bord Failte (1974) | B.T.A. and Country -side Commis- sion (1968) | B.T.A. and Country -side Commis- sion (1968) | B.T.A. and Country -side Commis- sion (1968) | Owen and Mears (1974b) | N.I.T.B. (1982) | E.T.B. Market Research Dept. (1982) | N.I.T.B. (1982) |
| | % | % | % | % | % | % | % | % | % | % |
| Age groups: | | | | | | | | | | |
| 16-24 | 24 | 24 | 19 | 14 | 15 | 14 | 18 | 12 | 20 | 23 |
| 25-34 | )49 | )49 | 19 | 16 | 17 | 18 | )47 | )57 | 31 | )59 |
| 35-44 | ) | ) | 22 | 23 | 21 | 24 | ) | ) | 26 | ) |
| 45-54 | )21 | )23 | 20 | 25 | 25 | 20 | )26 | )25 | 12 | )15 |
| 55-64 | ) | ) | 8 | 15 | 16 | 18 | ) | ) | )11 | ) |
| 65&+ | 6 | 4 | 5 | 7 | 6 | 6 | 8 | 6 | ) | 3 |

Note: under 16s are excluded from this table.

Source: As authors.

Table 2.6.
Age groups of visitors to heritage sites

| Site: | National Trust | | Historic gardens | National Trust for Scotland membership | National Trust membership / National Trust visiting sites | |
|---|---|---|---|---|---|---|
| Authors: | Mass Observations (UK) Ltd. (1978) | | Gallagher (1983) | McGrath (1982) | Mass Observations (UK) Ltd. | |
| | (1977) % | (1978) % | % | % | (1977) % | (1978) % |
| Age groups: | | | | | | |
| 16–20 | 5 | 4 | 7 | 2 | 2 | 2 |
| 20–29 | 16 | 18 | 19 | 4 | 11 | 12 |
| 30–39 | 19 | 21 | 21 | 11 | 15 | 18 |
| 40–49 | 18 | 20 | 17 | 17 | 17 | 19 |
| 50–59 | 21 | 18 | 15 | 22 | 24 | 22 |
| 60 and over | 22 | 18 | 21 | 44 | 31 | 27 |

Note: under 16s are excluded from this part of the table.

Cont ....

24

Table 2.6 cont .....
Age distribution of visitors to museums

| Site: | Victoria and Albert Museum, London | Science Museum, London | National Railway Museum, York |
|---|---|---|---|
| Authors: | Heady (1984) % | Heady (1984) % | Heady (1984) % |
| Age groups: | | | |
| Up to 10 years | 6 | 19 | 11 |
| 11-20 | 23 | 36 | 21 |
| 21-30 | 28 | 15 | 15 |
| 31-40 | 16 | 15 | 27 |
| 41-50 | 12 | 8 | 11 |
| 51-70 | 13 | 6 | 15 |
| 71 and over | 3 | 0 | 1 |

Note: under 10s are excluded from this part of the table.

Source: As authors.

Prentice and Prentice, 1987). Some caution is implied therefore in our conclusions about the social class mix of visitors to heritage sites.

Against this social class background of visitors to major sites, Cadw's visitors in the latter 1980s appear more consistently white collar, particularly persons visiting out of season (Table 2.2). Around two thirds of Cadw's visitors in this period were white collar workers, and over half were professional and intermediate workers. At most, skilled manual workers formed a fifth to a quarter of summer visitors, but fewer out of season visitors. Partly skilled workers and unskilled workers, and their families, were notably scarce amongst visitors. Skilled manual workers formed a disproportionate number of Heritage in Wales (club) members than did general visitors. In contrast, certain of Cadw's sites showed a disproportionate white collar bias amongst visitors (Table 2.3). At Tintern Abbey, Caernarfon Castle and Criccieth Castle a third of all Easter 1986 surveyed visitors were professional workers or their families. In the summer of 1986 upwards of a fifth of visitors surveyed at Tintern Abbey, Caerphilly Castle, Raglan Castle and Harlech Castle were professional workers and their families. In general, white collar workers formed fewer than six out ot ten surveyed visitors at only Conwy Castle and Caernarfon Castle of Cadw's sites in the summer of 1986. Skilled manual workers and their families, in contrast, formed at least a fifth of the visitors surveyed only at Castell Coch, Conwy Castle, Harlech Castle and Caernarfon Castle, and with the exception of Castell Coch, this was a summer feature of visiting. At only Conwy Castle in the summer did partly skilled or unskilled manual workers form at least one fifth of surveyed visitors. Cadw's market profile would thus appear exceptionally biased to white collar workers and, at particular sites, especially to the more affluent white collar worker. In part, the summer increase of skilled manual workers amongst Cadw's visitors reflects the holiday taking of skilled manual workers in North Wales and Mid Wales (Table 2.4). However, the more general point to be made from a comparison of holiday taking and visits to Cadw's sites is that professional and intermediate workers and their families are much more likely than others to make a visit to a Cadw site, either as a holiday maker or as a day tripper. In short, the social class bias in visits to Cadw's sites does not in large part reflect the social class breakdown of holiday makers and day trippers in Wales. Other explanations, such as access to a motor vehicle, pricing, other opportunities, promotion or taste must be sought for this pronounced social class bias.


Age groups of adult visitors to heritage sites

Previous research on heritage site visitors tentatively suggests that the age groups of visitors do vary by the type of site. Adult visitors to castles, folk parks, museums and galleries are on the whole younger than visitors to National Trust, and like historic houses (Tables 2.5 and 2.6).

Table 2.7.
Age groups of visitors to Cadw's sites

| | Easter 1986: survey inside site | Summer 1986: General survey inside site | Pricing survey inside site | Pricing survey outside site | Interpretation survey inside site | ALL surveys inside site |
|---|---|---|---|---|---|---|
| N = | 2,220 | 1,787 | 961 | 369 | 913 | 5,881 |
| | % | % | % | % | % | % |
| **Age groups:** | | | | | | |
| 15-29 | 39 | 27 | 22 | 27 | 27 | 31 |
| 30-39 | 34 | 32 | 34 | 31 | 26 | 32 |
| 40-49 | 17 | 23 | 23 | 21 | 18 | 20 |
| 50-59 | 7 | 11 | 11 | 11 | 13 | 10 |
| Over 59 | 3 | 7 | 10 | 9 | 16 | 7 |

Note: children under 15 years were not surveyed and, thus,
do not appear in this age distribution.

Source: Seren (1986a); Seren (1986b); Seren (1986c); Seren (1986d).

'Natural' sites vary: visitors to the Giant's Causeway were
found to be younger than visitors to gardens. However,
evidence from the Isle of Man of visitors to the Island's
National Glens suggests that adults aged over sixty are
least likely to visit the Glens (Prentice, 1986; Prentice
and Prentice, 1987). Three quarters of visitors to
Caernarfon and Chepstow Castles were found in the mid 1970s
to be persons aged 16-44 years; retired persons were notably
few amongst visitors. Likewise, more than two thirds of
visitors to St. Fagan's and the Ulster American Folk Park
were similarly aged. In contrast, around four out of ten
adult visitors to National Trust properties were aged under
forty years in the late 1970s, and the distribution of
members' ages was disproportionately older. Around three
out of ten National Trust members visiting sites were found
to be aged sixty years or over; and of the total National
Trust for Scotland membership in 1982, over four out of ten
were aged sixty or over. The physical characteristics of
properties can only in part explain these age differences:
castles may deter the elderly because of their steps and
stairways, but many historic houses likewise have stairs.
Like the social class profiles, these age profiles may need
to be explained by other attributes of the 'products'
offered, by promotional strategies and by tastes. It should
also be noted that some sites attract large numbers of
children. Over half of the visitors to the Science Museum
are aged under twenty years, as are a third of visitors to
the National Railway Museum (Heady, 1984). As visitor
surveys tend to include only adults as respondents, child
visitors may be under-recorded at sites.

The disproportionately young adult population of visitors
to Cadw's sites in the later 1980s can be seen in Table 2.7.
Only one in five visitors to Cadw sites in the summer of
1986 were aged fifty years or over; at Easter, only one in

Table 2.8.
Age groups of Heritage in Wales members

|  | Members who joined in 1985 |
|---|---|
| N = | 1,033 |
|  | % |
| Years: | |
| 16-25 | 12 |
| 26-35 | 21 |
| 36-45 | 32 |
| 46-55 | 13 |
| 56-65 | 10 |
| Over 65 | 11 |

Note: persons under 16 years are excluded from this table.

Source: Seren (1986e).

28

ten were found to be in this age group. In contrast, a
quarter of Cadw's visitors were aged 15 to 29 years, and at
Easter four out of ten were in this age category.
Membership of Cadw's club, Heritage in Wales, shows a
slightly older age profile to that of the visitors to their
sites (Table 2.8). However, this profile is not markedly
different, and the age structure of the membership is still
biased to persons aged 45 years or younger. Examined on a
site by site basis some of Cadw's sites differ markedly in
the age distribution of their visitors, summer compared to
Easter (Table 2.9). At Caernarfon Castle, at the most
extreme, the proportion of summer visitors aged under thirty
years was found to be one third of the proportion at Easter.
Harlech Castle, Conwy Castle and Tintern Abbey each showed a
reduction in the proportion of persons aged under thirty in
the summer, compared to Easter, but at Castell Coch the
opposite was the case. Promoted as a fairytale castle,
this anomaly may result from young families bringing
children to Castell Coch for a summer's day out. The sites
also differed one with the other in the age profile of their
visitors. In the summer, Tintern Abbey's, Caerphilly
Castle's and Caernarfon Castle's visitors were on the whole
older than those elsewhere, particularly when compared with
visitors at 'neighbouring' sites, namely the Caerleon sites
and Beaumaris Castle. The latter would imply the importance
of site specific characteristics in attracting adult
visitors of different ages. A comparison of Tables 2.7 and
2.10 suggests that Cadw's sites would appear in the summer
to be attracting a proportionate share of staying
holidaymakers in their fifties and over, but not a
proportionate share of day trippers in this age range. This
would imply a need to investigate this market segment
further. Otherwise, Cadw would appear to be receiving
visitors by age group in rough proportion to their mix
amongst staying visitors and day trippers.


Holiday status of visitors to heritage sites

It is of course to be expected that the proportion of
holiday makers compared to day trippers amongst visitors at
any single heritage site will depend on the regional
location of the site as regards main and 'second' holidays.
Wales is a destination for both types of holiday. Even at
Easter most of the surveyed visitors at Cadw's sites were
found to be holiday makers staying away from home, rather
than day trippers visiting from home (Table 2.11). In the
summer the recorded proportion of holiday makers staying
away from home exceeded three quarters of all surveyed
visitors at Cadw's sites. However, marked variations in the
holiday status of Cadw's visitors are to be expected from
the regional location of the sites within Wales; the South
Wales conurbation is a main source of day trips, whereas in
Mid Wales and North Wales comparable concentrations of
population do not exist. The expected variations in terms
of holiday status were in fact found by the surveys in 1986.
For example, four out of ten of the visitors surveyed at

Table 2.9.
Age groups of visitors to individual sites managed by Cadw, 1986

| Age: | Tintern Abbey | | Castell Coch | | Caerphilly Castle | | Kidwelly Castle | Caerleon Fort and Amphitheatre | Raglan Castle |
|---|---|---|---|---|---|---|---|---|---|
| | E % | S % | E % | S % | E % | S % | E % | E % | S % |
| N = | 273 | 232 | 290 | 254 | 349 | 202 | 120 | 181 | 237 |
| 15-19 years | 10 | 2 | 2 | 3 | 4 | 4 | 10 | 15 | 3 |
| 20-29 | 35 | 19 | 22 | 32 | 27 | 22 | 21 | 21 | 20 |
| 30-39 | 29 | 27 | 45 | 32 | 36 | 30 | 45 | 31 | 30 |
| 40-49 | 14 | 27 | 15 | 22 | 20 | 20 | 12 | 17 | 26 |
| 50-59 | 9 | 16 | 10 | 7 | 9 | 14 | 4 | 13 | 14 |
| 59 and over | 3 | 10 | 6 | 4 | 4 | 10 | 8 | 4 | 7 |

Cont .....

Table 2.9 cont ....

| | Conwy Castle | | Harlech Castle | | Caernarfon Castle | | Criccieth Castle | Valle Crucis Abbey | Beaumaris Castle |
|---|---|---|---|---|---|---|---|---|---|
| N = | 357 | 185 | 205 | 225 | 211 | 236 | 166 | 111 | 216 |
| | E | S | E | S | E | S | E | E | S |
| | % | % | % | % | % | % | % | % | % |
| Age: | | | | | | | | | |
| 15-19 years | 4 | 3 | 5 | 8 | 26 | 2 | 4 | 7 | 5 |
| 20-29 | 32 | 24 | 37 | 24 | 37 | 20 | 40 | 43 | 23 |
| 30-39 | 36 | 27 | 36 | 35 | 18 | 33 | 25 | 27 | 38 |
| 40-49 | 20 | 29 | 14 | 21 | 12 | 20 | 20 | 18 | 23 |
| 50-59 | 5 | 11 | 5 | 8 | 4 | 14 | 8 | 4 | 5 |
| 59 and over | 2 | 6 | 2 | 4 | 3 | 12 | 4 | 1 | 6 |

Note: E = Easter; S = Summer.

Source: Seren (1986a); Seren (1986b).

31

Table 2.10.
Age groups of holidaymakers and day-trippers in Wales

|  | Staying visitors: | | | | Day-tripper: | | | |
|---|---|---|---|---|---|---|---|---|
|  | North Wales | Mid Wales | South Wales | TOTAL | North Wales | Mid Wales | South Wales | TOTAL |
| N = | 1,405 % | 812 % | 1,004 % | 3,221 % | 352 % | 306 % | 416 % | 1,074 % |
| Age groups: | | | | | | | | |
| 16-34 | 43 | 24 | 35 | 36 | 37 | 24 | 33 | 32 |
| 35-44 | 22 | 32 | 27 | 26 | 20 | 26 | 21 | 22 |
| 45-54 | 16 | 20 | 15 | 17 | 13 | 15 | 19 | 16 |
| 55 and over | 17 | 24 | 22 | 21 | 30 | 35 | 28 | 31 |

Note: under 16s are excluded from this table.

Source: Marplan Ltd. (1984).

Table 2.11.
Holiday status of visitors to Cadw's sites

| | Easter 1985: survey | Easter 1986: survey | Summer 1986: General survey | Summer 1986: Pricing survey | | Interpretation survey | ALL surveys of 1986 |
|---|---|---|---|---|---|---|---|
| | inside site | inside site | inside site | inside site | outside site | inside site | inside site |
| | 3,137 | 2,243 | 1,811 | 961 | 369 | 913 | 5,928 |
| | % | % | % | % | % | % | % |
| **Holiday status:** | | | | | | | |
| On holiday, away from home | )68 | 66 | 77 | 79 | 75 | 77 | 73 |
| On holiday, at home | ) | 18 | 8 | 9 | 7 | 6 | 12 |
| Not on holiday | 32 | 16 | 15 | 12 | 18 | 17 | 15 |

Source: Seren (1986a); Seren (1986b); Seren (1986c); Seren (1986d); Seren (1986f).

Table 2.12.
Holiday status of visitors to individual Cadw sites, 1986

| | Tintern Abbey | | Castell Coch | | Caerphilly Castle | | Kidwelly Castle | Caerleon Fort and Amphi-theatre | Raglan Castle |
|---|---|---|---|---|---|---|---|---|---|
| | E | S | E | S | E | S | E | E | S |
| | % | | % | | % | | % | % | % |
| N = | 273 | 237 | 290 | 259 | 349 | 202 | 120 | 181 | 243 |
| On holiday away from home | 64 | 78 | 38 | 49 | 48 | 64 | 59 | 54 | 65 |
| On holiday at home | 23 | 10 | 22 | 20 | 23 | 9 | 15 | 29 | 12 |
| Not on holiday | 13 | 12 | 40 | 31 | 29 | 27 | 26 | 17 | 23 |

| | Conwy Castle | | Harlech Castle | | Caernarfon Castle | | Criccieth Castle | Valle Crucis Abbey | Beaumaris Castle |
|---|---|---|---|---|---|---|---|---|---|
| | E | S | E | S | E | S | E | E | S |
| | % | | % | | % | | % | % | % |
| N = | 357 | 186 | 205 | 227 | 211 | 236 | 166 | 111 | 221 |
| On holiday away from home | 77 | 86 | 93 | 93 | 88 | 94 | 89 | 62 | 93 |
| On holiday at home | 21 | 2 | 6 | 2 | 7 | * | 7 | 18 | 4 |
| Not on holiday | 2 | 12 | 1 | 4 | 5 | 5 | 4 | 20 | 3 |

Note: (i)  E = Easter; S = Summer.
      (ii) * indicates a percentage greater than 0 but less than 1.

Source: Seren (1986a); Seren (1986b).

34

Easter at Castell Coch were day trippers, not on holiday, and a further fifth were staying at home but on holiday (Table 2.12). With the exception of Valle Crucis in North Wales, accessible to day trippers from the English Midlands, Cadw's sites in South Wales had a much higher proportion of day trippers at both Easter and in the summer, than did the sites in North Wales. The sites in North Wales attracted mainly staying holiday makers, irrespective of main or secondary season. For example, at both Harlech and Caernarfon Castles nine out of ten visitors were staying holiday makers, both at Easter and in the summer of 1986.

In contrast to the Welsh sites were three historic sites surveyed in 1968. At Ragley Hall over half of surveyed visitors were day trippers not on holiday, as were nearly two thirds of visitors to Tatton Park (B.T.A. and Countryside Commission, 1968). The latter had hardly any holiday makers staying away from home as visitors. The visitors to Castle Howard were more varied by holiday status, but all the same, four out of ten were day trippers not on holiday. This survey of twenty years ago serves again to illustrate the importance of regional location in this regard.


Distance travelled to heritage sites by visitors on day of visit

The distances travelled to heritage sites by visitors can be expected, in part at least, to vary; firstly, by the comparative proximity of large concentrations of populations, both permanent, and in the case of holiday making, transient; and, secondly, by the extent of competing destinations for recreational trips. However, having noted these causal factors it is also of interest for marketing to see if any general patterns can be found. Surprisingly, particularly in view of its potential usefulness in target promotions, data on day of visit distances travelled is comparatively sparse. The information which does exist is largely for the more developed or substantial heritage sites. In particular, we do not know the distances people will travel to see field monuments. A particular example of the impression of localisation which will be given by much of this section, which would otherwise rely on evidence from major sites, is evidence from visits made to 'natural' heritage sites on the Isle of Man. Visits to many of the Manx National Glens can be very localised, especially visits made by rural residents. Whilst it must be remembered that the Island's size constrains trips to a maximum of about thirty miles, over a twelve month period half of the rural visitors to the less popular Glens were found to live within about seven miles of the site visited; a similar proportion of visitors to the popular Glens were found to live within eight miles of the site (Prentice, 1986; Prentice and Prentice, 1987). However, most visits to major sites are also of limited distances, although these distances are greater than those found for the sites on the Isle of Man. Data from the late 1960s and mid 1970s suggest an average

Table 2.13.
Distances travelled to heritage sites on day of visit in late 1960s

| Site: | Ragley Hall | Castle Howard | Tatton Park |
|---|---|---|---|
| Author(s): | B.T.A. and Countryside Commission (1968) | B.T.A. and Countryside Commission (1968) | B.T.A and Countryside Commision (1968) |
| | % | % | % |
| Distances travelled: | | | |
| 0-9 miles | 10 | 6 | 11 |
| 10-24 miles | 47 | 21 | 39 |
| 25-49 miles | 29 | 44 | 38 |
| 50-74 miles | 7 | 25 | 10 |
| 75-99 miles | 2 | 3 | 1 |
| 100 miles and over | 4 | 1 | 1 |
| Mean | 30 | 39 | 27 |

Source: As authors.

trip distance of under forty miles for major sites in Britain: in 1968 on average visitors to Ragley Hall, Castle Howard and Tatton Park had travelled respectively thirty, thirty-nine and twenty-seven miles (Table 2.13). Visitors to National Trust properties in the 1970s were found on average to have travelled thirty-two miles (Mass Observation (U.K.) Ltd, 1978). Likewise, all but sixteen per cent of day trippers visiting Powerscourt in Ireland in 1981 were found to have come from the neighbouring conurbation of Dublin, Dun Laghaire and Bray (Bord Failte, 1981). Similarly, all but one in twenty visitors to the Ulster American Folk Museum had travelled on their day of visit from either Northern Ireland or neighbouring County Donegal in the Irish Republic (N.I.T.B., 1982). This general pattern of localised trip making does however show some extensive variations. The 1968 study showed that visitors to Castle Howard were notably more likely to travel further than were visitors to Ragley Hall and Tatton Park (Table 2.13). Of the twenty five National Trust properties surveyed in 1977 and 1978, the average overall trip distance of thirty two miles conceals a wide range of average distances for the specific sites. Four sites had average trip distances of under twenty miles, and eight of under twenty five miles. In contrast, three sites had average trip distances of over forty miles, including the Treasurer's House at York, which had an average distance travelled of fifty two miles (Mass Observation (U.K.) Ltd, 1978). Trip distances of the order considered here for heritage sites are not uncommon for most day trips: most round trips (that is, out and back) were found in the 1980s

Table 2.14.
Distance travelled to Cadw sites on day of visit (all sites)

|  | Easter 1985: | Easter 1986: | Summer 1986: | | | | ALL |
|---|---|---|---|---|---|---|---|
|  | | | General | Pricing | | Interpretation | |
|  | survey inside site 3,780 % | survey inside site 2,191 % | survey inside site 1,745 % | survey inside site 961 % | survey outside site 369 % | survey inside site 913 % | surveys inside site 9,590 % |
| Under 6 miles | )56 | )63 | 17 | 20 | 21 | 21 | )57 |
| 6-20 miles | ) | ) | 35 | 37 | 32 | 33 | ) |
| 21-30 miles | )26 | 13 | 16 | 18 | 21 | )30 | )28 |
| 31-40 miles | ) | 8 | 11 | 10 | 9 | ) | ) |
| 41-50 miles | ) | 4 | 7 | 4 | 9 | ) | ) |
| 51-75 miles | )9 | 5 | 5 | 4 | 3 | 9 | )9 |
| 76-100 miles | ) | 3 | 4 | 3 | 2 | 2 | ) |
| Over 100 miles | 9 | 4 | 5 | 4 | 3 | 5 | 6 |

Source: Seren (1986a); Seren (1986b); Seren (1986c); Seren (1986d); Seren (1986f).

Table 2.15.
Distance travelled on day of visit by Easter visitors to individual sites managed by Cadw, 1986

|  | Tintern Abbey | Castell Coch | Caerphilly Castle | Kidwelly Castle | Caerleon Fort and Amphitheatre |
|---|---|---|---|---|---|
| N = | 273 | 290 | 349 | 120 | 181 |
|  | % | % | % | % | % |
| Under 21 miles | 51 | 68 | 67 | 70 | 64 |
| 21-30 miles | 21 | 9 | 10 | 12 | 13 |
| 31-40 miles | 7 | 12 | 12 | 2 | 7 |
| 41-50 miles | 3 | 4 | 3 | 2 | 7 |
| 51-75 miles | 7 | 3 | 2 | 7 | 1 |
| 76-100 miles | 3 | 1 | 3 | 2 | 2 |
| Over 100 miles | 8 | 2 | 4 | 5 | 6 |

|  | Valle Crucis Abbey | Conwy Castle | Harlech Castle | Criccieth Castle | Caernarfon Castle |
|---|---|---|---|---|---|
| N = | 111 | 357 | 205 | 166 | 211 |
|  | % | % | % | % | % |
| Under 21 miles | 51 | 66 | 65 | 77 | 48 |
| 21-30 miles | 18 | 2 | 16 | 6 | 32 |
| 31-40 miles | 13 | 13 | 6 | 2 | 2 |
| 41-50 miles | 9 | 4 | 3 | 2 | 3 |
| 51-75 miles | 3 | 11 | 3 | 3 | 7 |
| 76-100 miles | 4 | 2 | 5 | 5 | 3 |
| Over 100 miles | 3 | 2 | 2 | 4 | 6 |

Source: Seren (1986a).

Table 2.16.
Distances travelled on day of visit by summer visitors to individual sites managed by Cadw, 1986.

| | Tintern Abbey | Castell Coch | Caerphilly Castle | Raglan Castle | Caernarfon Castle | Conwy Castle | Harlech Castle | Beaumaris Castle |
|---|---|---|---|---|---|---|---|---|
| N = | 233 | 253 | 194 | 241 | 216 | 178 | 221 | 209 |
| | % | % | % | % | % | % | % | % |
| Under 6 miles | 18 | 17 | 11 | 3 | 25 | 38 | 14 | 14 |
| 6-20 miles | 24 | 39 | 44 | 32 | 36 | 21 | 38 | 47 |
| 21-30 miles | 18 | 9 | 12 | 22 | 17 | 19 | 15 | 19 |
| 31-40 miles | 17 | 10 | 8 | 16 | 11 | 6 | 12 | 10 |
| 41-50 miles | 6 | 9 | 11 | 5 | 4 | 5 | 7 | 5 |
| 51-75 miles | 3 | 7 | 5 | 8 | 3 | 4 | 7 | 2 |
| 76-100 miles | 3 | 4 | 5 | 6 | 1 | 3 | 3 | 1 |
| Over 100 miles | 11 | 5 | 3 | 7 | 2 | 2 | 4 | 1 |

Source: Seren (1986b).

in Scotland to be under a hundred miles, and on average between fifty and seventy three miles across the regions of Scotland (Countryside Commission for Scotland, 1985).

The distances travelled to Cadw's sites are overall less than those found from elsewhere (Table 2.14). Most visitors to Cadw's sites were found to have started their journey within twenty miles of the site at which they were interviewed. This was much the same main season compared to secondary season. Variation between specific sites was mainly in the extent of this localisation of trip making. For example, at Easter upwards of seven out of ten visitors to Kidwelly Castle and Criccieth Castle were found to have travelled twenty miles or less, and in the summer a quarter and over a third, respectively, of visitors to Caernarfon Castle and Conwy Castle were found to have travelled under six miles to the site (Tables 2.15 and 2.16). Visits to Cadw's sites appear to be more localised than general day trips in and to Wales, which on average take around an hour in North and South Wales (Table 2.17). Likewise, only a

Table 2.17.
Travel time of day visitors in Wales

|  | North Wales | Mid Wales | South Wales | TOTAL |
|---|---|---|---|---|
| N = | 352 | 306 | 416 | 1,074 |
|  | % | % | % | % |
| Travel time: |  |  |  |  |
| Under 1 hour | 41 | 23 | 63 | 45 |
| 1-2 hours | 34 | 42 | 24 | 35 |
| 2-3 hours | 13 | 40 | 8 | 13 |
| Over 3 hours | 12 | 13 | 3 | 9 |

Source: Marplan Ltd. (1984).

third of day visitors to Gwynedd were found in 1980 to have started their journeys in the neighbouring counties of Wales (Gwynedd County Planning Department, 1981). It would seem therefore that visitors to monuments in Wales either do not need to travel as far to visit a site or are not prepared to do so, compared to general day trip making in Wales.

Regions of visitor origins at heritage sites

Whereas the previous section considered visitor origins on their day of visit, this section considers their location of residence. For day trippers visiting from home, this is of course the same, but not for holiday makers. The regional, or national, origins of visitors are as varied as the structure of the holiday industry in a locality. For example, visitors to the major Irish monuments in 1974 were found not only to be mostly foreign visitors, but at some

Table 2.18.
Region of origin of holiday visitors to Wales at three
heritage sites in the 1970s

| Site: | Caernarfon Castle | Chepstow Castle | St Fagans Welsh Folk Museum |
|---|---|---|---|
| Author(s): | Owen and Mears | Mears | Owen and Mears |
| | (1974a) | (1976) | (1974b) |
| | % | % | % |
| Northern England | 2 | * | 1 |
| Yorks/Humberside | 3 | 3 | 3 |
| East Midlands | 4 | 4 | 4 |
| East Anglia | * | * | * |
| South East | 14 | 15 | 13 |
| South West | 4 | 2 | 4 |
| West Midlands | 21 | 16 | 19 |
| North West | 17 | 19 | 19 |
| Scotland | * | * | * |
| Wales | 15 | 19 | 14 |
| Elsewhere | 20 | 19 | 25 |

Note: * indicates a percentage of less than 1%.

Source: As authors.


sites, largely so. At the State Appartments, Cashel,
Monasterboice and Cahir fewer than one in five surveyed
visitors were Irish residents (Bord Failte, Research
Section, 1974). In contrast, at Mellifont and Ballintubber
more than four out of ten surveyed visitors were Irish
residents. Likewise, at Bunratty Folk Park in the years
1982 to 1984 fewer than a quarter of visitors were resident
in Ireland: at this site, over half the visitors in 1984
were from the United States of America (Shannon Free Airport
Development, 1984). These Irish surveys, and that at
Bunratty in particular, are indicative of the importance of
international tourism to many Irish heritage attractions.
    Welsh heritage sites have not attracted such large
proportions of foreign visitors as have the Irish sites
(Table 2.18). In the mid 1970s the main markets were not
overseas but the West Midlands, North West and South East of
England, and Wales itself. Reliance on the British market
has remained the case in the 1980s for most of the Welsh
monuments. Dependent on the regional location of the sites
the origins of visitors vary within Great Britain, rather
than between British and overseas visitors (Tables 2.19 and
2.20). For example, both Castell Coch and Kidwelly Castle
attract large numbers of visitors resident in Wales, whereas
the sites in North Wales attract visitors disproportionately
from Northern England. Generally, South East England is a
consistent market for visitors across all of Cadw's sites.
However, having noted the general predominance of British
visitors to the Welsh monuments, at some sites overseas

Table 2.19.
Home location of visitors to Cadw's sites at Easter 1985

| | Caernarfon Castle | Conwy Castle | Denbigh Castle | Valle Crucis Castle | Kidwelly Castle | Castell Coch | Caerphilly Castle | Tintern Abbey | ALL sites |
|---|---|---|---|---|---|---|---|---|---|
| N = | 353 | 309 | 382 | 220 | 406 | 574 | 229 | 664 | 3137 |
| | % | % | % | % | % | % | % | % | % |
| **Home location:** | | | | | | | | | |
| Wales: under 20 miles | 4 | 5 | 22 | 10 | 35 | 41 | 25 | 7 | 20 |
| Wales: 20 to 50 miles | 4 | 1 | 5 | 6 | 11 | 12 | 7 | 8 | 7 |
| Elsewhere in Wales | 5 | 3 | 3 | 3 | 5 | 4 | 2 | * | 3 |
| Total: Wales | 12 | 9 | 29 | 18 | 51 | 56 | 33 | 16 | 30 |
| North West England | 19 | 20 | 23 | 27 | 2 | 2 | 3 | 5 | 11 |
| West Midlands | 20 | 9 | 7 | 16 | 7 | 3 | 5 | 6 | 8 |
| East Midlands, Yorkshire and Humberside | 12 | 14 | 8 | 5 | 3 | 3 | 5 | 4 | 6 |
| Northern England and Scotland | 3 | 4 | 2 | 2 | * | * | 1 | 2 | 2 |
| South East England and East Anglia | 24 | 28 | 17 | 19 | 21 | 16 | 26 | 31 | 23 |
| South West England | 3 | 5 | 4 | 4 | 10 | 11 | 15 | 20 | 10 |
| Elsewhere | 6 | 11 | 10 | 9 | 6 | 7 | 11 | 16 | 10 |

Note: *indicates a percentage less than 1% but greater than zero.

Source: Seren (1986f).

visitors are undoubtedly significant in the main season, notably at Tintern Abbey, Caerphilly Castle and Caernarfon Castle. Of the surveyed sites in 1986, overseas visitors formed upwards of a fifth of all visitors at these latter sites. The international proportion of visitors to Cadw's sites is akin to that of all staying visitors in Wales, fewer than one in ten of whom come from overseas (Marplan Ltd., 1984). Regional variations do however, occur within the domestic tourist market, and in particular the Gwynedd monuments attract substantially more visitors from the South East of England than the proportion of staying visitors from this region in Gwynedd would suggest. Visitors from South East England comprised fewer than one in ten staying summer visitors surveyed in Gwynedd in 1980 (Gwynedd County Planning Department, 1981), but reference to Table 2.20 shows their higher proportion amongst visitors to Cadw's sites in the mid 1980s. This may well reflect socio-economic differences in tourists' preferences, rather than any marked change in regional holiday-taking.

The location of the major British museums has a clear effect on the origins of their visitors. Whereas eight out of ten and two thirds respectively of visitors to the Victoria and Albert Museum and the Science Museum in London have been found to come from South East England, fewer than one in ten of visitors to the National Railway Museum at York were found to come from this region (Heady, 1984). In contrast, three out of ten visitors to the National Railway Museum were found to have come from Yorkshire and Humberside (the region in which it is located) and a further quarter from North and North West England. These regional variations in visitor hinterlands have important implications for the location of museums by the public sector.


Modes of travel to heritage sites

Irrespective of the location of sites in urban or rural areas the most prevalent mode of travel to heritage sites is by private car. Even fifteen years ago the Wales Tourist Board's studies of visitors at Caernarfon Castle, Chepstow Castle, and the Welsh Folk Museum, found that only at Caernarfon Castle were coach or bus passengers significant in proportion: visitors travelling by car represented three quarters of visitors at the other two sites (Owen and Mears, 1974b). At Caernarfon one in ten visitors were found to have arrived on a coach excursion. The private car was confirmed in 1984 as the dominant mode of transport for staying visitors in Wales, with between eight and nine out of ten staying visitors from Britain arriving by car (Marplan Ltd., 1984). Only overseas visitors arrived by other modes in any significant proportion; but even so, four out of ten overseas staying visitors to Wales arrived in Wales by car. Of day visitors, the same survey found that over three quarters arrived by car; fewer than one in twelve came by coach, and half this proportion by train. However, of the minority of day excursionists who had travelled over

Table 2.20.
Home location of visitors to Cadw's sites and Heritage in Wales members, 1986

| | Tintern Abbey | | Castell Coch | | Caerphilly Castle | | Kidwelly Castle | Caerleon Fort and Amphitheatre | Raglan Castle | Conwy Castle | |
|---|---|---|---|---|---|---|---|---|---|---|---|
| | E | S | E | S | E | S | E | E | S | S | E |
| N = | 273 | 237 | 290 | 259 | 349 | 202 | 120 | 181 | 243 | 357 | 186 |
| | % | % | % | % | % | % | % | % | % | % | % |
| Wales: under 20 miles | 8 | 5 | 42 | 33 | 36 | 22 | 29 | 32 | 8 | 6 | 3 |
| Wales: 20 to 50 miles | 7 | 6 | 11 | 12 | 8 | 4 | 8 | 10 | 12 | 3 | 2 |
| Elsewhere in Wales | 3 | 2 | 1 | 4 | 1 | * | 4 | 0 | 4 | 1 | 3 |
| Total: Wales | 17 | 13 | 54 | 49 | 46 | 27 | 41 | 41 | 23 | 10 | 7 |
| North West England | 7 | 5 | 3 | * | 2 | 4 | 3 | 2 | 3 | 34 | 27 |
| English West Midlands | 10 | 6 | 5 | 3 | 5 | 4 | 8 | 3 | 6 | 10 | 18 |
| English East Midlands | 1 | 2 | 1 | 2 | 1 | 2 | 2 | 6 | 4 | 8 | 7 |
| Yorks and Humberside | 1 | 2 | 2 | 2 | 3 | 3 | * | 3 | 2 | 6 | 5 |
| Northern England | 0 | * | 2 | * | 1 | * | 0 | * | 0 | 1 | 3 |
| South West England | 18 | 11 | 9 | 5 | 6 | 7 | 8 | 7 | 16 | 4 | 4 |
| South East England | 35 | 30 | 20 | 25 | 23 | 28 | 27 | 31 | 28 | 16 | 17 |
| East Anglia | 1 | 4 | 2 | 2 | 2 | 3 | * | * | 3 | 1 | 2 |
| Scotland | 1 | * | 0 | * | 1 | 0 | * | 0 | 0 | 1 | 2 |
| Elsewhere | 8 | 26 | 3 | 10 | 10 | 22 | 9 | 6 | 16 | 9 | 9 |

Cont ....

44

Table 2.20 cont ....

| | Harlech Castle | | Caernarfon Castle | | Criccieth Castle | Valle Crucis Abbey | Beaumaris Castle | ALL sites | | Heritage in Wales members (1985) |
|---|---|---|---|---|---|---|---|---|---|---|
| N = | 205 | 227 | 211 | 236 | 166 | 111 | 221 | 2263 | 1811 | 1051 |
| | E % | S % | E % | S % | E % | E % | S % | E % | S % | % |
| Wales: under 20 miles | 2 | * | 4 | 1 | 5 | 10 | 2 | 18 | 10 | – |
| Wales: 20 to 50 miles | 3 | 2 | 3 | 1 | 3 | 5 | 2 | 6 | 5 | – |
| Elsewhere in Wales | 3 | 6 | * | 6 | 2 | 6 | 5 | 2 | 4 | – |
| Total: Wales | 8 | 9 | 7 | 9 | 10 | 20 | 9 | 26 | 19 | 60 |
| North West England | 16 | 14 | 22 | 14 | 27 | 29 | 25 | 14 | 11 | 7 |
| English West Midlands | 15 | 26 | 8 | 13 | 12 | 10 | 13 | 8 | 11 | 6 |
| English East Midlands | 7 | 7 | 6 | 6 | 10 | 6 | 5 | 4 | 5 | 2 |
| Yorks and Humberside | 5 | 3 | 9 | 7 | 6 | 4 | 11 | 4 | 4 | 2 |
| Northern England | * | 2 | 2 | 1 | * | 0 | * | * | * | 1 |
| South West England | 7 | 6 | 6 | 6 | 3 | 2 | 5 | 7 | 8 | 7 |
| South East England | 26 | 17 | 33 | 20 | 25 | 19 | 18 | 25 | 23 | 10 |
| East Anglia | 3 | 1 | 4 | 3 | 1 | 1 | 2 | 2 | 3 | 2 |
| Scotland | 1 | * | 2 | 1 | 1 | 1 | 0 | * | * | * |
| Elsewhere | 11 | 15 | 5 | 19 | 3 | 8 | 11 | 7 | 16 | 4 |

Note: (i)  E = Easter; S = Summer;
      (ii) * indicates a percentage of under 1% but greater than zero.

Source: Seren (1986a); Seren (1986b); Seren (1986f).

45

Table 2.21.
Repeat visiting at heritage sites

| Site: | Glendalough | Ragley Hall | Castle Howard | Bunratty Folk Park | | Powerscourt Gardens |
|---|---|---|---|---|---|---|
| Author: | Bord Failte (1976) | B.T.A. and Countryside Commission (1968) | B.T.A. and Countryside Commission (1968) | Shannon Free Airport Development (1984) | | Bord Failte (1981) |
| | | | | (1983) | (1984) | |
| | % | % | % | % | % | % |
| First visit | 31 | 77 | 76 | 86 | 79 | 63 |
| Second visit | 12 | 14 | 14 | )14 | )21 | 15 |
| Third visit, or more | 57 | 9 | 10 | ) | ) | 21 |

46

Table 2.21 cont ....

| Site: | National Trust | | Museums and Galleries | Victoria and Albert Museum, London | Science Museum, London | National Railway Museum, York |
|---|---|---|---|---|---|---|
| Author: | Mass Observation (UK) Ltd. (1978) | | E.T.B. Market Research Dept. (1982) | Heady (1984) | Heady (1984) | Heady (1984) |
| | (1977) | (1978) | | | | |
| | % | % | % | % | % | % |
| First visit | 73 | 76 | 33 | 47 | 46 | 64 |
| Second visit | 11 | 11 | ) 67 | 8 | 12 | 12 |
| Third visit, or more | 16 | 13 | ) | 45 | 42 | 24 |

Source: As authors.

47

ee hours, a third were coach passengers, indicating the
proportionate importance of coach travel to longer
stance day trips.

## Repeat visiting at heritage sites

Repeat visiting of the same heritage site is comparatively
unusual, other than at museums and galleries, and generally
upwards of eight out of ten visitors have been found to be
on their first or second visit to a historic site. Most
visitors are usually first time visitors (Table 2.21). A
notable exception was found at Glendalough in Ireland, a
site combining both historical and natural heritage. At
Glendalough over half of the visitors surveyed in 1975 were
visitors on at least their third visit. Two thirds of Irish
visitors surveyed were found to be in on at least their
fifth visit; while a quarter of overseas visitors to the
site were also repeat visitors. Repeat visiting of this
order at out of door sites should be regarded as highly
exceptional. Museums and galleries are, however, clearly
different in terms of repeat visiting to other types of
heritage sites. Over half of the visitors to the Victoria
and Albert Museum and the Science Museum are repeat
visitors. However, in contrast, nearly two thirds of
visitors to the National Railway Museum are first time
visitors.
   Most visitors to Cadw's sites in the mid 1980s were found
to be on their first visit, both at Easter and in the main
season (Table 2.22). Generally, around two thirds of
visitors were on their first visit to the sites, although
visitors interviewed turning away at the gates of sites were
notably more likely to be repeat visitors. However, even of
those who did not enter the sites, over half were on their
first visit, and so this effect should not be overstated.
At Easter both Caernarfon and Criccieth Castles were
exceptions to the general picture (Table 2.23). At these
sites around half of the Easter visitors had been before.
It is noticeable that at Easter repeat visitors generally
are slightly more common than in the main season, although
Harlech Castle is an exception.

## Other heritage sites visited

The historic houses surveys of 1968 asked respondents when
they had last visited any other country house. The results
varied by site (B.T.A. and Countryside Commission, 1968).
At Ragley Hall one in five respondents claimed to have
visited another country house in the previous week, and
three out of ten in the previous three weeks. At Castle
Howard the corresponding proportions were not so great, one
in eight and one in five respondents respectively.
Similarly, while at Castle Howard more recent visiting had a
direct relationship with social class, this was not the case
at Ragley Hall. Respondents were also asked how often they
had visited other historic houses in the previous two years.

Table 2.22.
Visitors' previous visits to Cadw sites at which interviewed

| | Easter 1985: survey inside site | Easter 1986: survey inside site | Summer 1986: General survey inside site | Pricing survey inside site | Pricing survey outside site | ALL surveys inside site |
|---|---|---|---|---|---|---|
| N = | 3,137 % | 2,236 % | 1,796 % | 961 % | 369 % | 8,130 % |
| Previous visits: | | | | | | |
| No previous visit | 69 | 64 | 69 | 73 | 57 | 68 |
| One previous visit | 15 | 16 | 15 | 17 | 16 | 16 |
| More than one previous visit | 16 | 20 | 16 | 10 | 27 | 16 |

Source: Seren (1986a); Seren (1986b); Seren (1986f).

Table 2.23.
Visitors' previous visits to Cadw sites at which interviewed (individual sites), 1986

| | Tintern Abbey | | Castell Coch | | Caerphilly Castle | | Kidwelly Castle | Caerleon Fort and Amphi- theatre | Raglan Castle |
|---|---|---|---|---|---|---|---|---|---|
| N = | 273 | 236 | 290 | 255 | 349 | 202 | 120 | 181 | 242 |
| | E | S | E | S | E | S | E | E | S |
| | % | | % | | % | | % | % | % |
| No previous visit | 60 | 73 | 65 | 70 | 68 | 75 | 70 | 78 | 75 |
| One previous visit | 21 | 15 | 15 | 17 | 14 | 10 | 18 | 13 | 14 |
| More than one previous visit | 19 | 12 | 20 | 13 | 18 | 15 | 12 | 9 | 11 |

| | Conwy Castle | | Harlech Castle | | Caernarfon Castle | | Criccieth Castle | Valle Crucis Abbey | Beaumaris Castle |
|---|---|---|---|---|---|---|---|---|---|
| N = | 357 | 178 | 205 | 226 | 211 | 236 | 166 | 111 | 221 |
| | E | S | E | S | E | S | E | E | S |
| | % | | % | | % | | % | % | % |
| No previous visit | 61 | 70 | 67 | 65 | 54 | 64 | 48 | 79 | 65 |
| One previous visit | 21 | 18 | 12 | 19 | 20 | 15 | 15 | 11 | 14 |
| More than one previous visit | 18 | 12 | 21 | 16 | 26 | 21 | 37 | 10 | 21 |

Note:  E = Easter;  S = Summer.

Source: Seren (1986a); Seren (1986b).

These responses also differed by site. At Ragley Hall more than four out of ten respondents claimed to have visited five or more historic houses in the previous two years, but at Castle Howard, only three out of ten visitors indicated a comparable rate. At both sites respondents making over twenty visits in the previous two years to historic sites represented only one in twenty of all visitors. Museum visitors of the 1980s also demonstrate patterns of joint visiting. Over a quarter of visitors to the Victoria and Albert Museum were found to have visited ten or more other museums and galleries in the previous twelve months (Heady, 1984). This is perhaps exceptional, but only a fifth of visitors at the Science Museum and the National Railway Museum had not visited at least one other museum or gallery in the previous twelve months.

Two Irish studies have indicated significant, if not extensive, joint visiting of major heritage sites in Ireland. In 1974 visitors at ten of Ireland's major monuments were interviewed to see if they had ever visited any other of the ten (Bord Failte, Research Section, 1974). As would be expected, Irish visitors had more extensively visited the other sites, than had overseas visitors, although Glendalough and Cashel had clear international importance (Table 2.24). These sites were particularly popular amongst Irish visitors too. More importantly, a national market for monuments in Ireland was implied. A subsequent study at Powerscourt included a longer list of previous destinations, but the survey was not implemented at these other sites, unlike the 1974 study. Thus, the full impact of past visiting is unrecorded in this subsequent study. However, the national importance of certain other Irish sites was made clear from the Powerscourt survey. Three out of ten visitors had previously visited Bunratty

Table 2.24.
Visitors to Irish monuments previous visits to other monuments

|  | Irish visitors % | Foreign visitors % | All visitors % |
|---|---|---|---|
| Had visited: |  |  |  |
| Newgrange | 32 | 13 | 19 |
| Monasterboice | 29 | 16 | 20 |
| Mellifont | 38 | 14 | 22 |
| Glendalough | 67 | 35 | 46 |
| Clonmacnoise | 28 | 14 | 18 |
| Cashel | 54 | 23 | 28 |
| Cahir | 20 | 10 | 13 |
| State Apartments | 31 | 14 | 19 |
| Ballintuller Abbey | 16 | 5 | 9 |
| Jerpoint Abbey | 16 | 6 | 10 |

Source: Bord Failte, Research Section (1974).

Folk Park, a quarter had previously visited Blarney Castle, and a similar proportion had previously visited Muckross.

Joint visiting of Cadw's sites is known only for its club members, members of Heritage in Wales. This group cannot be assumed to be generally representative of all visitors. Members joining in 1985 generally visited between two and five sites in their first year of membership. Fewer than one in seven visited more than ten sites (Seren, 1986e). Joint visiting in the first year of membership shows two patterns: firstly, local spatial interlinkage, and, secondly, a number of nationally important sites. One site stood out in 1986 as particularly popular, Caernarfon Castle, with extensive spatial interlinkage in visiting. Upwards of eight out of ten new Heritage in Wales members who visited other sites in North West Wales and Anglesey had also visited Caernarfon Castle (Seren, 1986e). Linkages to the North Western coastal monuments were also apparent from North East and Southern Gwynedd. For example, eight out of ten new members visiting Harlech Castle had in their first year of membership also visited Caernarfon Castle, and seven out of ten had visited Beaumaris or Conwy Castles. From the visiting patterns of new members two clearly integrated markets were apparent. One in the North along the coast from Harlech to Rhyddlan, the second in the South and South East from Kidwelly to Tintern. Cadw's sites in West Wales were integrated by joint visiting into both these markets: north along the coastal corridor to Gwynedd, and east to Gwent. The extent to which these visiting patterns are representative of other visitors is unknown, and should not be assumed. However, these interlinkages demonstrate, at least for a minority of visitors, substantial spatial markets for monuments in Wales.


Length of stay by visitors at heritage sites

The length of time visitors spend at sites is clearly related, at least in part, to the types of site, and in particular, to the extent to which a site is 'developed' with interpretation and visitor facilities. As most heritage site visitor surveys are of the more popular and 'developed' sites, figures on length of visits may be unrepresentative of a full portfolio of heritage sites. The Powerscourt survey of 1981 also reminds us that visitors may spend different times at a site if they come to visit different parts of the site, or if they come for different reasons. At Powerscourt the length of stay for visitors at the waterfall was much more varied than for those visiting the gardens; likewise tourists at the waterfall spent notably less time at the site than did day trippers (Table 2.25). In this case averages would be meaningless. Bunratty Folk Park provides an example of a 'developed' heritage site. In 1984 nearly half of all visitors spent between one and two hours at the site, and a further four out of ten spent over two hours (Shannon Free Airport Development, 1984). However, very few visitors in tour groups spent over two hours at the site, calling into

Table 2.25.
Length of stay at Powerscourt

| Length of stay: | Gardens: | | | Waterfall: | | |
|---|---|---|---|---|---|---|
| | Tourists % | Day trippers % | ALL % | Tourists % | Day trippers % | ALL % |
| Less than one hour | 4 | 8 | 5 | 33 | 6 | 16 |
| 1-2 hours | 46 | 43 | 45 | 37 | 29 | 32 |
| 2-3 hours | 34 | 40 | 36 | 17 | 19 | 19 |
| 3-4 hours | 13 | 7 | 12 | 7 | 21 | 16 |
| Over 4 hours | 2 | 2 | 2 | 6 | 25 | 17 |

Source: Bord Failte (1981).

Table 2.26.
Length of stay of visitors to Cadw's sites

|  | Easter 1986 inside site | Summer 1986 general survey inside site | Summer 1986 interpretation survey inside site |
|---|---|---|---|
| N = | 2,263 | 1,809 | 894 |
|  | % | % | % |
| Under 30 minutes | 12 | 9 | 5 |
| 30-59 minutes | 49 | 30 | 28 |
| 60-90 minutes | 24 | 40 | 39 |
| Over 90 minutes | 15 | 21 | 28 |

Sources: Seren (1986a); Seren (1986b).

question whether tour groups were being given sufficient time at the Park by tour operators. Seasonality is also important in time spent, as most monuments are open air sites and less attractive in wet weather. Cadw's sites show a marked seasonality in length of stay: at Easter the modal frequency is thirty minutes to fifty-nine minutes but in the summer one hour to ninety minutes (Table 2.26). Compared to Bunratty and Powerscourt gardens, Cadw's sites on the whole do not show such lengthy stays. Caernarfon Castle is a notable exception to many other of Cadw's sites (Table 2.27), further confirming the link between product 'development' and visitor stay. At Caernarfon Castle, irrespective of summer or Easter season, half of all visitors surveyed in 1986 had stayed over ninety minutes at the site. At Caernarfon there is plenty to see. Caerphilly Castle, similarly, had above average length of stays by visitors, somewhat in contrast to Tintern Abbey which had a similar display as its major interpretative provision.

Visitor group characteristics at heritage sites

In the 1970s family groups were found to predominate at surveyed Welsh heritage sites (Table 2.28). This was particularly so at the Welsh Folk Museum and amongst holiday visitors at the two surveyed castles. Day visitors included a disproportionate share of visitors in organised parties at all three surveyed sites. More recent surveys at Cadw's sites have shown the importance both of two person groups and of larger groups of four persons or more (Table 2.29). This is irrespective of summer or Easter season. Few of Cadw's visitors have pre-school age children in their personal groups. At Easter 1986 only one in ten had a pre-school age child in their group, although in the summer this proportion rose to nearly one out of five visitor groups. School age children are more common amongst visitor groups at Cadw's sites: the 1986 surveys showed that irrespective of season four out of ten visitors had school age children in their group. It should, however, be noted that in the

Table 2.27
Length of stay of visitors at individual Cadw sites, 1986

| | Tintern Abbey | | Castell Coch | | Caerphilly Castle | | Conwy Castle | | Harlech Castle | | Caernarfon Castle | |
|---|---|---|---|---|---|---|---|---|---|---|---|---|
| N = | 252 | 237 | 290 | 259 | 341 | 202 | 356 | 186 | 205 | 226 | 180 | 235 |
| | E | S | E | S | E | S | E | S | E | S | E | S |
| | % | % | % | % | % | % | % | % | % | % | % | % |
| Length of stay: | | | | | | | | | | | | |
| Under 30 minutes | 9 | 9 | 6 | 10 | 3 | 0 | 10 | 13 | 27 | 7 | 4 | 3 |
| 30-59 minutes | 54 | 29 | 62 | 37 | 35 | 12 | 54 | 50 | 49 | 39 | 16 | 9 |
| 1 hour to 90 minutes | 25 | 42 | 23 | 45 | 36 | 46 | 27 | 31 | 19 | 47 | 29 | 35 |
| Over 90 minutes | 13 | 20 | 10 | 8 | 26 | 42 | 10 | 6 | 5 | 7 | 50 | 53 |

Note: E = Easter; S = Summer.

Source: Seren (1986a); Seren (1986b).

Table 2.28.
Visitor groups at Welsh heritage sites in 1970s

| Site: Authors: | Caernarfon Castle Owen and Mears (1974a) | | Chepstow Castle Mears (1976) | | St Fagans Welsh Folk Museum Owen and Mears (1974b) | |
|---|---|---|---|---|---|---|
| | Day visitors % | Holiday visitors % | Day visitors % | Holiday visitors % | Day visitors % | Holiday visitors % |
| Group type: | | | | | | |
| Alone | 7 | 2 | 8 | 8 | 2 | 2 |
| Family group | 43 | 67 | 51 | 63 | 64 | 67 |
| Friends | 17 | 14 | 14 | 19 | 11 | 14 |
| Family/friends | 12 | 8 | 11 | 6 | 8 | 7 |
| Organised party | 21 | 10 | 17 | 4 | 16 | 11 |

Source: As authors.

56

Table 2.29.
Group sizes of visitors to Cadw's sites

|  | Easter 1986 inside site | Easter 1986 inside site | Summer 1986 general survey inside site |
|---|---|---|---|
| N = | 3,137 | 2,263 | 1,811 |
|  | % | % | % |
| Number of persons in personal group: |  |  |  |
| 1 person | 5 | 4 | 3 |
| 2 persons | 36 | 35 | 36 |
| 3 persons | 16 | 14 | 16 |
| 4 persons | 23 | 25 | 24 |
| 5 persons or more | 20 | 22 | 21 |

Sources: Seren (1986a); Seren (1986b); Seren (1986f).


Table 2.30.
Visitor groups at three major British museums in 1980

|  | Victoria and Albert Museum % | Science Museum % | National Railway Museum % |
|---|---|---|---|
| Visitor group type: |  |  |  |
| Alone | 26 | 10 | 5 |
| With friends but not members of family | 24 | 20 | 11 |
| With members of family | 38 | 45 | 64 |
| With a school party | 6 | 19 | 14 |
| With another type of organised party | 6 | 6 | 6 |

Source: Heady (1984).


1980s many visitors to Welsh monuments do not have children
in their groups and that the family group is not the
dominant visitor group at many sites. Further variety in
visitor group types is apparent from visitors to major
British museums (Table 2.30). Family groups predominate at
the National Railway Museum, and represent a substantial
minority of visitors to the Victoria and Albert Museum and
to the Science Museum. However, the Victoria and Albert
Museum is a notable exception to the other two museums
described in Table 2.30, for half of its visitors are either
on their own or with friends. This variety in group type is

perhaps best summarised by saying that we should not necessarily assume that family groups predominate in visits to heritage sites.


## Conclusions

Visitors to the major heritage sites in the British Isles show some consistencies in terms of their social characteristics irrespective of the location of the site. In particular, the social class profile of visitors, the distances that they have travelled, their mode of travel, patterns of repeat and joint visiting, and group profiles all show some consistency. Visitors are generally unrepresentative of the social class breakdown of the British population. Visitors to heritage sites are disproportionately from white collar groups, and particularly from professional and intermediate white collar groups. Visitors to monuments in Wales are disproportionately unrepresentative of the population in terms of social class, and this market profile can only be attributed partly to the social class breakdown of holiday makers in Wales. Explanations of the social class bias in visits to heritage sites must be sought in access to motor vehicles, pricing, other opportunities, promotion or tastes. Distances travelled on the day of visit to the major sites likewise show consistencies. Most visitors travel under fifty, often under forty, miles to heritage sites, although specific site variations do occur. In Wales trip distances appear to be more localised still, and most visitors to Cadw's sites in the 1980s appear to have travelled twenty miles or under. Moreover, modes of travel show greater consistency than distance travelled: most visitors to major heritage sites arrive by car. Repeat visiting is unusual at heritage sites, other than at museums and galleries. Specific sites are again exceptions, but repeat visiting, where it occurs, is usually infrequent. However, a sizeable segment of visitors also visit other heritage sites, confirming the importance of general taste or interest in determining visits. Finally, it should not be assumed that family groups dominate amongst visitors to heritage sites: equally, groups of this type are often in substantial proportion amongst visitors.

Other characteristics, in contrast, are not so consistent. The ages of visitors vary by type of heritage site. Adult visitors to castles, folk parks, museums and galleries are on the whole younger than visitors to historic houses, particularly visitors to houses owned by the National Trust. Some sites attract disproportionate numbers of children, notably the Science Museum in London. Visitors at 'natural' sites appear to vary in age, with visitors to gardens generally being older. Dependent on the regional location of heritage sites the regional, and national, origins of visitors also differ. The visitor mix in terms of origins at a site depends on the proportion of day trippers it receives amongst its visitors, the regional origins of holiday makers staying in its vicinity, whether, or not, it is on an international tourism circuit, and whether, or not, its region is successful in attracting overseas tourists. Many heritage sites are determined by the location of the original resource, such as a mediaeval castle. Others are largely 'man- made', such as many folk parks and museums. Similarly, the extent to which a site is developed and promoted is often a commercial or public decision. In that even national museums can demonstrate a significant regional bias in visiting, location, at least for 'man made' sites, appropriately becomes a policy decision. Length of stay at sites is also in part related to what a site has to offer a visitor, and, in particular, how it has been developed as a leisure or tourist attraction. However, it would be foolish to assume that increased provision at a site necessarily increases the length of visitors' stays. Other factors intervene, such as whether interest can be sustained. Length of stay should also be considered in terms of repeat visiting, and aggregated over visits previously made, if any.

Sufficient has been discussed to indicate the need for site operators and developers to monitor or anticipate their market profile of visitors in terms of social characteristics. The general need in tourism studies is to integrate what are often commercially sensitive, and thus initially confidential, surveys into a common framework. As the 'heritage product' is continually differentiated into a series of products the need for comparison becomes essential if consistencies in market segmentation are to be identified for the products.


References

Bord Failte (Research Section) (1974). National monuments survey. Dublin: Bord Failte.
Bord Failte (1976). Report on a survey of Glendalough 1976. Dublin: Bord Failte.
Bord Failte (1981). Powerscourt visitor survey 1981. A research and planning report. Dublin: Bord Failte.
British Tourist Authority and the Countryside Commission (1968). Historic houses survey. London: British Tourist Authority.
Countryside Commission for Scotland (1985). Patterns of countryside recreation trips. Scottish Leisure Survey report no 4. Perth: Countryside Commission for Scotland.
English Tourist Board, Market Research Department, and NOP Market Research Ltd. (1982). Visitors to museums survey of 1982. London: English Tourist Board.
Frain, J. (1986). Principles and practice of marketing. London: Pitman.
Gallagher, J. (1983). Visiting historic gardens. Research report no. 41. (A report on contemporary garden visiting and its literature). Leeds: School of Planning and Environmental Studies, Leeds Polytechnic.
Gwynedd County Planning Department (1981). Gwynedd tourism survey 1980. Caernarfon: Gwynedd County Council.

Heady, P. (1984). Visiting museums. Office of Population Censuses and Surveys, Social Survey Division, SS1147. London: Her Majesty's Stationery Office.

Marplan Ltd. (1984). A survey of non-business visitors to Wales, 1984. (And 3 appendix volumes). London: Marplan Ltd.

Mass Observation (U.K.) Ltd. (1978). National Trust visitors' survey, 1978. Part 1: Report of principal findings. Part 2: Appendix of tables and comments on properties. London: Mass Observation (U.K.) Ltd.

Mears, W. (1976). Survey of visitors to tourist attractions 1974. Report 6, Chepstow Castle. Cardiff: Wales Tourist Board.

McGrath, C. (1982). Survey of members' attitudes and interests. Edinburgh: The National Trust for Scotland.

Northern Ireland Tourist Board (1982). Survey of visitors to Ulster - American Folk Park. Belfast: Northern Ireland Tourist Board.

Owen, E. and Mears, W. (1974a). Survey of visitors to tourist attractions 1973. Report 3, Caernarfon Castle. Cardiff: Wales Tourist Board.

Owen, E. and Mears, W. (1974b). Survey of visitors to tourist attractions 1973. Report 5, Welsh Folk Museum, St. Fagans. Cardiff: Wales Tourist Board.

Prentice, R. C. (1986). Rural residents' leisure use of Manx National Glens. St. Johns, Isle of Man: Isle of Man Forestry, Mines and Lands Board.

Prentice, R. C. and Prentice, M. M. (1987). Urban residents' leisure use of Manx National Glens. St. Johns, Isle of Man: Isle of Man Department of Agriculture, Fisheries and Forestry.

Seren (1986a). Herbert, D. T., Prentice, R. C., Thomas, C. J., Edwards, J. A., Humphrys, G. and Prentice, M. M. Easter 1986 visitor survey. Final report. Swansea: Social Economic Research and Environment, Department of Geography, University College of Swansea.

Seren (1986b). Herbert, D. T., Prentice, R. C., Thomas, C. J. and Prentice, M. M. General survey at Cadw sites. Summer 1986. Swansea: Social Economic Research and Environment, Department of Geography, University College of Swansea.

Seren (1986c). Herbert, D. T., Prentice, R. C., Thomas, C. J., and Prentice, M. M. Pricing policy and visitors' satisfaction at Cadw's sites. Swansea: Social Economic Research and Environment, Department of Geography, University College of Swansea.

Seren (1986d). Herbert, D. T., Thomas, C. J., Prentice, R. C. and Prentice, M. M. Interpretation at Cadw's sites. Swansea: Social Economic Research and Environment, Department of Geography, University College of Swansea.

Seren (1986e). Prentice, R. C. Heritage in Wales membership. Swansea: Social Economic Research and Environment, Department of Geography, University College of Swansea.

Seren (1986f). Herbert, D. T., Thomas, C. J. Visitor survey report. Easter 1985. Swansea: Social Economic Research and Environment, Department of Geography, University College of Swansea.

Shannon Free Airport Development Co. Ltd. (1984). <u>Report on</u> ·
<u>survey</u> of <u>day</u> visitors <u>at</u> <u>Bunratty</u> <u>Folk</u> <u>Park</u>. Limerick:
Shannon Free Airport Development Co Ltd.
Welsh Office (1987). <u>Welsh</u> <u>inter-censal</u> <u>survey,</u> <u>1986</u>.
Cardiff: Welsh Office.

# 3 The roles of historic sites and reasons for visiting

COLIN J THOMAS

## Introduction

The management and marketing of historic sites requires a knowledge of the general roles they play in leisure and recreational activities, as well as the specific behavioural motivations, or reasons, for the visits. It is only by reference to such information that those responsible for the control and development of historic sites can adequately judge the success and potential of the various strategies they adopt. Such information, however, is not available in an easily interpretable form. Studies of the leisure and recreational roles of historic sites and the reasons expressed for undertaking visits are available in a multitude of reports produced for official agencies and private organisations concerned with the conservation of historic monuments, as well as with their potential for recreation and tourism. Of particular importance in this respect have been the various Tourist Boards and the National Trust. Such studies have been undertaken, either by market research companies or by academics, with the object of providing information on broad issues defined by the particular client. For this reason the body of information is variable in quality and content. Nevertheless, it is possible to recognise some consistent findings concerning the roles of historic monuments in leisure activities and the specific reasons associated with the decision to undertake a visit. This chapter provides a review and synthesis of the literature which examines these issues. The discussion is elaborated by reference to data

obtained from site survey analyses undertaken by the authors
for Cadw over the period 1985-87.


## Historic sites: their significance and roles in leisure activities

The significance of visits to historic buildings to the
overall pattern of recreational activities in England and
Wales appears at first sight to be relatively slight. A
Countryside Commission survey of the recreational behaviour
of 1000 people for the four weeks prior to the survey
revealed that of the total urban and countryside
recreational activity reported, only 3% consisted of visits
to historic buildings (Phillips and Worth, 1985). The
pattern was dominated by informal visits to the countryside
(49%), visits to urban parks (20%) and to seaside resorts
(11%). Most of such visits were informal and designed to
provide days-out involving activities such as walking and
picnics rather than visits to specific attractions such as
castles. In many of these countryside visits people did not
venture very far from their cars, and parking and
refreshment facilities are often the priority. Similar
findings were reported by Mackenzie (1985) for Scotland. Of
2061 respondents only 7% identified stately homes, historic
buildings or museums as places where main recreational stops
were made, while just 1% cited ruins, earthworks, or ancient
monuments as venues.
   Surveys of this kind can, however, understate the true
recreational significance of 'managed' activities such as
visits to historic buildings, country parks and organised
sporting events. In the first study, for example, the
analysis appears to equate a visit to a local park or to a
friend or relative with a visit to a historic building or a
country park. The former types of activities are probably
more likely to require less organisational effort than the
latter and will tend to be relatively frequent events
compared with the occasional visit to specific recreational
attractions. In fact, the latter types of activities are
more likely to involve a long day-out than the former. Thus
it could be argued that the two types of activities are not
really quantitatively equivalent in the context of the
totality of an individual's leisure behaviour.
Consequently, the importance of visits to such specific
attractions as historic buildings may well be underestimated
in analyses of this type.
   Similarly, in the Scottish study the figures recorded
relate to 'main' recreational stops. Visits to particular
attractions could well form a 'subsidiary' but important
element of a day-out primarily undertaken for some other
main purpose, and as such would not be recorded. This would
also have the effect of understating the recreational
significance of 'managed sites'.
   In fact, other studies which focus more specifically on
day-trips suggest that the recreational importance of visits
to historic sites is somewhat greater than the situation
noted above. The National Survey of Recreation in the

Table 3.1.
Attractions visited by day-trippers in Wales

| | Total respondents 1074 % | North Wales 352 % | Mid Wales 306 % | South Wales 416 % |
|---|---|---|---|---|
| N = | 1074 | 352 | 306 | 416 |
| Attractions visited: | | | | |
| Beauty spots in the countryside | 34 | 40 | 46 | 21 |
| Seaside resorts | 32 | 36 | 44 | 21 |
| Traditional Welsh towns and villages | 21 | 26 | 30 | 10 |
| Castles | 15 | 13 | 18 | 15 |
| Old slate quarries etc. | 10 | 8 | 7 | 13 |
| Steam railways | 8 | 7 | 19 | 2 |
| Historic houses or stately homes | 6 | 11 | 4 | 2 |
| Cathedrals, churches, religious sites | 6 | 3 | 5 | 10 |
| Zoos, wildlife parks, nature reserves | 6 | 4 | 2 | 10 |
| Fun fairs, entertainment parks | 6 | 9 | 1 | 7 |
| Museums, art galleries | 4 | 2 | 5 | 6 |

Source: Adapted from Marplan (1984), Table 7, p. 35.

Countryside undertaken by the Countryside Commission (Fitton, 1979), for example, indicated that 13% of the 4342 respondents recorded that the main destination of their last trip to the countryside was to visit a historic building or a stately home. Again, however, the more casual activities of drives, picnics and walks in the countryside or at the seaside dominated trip types (70%). Closely similar findings were recorded by the Countryside Commission for Scotland's survey of countryside recreation trips (1985). Drives, picnics, walks and visits to lochs and riversides were the main destinations for the pleasure trips of two thirds of respondents, while those indicating a visit to historic buildings, stately homes, museums, gardens and parks comprised only 9%.

Broadly consistent results have also been recorded for Wales although the percentage of visits to historic sites were significantly higher (Marplan, 1984). A survey of 1074 day-trippers interviewed throughout Wales indicated that 15% visited a castle, 6% a historic house and a further 6% a religious site. Again, the more casual activities associated with trips to beauty spots (34%), seaside resorts (32%), and towns and villages (21%) were more important (Table 3.1). Clearly, however, the differential between the casual activities and visits to 'managed sites' were not as great as those demonstrated in the earlier studies. This reflects a different survey design. Respondents were asked in which of an array of activities they had participated on the day of the interview (Table 3.1). Consequently, the element of under-reporting of trip behaviour associated with the recording of a single 'main' destination was avoided. In fact, the results of this survey suggest that a visit to a historic site, at least in Wales, is around half as important as visits of a more casual recreational type. This is substantially greater than the situation suggested by the surveys previously quoted.

Surveys of tourists consistently recorded even higher levels of interest in and visits to historic sites as part of their holiday activities. An early survey of visitors interviewed at five Scottish centres declared particularly high levels of interest in castles (Gore and Huggins, 1968). Between 60% and 80% of those interviewed indicated an interest in castles, which was only superceded by 'scenery' (91%-97%) out of a list of ten leisure based activities. Levels of actual visits, however, appear to be lower than these figures, although significantly higher than those noted in the earlier studies. For example, a recent study of 3221 holiday-makers to Wales (Marplan, 1984) demonstrated that 41% visited a castle, and for those who stayed longer than a week this rose to over 50%. In addition, 25% visited an industrial heritage attraction, 20% a religious site and 13% a historic house (Table 3.2). Again, these levels of visits are of a lower order than those associated with the more informal recreational venues such as seaside resorts (62%), countryside beauty spots (61%) and traditional towns and villages (44%). Nevertheless, visits to historic sites are obviously an important element of the holiday experience.

Table 3.2.
Attractions visited by holidaymakers to Wales by length of holiday

| | Length of stay: | | | | | |
|---|---|---|---|---|---|---|
| | Total | 1 night | 2-3 nights | 4-7 nights | 8-14 nights | 15+ nights |
| N = | 3221 % | 147 % | 880 % | 1586 % | 549 % | 55 % |
| **Attractions visited:** | | | | | | |
| Seaside resorts | 63 | 32 | 51 | 69 | 74 | 78 |
| Countryside beauty spots | 61 | 40 | 56 | 62 | 70 | 67 |
| Traditional towns and villages | 44 | 32 | 35 | 46 | 54 | 64 |
| Castles | 41 | 39 | 37 | 39 | 50 | 52 |
| Industrial sites, mines | 25 | 7 | 14 | 29 | 35 | 44 |
| Steam railways | 23 | 7 | 15 | 25 | 36 | 35 |
| Religious sites | 20 | 12 | 21 | 18 | 26 | 31 |
| Zoos, wildlife parks, nature reserves | 20 | 6 | 13 | 22 | 28 | 29 |
| Fun fairs, entertainment parks | 17 | 17 | 11 | 10 | 19 | 19 |
| Museums and galleries | 16 | 7 | 14 | 16 | 21 | 33 |
| Historic houses, stately homes | 13 | 2 | 12 | 13 | 19 | 31 |

Source: Marplan (1984), Table 12, p. 15.

These are not isolated results. Similar findings emerge
from a number of other studies undertaken in Wales and
throughout Britain. An investigation by the Wales Tourist
Board (1979) of their resort advertising campaign reported
remarkably similar results with 42% of respondents visiting
an historic building or monument compared with 74%
sightseeing and 70% sunbathing. Even 28% of those primarily
undertaking a seaside-based holiday at Rhyl were intending
visiting a castle or stately home, despite their strong
predisposition towards town-based entertainments such as
hotels and restaurants (92%), amusement arcades (83%) and
funfairs (76%) (Peat, Marwick, Mitchell, 1984). Similarly,
an earlier study of caravanners and campers in Northern
Ireland indicated that 31% had visited a historic site
compared with 66% taking part in casual walks and 62%
sightseeing (N.I.T.B., 1971). More recently, a survey of
the Northern Ireland holiday market reported rather lower
levels of visits to historic sites (N.I.T.B., 1980). Only
10% of holiday-makers visited a stately home and 8% a place
of historic interest, compared with 65% participating in
beach-based activities, 48% in country walks and 45%
picknicking. Visits to historic sites were clearly of
secondary significance to holiday-makers in Northern
Ireland, but were, nonetheless, the most popular of the
formal activities undertaken. A similar point emerged from
a visitor survey of the sixth century monastic site of
Clonmacnoise in Ireland. Kneale and Turbridge (1984) argued
that Clonmacnoise was not a specific destination for most of
its visitors but was rather a place to call at in a more
general recreational round.

By contrast, a survey of visitors to the Orkney Islands
reported that a substantial 88% of main holiday visitors and
75% of touring visitors had been to a site of historical or
archaeological interest. These figures compared favourably
with participation rates in informal sightseeing (91% and
87% respectively) (Orkney Islands Council, 1982).
Obviously, the nature of the leisure opportunities offered
by the Orkney Islands centres on the landscape and heritage.
Thus, it is not surprising that historic sites formed a
more substantial element of the holiday experience than
noted in the other cases.

Together, the evidence provided by these studies suggests
that the leisure and recreational behaviour of the
population in general, of day-trippers, and even of staying
holiday-makers is dominated by informal activities such as
drives through the countryside or to seaside resorts,
involving sightseeing, casual walks and picnics. For the
most part, people's ideas of leisure and recreation appear
to involve relaxation associated with the gentle stimuli of
attractive scenery, open space, peace and quiet, and the
opportunity to enjoy the outdoors in non-organised ways.
Nevertheless, there is sufficient evidence to suggest that
visits to specific attractions or 'managed sites' constitute
an important, albeit secondary, element of leisure
behaviour. Amongst such attractions visits to various kinds
of historic sites rank high. Either they serve the purpose
of occasionally offering a more specific destination in the

context of a general day-trip, or they provide an alternative, and usually subsidiary, recreational activity to those on holiday in their vicinity. In either event the role of such activities is of secondary recreational significance, but nevertheless appears to constitute an important element of leisure-based behaviour. The next section will examine whether the reasons expressed by visitors to historic sites for their visits reflects the apparently general recreational context of their visit, or whether the visit is fulfilling some other or additional purposes.


Historic sites: the reasons for visits

The analysis of the reasons or motivations for visits to historic sites is problematic. This reflects the considerable variability of research design adopted.
     Some investigations adopt an open-ended approach whereby visitors are asked to state their reasons for undertaking the visit. The responses are subsequently coded into a smaller number of appropriate summary categories. Others present respondents with a list of reasons derived intuitively . or with the aid of earlier studies, or via a pilot survey. The list is sometimes small so that the subtleties of the decision-making process may be lost. Frequently, the structured survey also offers the additional open-ended category of 'any other reason', while occasionally the respondent is asked to list their reasons in rank order. Further variability is introduced by the use of prompts in any of the types of survey mentioned.
     The inconsistency of survey design presents problems for the development of a strong synthesis of the behavioural motivations associated with visits to historic sites. Nevertheless, some recurrent themes emerge and the following discussion is offered as an exploratory review of this topic.
     An early study of visitors to three historic houses by the British Tourist Authority and Countryside Commission (1968) provides a base for the discussion. All visitors who had 'planned' their visit (85%) were asked to give their reasons, without prompting 'for coming here today'. Table 3.3 indicates the importance of broad recreational motivations. These are expressed in terms of a general interest or curiosity in old houses combined with a day out in pleasant surroundings. The study concluded that:

     .... the great majority of visitors to historic houses
     have few specific objectives in mind when planning their
     visit; they are mainly concerned with finding a
     destination for a 'recreation or holiday' trip. (p. 8).

The generality of visits clearly predominated, but a note of caution is appropriate on this point. For example, at Ragley Hall 14% of visitors expressed specifically historical reasons and 9% an interest in art and decor. Equivalent figures for Castle Howard were 10% and 6%

Table 3.3.
Reasons for visiting historic houses

| Reasons: | Ragley Hall (Warwickshire) 185 % | Castle Howard (Yorkshire) 127 % | Tatton Park (Chesire) 140 % |
|---|---|---|---|
| N = | 185 | 127 | 140 |
| | % | % | % |
| General interest in old houses | 27 | 14 | 12 |
| Curiosity and general interest | 22 | 22 | 26 |
| Nice day out | 20 | 19 | 28 |
| Location | 20 | 9 | 6 |
| Reputation | 15 | 12 | 21 |
| Brought friend/relative | 14 | 13 | 16 |
| Organised outing | 10 | 5 | 4 |
| Historical interest | 14 | 10 | 5 |
| Art and decor | 9 | 6 | 4 |
| Architectural interest | 3 | 2 | 1 |
| Scenic reasons | 7 | 4 | 10 |
| Gracious living | 3 | 0 | 1 |
| Seen advertisement | 6 | 7 | 7 |
| All others | 11 | 33 | 7 |

Source: B.T.A., Countryside Commission (1968), p.8.

respectively. While these figures were small, so too were all responses in an unstructured and unprompted survey of this kind. In fact, relative to the most commonly expressed reasons they were still secondary, but it may well be that, at least, general historical interests in the specific characteristics of a site were important to a significant proportion of visitors.

A series of surveys of visitors to the Natural History Section of the British Museum over the period 1976-81 yielded comparable findings. The primary importance of visiting the museum for general interest (28-40%) or 'to bring the children' (16-21%), relative to those who had come to 'see something specific' (8-14%) suggests a general educational or recreational motivation for the majority of visits and the secondary significance of more particular interests (Griggs and Alt, 1982-83).

Other evidence is available, however, which suggests that the particular characteristics of a site are a more important contributory reason for visits than emerges from the previous studies. A survey of visitors to Irish National Monuments (1974) again stressed the general recreational reasons for visits, with only around 10% citing the historical connotations of the site as the reason for a visit. However, the figures increased dramatically when prompts were used. In this situation as many as 55% stated that culture and heritage were very important for the enjoyment of a visit, and 39% placed art and architecture in that category. It is probable, therefore, that at least a general interest in history and culture contributed to the decision-making process. This contention is supported by the Glendalough visitor survey (1976), also from Ireland. The site is located in a scenically attractive area and includes historic monuments, lakes, nature trails, and walks through a wooded valley. The features which were considered particularly attractive by the vast majority of visitors (84%) were a combination of the scenery and landscape, while 35% also cited peace and quiet under this heading. Again these findings were indicative of the general recreational context of the visit. However, 21% of visitors also quoted the historical character of the site or its antiquity as features they particularly liked. In fact, 49% visited the main monument and 44% the round tower, which compared favourably with the other principal attractions of the upper lake (51%) and the picnic area (42%). The general historical character of the site was obviously of considerable significance to the decision to visit.

Similar evidence is provided by a recent investigation undertaken for English Heritage at a number of castles, abbeys, houses and monuments (PAS,1985). In this study 54% of visitors expressed a general sightseeing interest, but 40% also declared an interest in history and 10% a particular interest in the monuments (Table 3.4). The survey noted the importance of the recreational context of visits but also considered that visitors had a prior interest in either the historic buildings in general, or in the particular site.

70

Table 3.4.
Reasons for visiting fourteen historic sites

|  | visitors % |
|---|---|
| Reasons: |  |
| General interest/sightseeing | 54 |
| Interest in history/historical places | 40 |
| To bring family/friends/relatives/children | 13 |
| To see the house/building/abbey/castle | 10 |
| Just passing/en route | 8 |
| For a day out | 7 |
| On an organised tour | 5 |
| Recommended | 3 |
| Like the place/been before/often | 3 |
| Close to home/holiday location | 2 |
| To see gardens/scenery/grounds | 1 |
| Educational/academic reasons | 1 |

Source: P.A.S. (1985), p.18.


Evidence from a series of visitor surveys undertaken at a number of historic and other attractions by the Wales Tourist Board in the mid 1970s provides broadly consistent findings. Visitors were asked to indicate which of a list of reasons were important to their decision to visit. For Caernarfon Castle (Owens and Mears, 1974a), Chepstow Castle (Mears, 1976a) and St. Fagans Welsh Folk Museum (Owens and Mears, 1974b), the recreational reasons of 'general interest' and 'somewhere to go' on a day out were of considerable importance in each case (Table 3.5). These were associated with the subsidiary reasons of visiting somewhere 'to interest the children' or 'an alternative to the beach' in inclement weather. Again the central significance of the recreational context of the visits was confirmed. It is also notable that this array of reasons was not confined to historic sites but was even more marked at explicitly leisure facilities such as the Penscynor Bird Gardens near Neath (Mears, 1976b; Table 3.5), at the Dan-yr-Ogof caves in the Swansea Valley (Mears, 1976c); and, more recently, at the Liverpool Garden Festival (NOP, 1985).

For the three historic sites, however, a 'particular interest in the site' was the most important reason indicated for the visit. At Chepstow Castle, for example, this was by far the most important reason (47%), while a figure of 30% was recorded at Caernarfon Castle (Table 3.5). Likewise, 27% of visitors to St. Fagans cited an interest in folk museums and 19% an interest in Welsh history and life. Even at the explicitly recreational sites significant minorities of visitors indicated that a particular interest contributed to their decision to visit. At Penscynor Bird Gardens 10% recorded an interest in ornithology and 7% in animals, while caves and geology were of particular interest to similar numbers of visitors to Dan-yr-Ogof Caves.

Table 3.5.
Reasons for visiting historic sites and attractions in Wales

| Reasons: | Caernarfon Castle (1) % | Chepstow Castle (2) % | St. Fagans Folk Museum (3) % | Pensycynor Bird Gardens (4) % |
|---|---|---|---|---|
| Particular interest in site | 30 | 47 | 27 | 10 |
| General interest | 23 | 9 | 25 | 13 |
| In area/passing | 15 | 24 | - | 7 |
| Weather | 14 | 5 | 7 | 19 |
| Site specific reason | 10(a) | - | - | 7(b) |
| Interest Welsh history | 10 | 6 | 19 | - |
| Day out/somewhere to go | 9 | 15 | 25 | 39 |
| Somewhere to take children | 9 | 10 | 9 | 28 |
| Organised tour | 8 | 4 | 8 | 12 |
| Educational | - | 5 | 12 | 2 |
| Somewhere different | - | - | 5 | 9 |

Note: (a) Investiture;
      (b) Animals.

Sources: (1) Owens, Mears (1974a), Table 9, p. 13.
         (2) Mears (1976a), Table 9, p. 9.
         (3) Owens, Mears (1974b), Table 8, p. 12.
         (4) Mears (1976b), Table 8, p. 9.

Table 3.6.
Main reasons for visiting a museum or gallery in England

|  | All respond- ents 1347 % | At local authority sites 608 % | At national sites 739 % |
|---|---|---|---|
| N = | | | |
| Reasons: | | | |
| General interest/ sightseeing | 30 | 36 | 28 |
| Specific interest in item/ collection | 34 | 25 | 35 |
| Educational | 9 | 3 | 11 |
| Brought children | 14 | 21 | 13 |
| Special exhibition | 18 | 4 | 21 |
| Recommended | 2 | 10 | 1 |

N.B.: Columns can total >100% as some respondents gave more than one main reason for the visit.

Source: E.T.B. (1982).


Similarly, at Fota Island Wildlife Park in Ireland, 31% of visitors professed a particular interest in wildlife as a reason for their visit (Research Surveys of Ireland Ltd., 1983). Clearly, the 'particularities' of a site may well contribute more to the decision to visit historic and recreational sites than was suggested by the earlier literature, even if in a non-specialist manner.

The apparent increase in the importance of specific site characteristics as a factor influencing the decision to visit historic sites also emerges from surveys of other 'heritage'sites. An English Tourist Board investigation of 1347 visitors to fourteen museums and galleries indicated that 34% recorded a 'specific interest in an item or the collection' as the main reason for the visit, while 18% indicated that a 'special exhibition' had determined their visit (ETB, 1982). This supercedes the broader recreational reasons such as a 'general interest or sightseeing (30%). or for the benefit of 'the children' (14%) (Table 3.6). Similar findings were reported by the Wales Tourist Board for visitors to the Big Pit Mining Museum at Blaenafon in South Wales (WTB, 1984). This is a highly specific heritage attraction which takes suitably equipped visitors on a tour through abandoned coal workings, three hundred feet underground. A high percentage of visitors would obviously be expected to have an interest in the heritage of coal-mining. In fact, 41% of visitors spontaneously quoted the 'appeal of the coal mine' as the main reason for their visit, while the same percentage indicated a 'curiosity or general interest' in Big Pit as their prime motivation. Visitors were also presented with a prompt card and asked if any of six listed reasons contributed to their decision to visit Big Pit. The following results were obtained:

| Reason for visiting Big Pit (Prompted) | Visitors % |
|---|---|
| To see how coal is mined | 73 |
| To find out about Welsh history and life | 27 |
| Educational reasons | 27 |
| Interested in industrial archaeology | 15 |
| A place to take the children | 13 |
| Saw it in 'Have a fine day in Wales' leaflet | 1 |
| None of them | 2 |

Source: WTB, 1984.

Despite the limited array of reasons arbitrarily included in this list, it is interesting to note that the particularities of the site were important to the vast majority of visitors, and that the acquisition of heritage information looms large as a motivational factor.

The previous section concluded that recreational activities tend to be dominated by informal pursuits, frequently associated with a visit to the countryside. Visits to historic sites emerged as a secondary but important element of leisure behaviour which frequently provided a more specific focus in the context of casual countryside recreation. Consistent with these findings, the early studies of the reasons behind the decision to visit historic or heritage sites stressed the general recreational significance of the trip. A closer examination, however, of more recent evidence suggests that, at least, a general interest in history and culture may be equally as important a determinant of the decision to undertake a visit. There is also some evidence to suggest that a significant proportion of visitors actively pursue heritage information or education. Furthermore, for a minority of visitors the specific historical or cultural characteristics of sites appear central to their decision-making process. These conclusions will be examined in greater detail with respect to evidence provided by analyses undertaken by the authors for Cadw over the period 1985-87.

Cadw, Welsh Historic Monuments: visitor surveys 1985-86

An extensive survey of 2263 visitors to 10 Cadw sites comprising 7 castles, 2 abbeys and the Roman baths, amphitheatre and fort at Caerleon was undertaken during the Easter holiday period, 1986 (Seren, 1986a). This included investigations of the recreational context of the trips, the reasons and functions of the visits, as well as the expectations of, and reactions of the visitors to the experiences offered. This information provided additional insight into both the role of historic sites in leisure and recreational behaviour and the specific reasons for visits.


The role of the visit: other sites visited and activities undertaken by visitors to Cadw sites

At four sites respondents were presented with a comprehensive checklist of 19 activities which might also have been undertaken on the day of the interview. The question was designed to elicit the general characteristics of the leisure trip associated with a visit to an historic site. A total 1201 respondents generated 2545 additional activities or 2.12 per visitor. That is, the typical visitor to a Cadw site combined the visit with another two activities.

The most popular associated activity was a visit to a restaurant-cafe-pub (39%), followed by a visit to a nearby town (34%) and a drive through the surrounding countryside (30%) (Table 3.7). Of lesser but related significance were combined visits to a beach (16%) or associated with a country walk. Together, these figures suggest the majority of visits to historic sites are undertaken in the general recreational context of a day-trip, a notion which is lent further support by the wide array of other leisure activities visited by small percentages of respondents.

Notable linkages, however, were recorded with another castle or abbey (20%), while a further 11% reported a visit to another historic site. Clearly, a significant proportion of visitors to Cadw sites have more than a casual historical or heritage interest, and are likely to make this the basis of a day-trip.

An examination of the patterns of combined visits broken down for each of the four castles provides additional interesting information. While the typical visitor to a Cadw site characteristically combined the visit with two other activities, this generalisation obscures an important variation. For Castell Coch and Caerphilly Castle visitors generated only 1.30 and 1.76 additional activities respectively. This stands in marked contrast with the 2.77 and 2.71 additional activities undertaken by the visitors to Conwy and Harlech Castles. This reflects the stronger home-based day-trip context of the visits to the urban South Wales sites (62% and 52% respectively), compared with the predominantly 'tourist' visitor to the North Wales sites (78% and 93% respectively). The difference, however, is related to the more extensive general recreational activities of the holiday-maker, involving drives and walks in the surrounding countryside, visits to nearby towns, catering facilities and beaches (Table 3.7). In fact, the incidence of visits to additional historical or heritage sites is similar for visitors to both the North and South Wales sites.

Table 3.7.
Other sites visited or activites undertaken by visitors at Cadw sites, 1986

| | All sites 1201 % | Castell Coch 290 % | Caerphilly Castle 349 % | Conwy Castle 357 % | Harlech Castle 205 % |
|---|---|---|---|---|---|
| **Other sites or activities:** | | | | | |
| Restaurant/cafe/pub | 39 | 30 | 38 | 53 | 41 |
| Nearby town/shops | 34 | 21 | 23 | 52 | 49 |
| Drive, surrounding country | 31 | 20 | 32 | 35 | 46 |
| Another castle/abbey | 20 | 19 | 30 | 18 | 20 |
| Beach | 16 | 4 | 6 | 30 | 29 |
| Walk, surrounding country | 14 | 10 | 15 | 14 | 27 |
| Another historic site | 12 | 5 | 12 | 17 | 15 |
| Museum/art gallery | 6 | 4 | 7 | 7 | 5 |
| Gardens | 5 | 1 | 5 | 9 | 6 |
| Tourist railway | 5 | 1 | 3 | 4 | 15 |
| Waterfalls | 4 | 1 | 3 | 9 | 4 |
| Country park/centre | 4 | 4 | 6 | 3 | 4 |
| Funfair/amusement park | 3 | 2 | 3 | 7 | 1 |
| Caves | 3 | 1 | 2 | 3 | 9 |
| Industrial museum | 3 | 1 | 5 | 3 | 3 |
| Leisure centre | 2 | 2 | 4 | 4 | 0 |
| Swimming baths | 2 | 1 | 4 | 3 | 0 |
| Wildlife Park | 1 | 0 | 3 | 2 | 1 |
| Power station | 1 | 0 | 0 | 1 | 1 |
| Other | 6 | 5 | 6 | 6 | 6 |

Source: Seren (1986a), Table 15, p. 58.

Other noteworthy variations appear to reflect site specific considerations. The limited recreational appeal of the Caerphilly shopping centre and the presence of other historic sites in the general vicinity are reflected in lower levels of linkages with the local shops (22%) and a high level of linkages with other castles or abbeys (30%). By contrast, the location of Conwy Castle adjacent to an attractive historic town centre near to the coast has resulted in strong linkages with catering facilities (53%) and shops (51%), and to the nearby beaches (29%). Proximity to the recreational opportunities of the Conwy Valley is also reflected in visits to waterfalls (9%) and gardens (5%). A similar pattern is noted for Harlech Castle. Again, proximity to an attractive small town is reflected in strong associations with catering establishments and shops (41% annd 48% respectively). The coastal location and rural situation is further reflected in strong associations with visits to beaches (29%), country drives (46%) and walks (27%). Even more specifically, proximity to a tourist railway is also evident for this site (15%).

These variations serve to confirm the broad recreational role of most visits to historic sites, They also demonstrate the importance of the specific set of recreational opportunities available in the vicinity of the sites to the detailed nature of the linkages which develop.

The investigation of other activities undertaken by visitors to Cadw sites was repeated in the summer survey, 1986 (Seren, 1986c). All 1811 respondents at 8 sites were presented with a checklist of the 10 activities earlier identified as most likely to be linked with a visit to an historic site. Overall, the patterns of combined leisure activities were remarkably similar to those noted in the Easter survey, although the absolute levels were substantially higher. This reflects the greater importance of the holiday-maker in the summer survey. They are likely to have more time in the leisure area compared with the home-based day-tripper who forms a more substantial element of the Easter visitors. Also, the better weather and longer summer days serve to increase the level of combined leisure activities.

Again, the most popular activity associated with a visit to a Cadw site was a visit to a nearby town or shops (52%), closely followed by a refreshment stop (51%) and a drive or walk in the country (44%). Likewise, the next most significant linkage was with another historic site (35%), while a museum visit also recorded a 11% linkage. At a lower level a wide array of other leisure facilities such as a beach (13%), funfair (10%) and country park (7%) reasserts the importance of leisure activities. This evidence confirms the importance of the recreational role of a visit to a Cadw site, although an important minority of visitors appear to have more specifically historical interests which are liable to determine their pattern of leisure behaviour. Similarly, the evidence of the summer survey confirms that the detailed locational situation of each site has a significant effect on the particular combination of leisure activities undertaken by visitors.

77

The reasons for visits

The Easter visitor survey, 1986 included an extensive analysis of the reasons for visits (Seren, 1986a). Respondents were presented with a list of sixteen reasons and invited to indicate those they considered important to their decision to visit the site. The list was compiled from earlier investigations and from 1490 responses to an open-ended question included in an exploratory self-administered visitor survey undertaken by Cadw at Easter 1985 (Seren, 1986b).

The findings were broadly consistent with the analysis of reasons for visits to historic sites derived from the earlier literature (Table 3.8). Again, the recreational motives of a 'general interest' in the site (67%) and sightseeing (66%) emerged as the most important reasons for the visits. These, however, were closely followed by interests in castles (62%) and history (61%). Apparently, the historical connotations of the sites were nearly as important as the recreational opportunities that they offered.

A similar duality between the recreational and informational functions of visits recur throughout the lower levels of the table. A significant proportion of visitors indicate an educational interest (46%) and an interest in monuments (46%). These reasons are matched by the 42% indicating that a 'day out' was important to their decision. At even lower levels, an architectural (39%) or cultural (36%) interest is equalled by those simply undertaking a visit for a 'change' (39%) while child-related reasons (26% and 24%) are closely matched by those indicating an archaeological interest (26%). Finally, visits undertaken primarily for the benefit of friends or relatives were important for only a minority of visitors, and even fewer had been attracted to the sites by family origins or to revisit localities in which they had previously lived.

The fact that leisure orientated reasons are matched by more specific heritage interests throughout Table 3.8 tends to support the contention that visits are not exclusively recreational but incorporate a substantial, and near to equivalent, historical-educational dimension. The latter dimension, however, probably comprises general rather than specialist heritage interests since the increasingly specific site characteristics are noted as important by progressively smaller percentages of respondents. It is, nevertheless, apparent that a significant minority of visitors are motivated by a particular interest in the historical or heritage characteristics of the sites.


Variations by survey site, social class, holiday status, age, and season

The general pattern of responses noted above are repeated broadly for each of the 10 survey sites, although subtle variations are apparent. Some are worthy of additional consideration (Table 3.8). For example, a distinct north-

Table 3.8.
Reasons for visiting historic sites in Wales, Easter 1986

Key:
Tint = Tintern Abbey
Coch = Castell Coch
Clly = Caerphilly Castle
Kidw = Kidwelly Castle
Carl = Caerleon Fort and Amphitheatre

Vall = Valle Crucis Abbey
Conw = Conwy Castle
Harl = Harlech Castle
Cric = Criccieth Castle
Cfon = Caernarfon Castle

| | All sites | Tint | Coch | Clly | Kidw | Carl | Vall | Conw | Harl | Cric | Cfon |
|---|---|---|---|---|---|---|---|---|---|---|---|
| N = | 2263 | 273 | 290 | 349 | 120 | 181 | 111 | 357 | 205 | 166 | 211 |
| | % | % | % | % | % | % | % | % | % | % | % |
| **Reasons rated very important or important:** | | | | | | | | | | | |
| General interest | 67 | 54 | 69 | 58 | 72 | 65 | 64 | 72 | 93 | 63 | 63 |
| Enjoy sightseeing | 66 | 58 | 53 | 65 | 61 | 64 | 66 | 74 | 85 | 71 | 64 |
| Interest in castles/abbeys | 62 | 52 | 61 | 67 | 78 | 55 | 74 | 62 | 68 | 61 | 56 |
| Historical interest | 61 | 57 | 52 | 60 | 73 | 69 | 71 | 66 | 67 | 57 | 53 |
| Educational interest | 46 | 40 | 34 | 45 | 55 | 53 | 51 | 51 | 54 | 42 | 50 |
| Ancient monuments interest | 46 | 45 | 25 | 44 | 44 | 54 | 62 | 52 | 54 | 50 | 47 |
| Day out in the country | 43 | 48 | 53 | 32 | 62 | 30 | 58 | 40 | 47 | 34 | 38 |
| Change of scene | 39 | 37 | 43 | 34 | 42 | 35 | 41 | 49 | 29 | 36 | 44 |
| Architectural interest | 39 | 43 | 32 | 38 | 40 | 44 | 61 | 41 | 28 | 37 | 41 |
| Interest Welsh culture/history | 36 | 24 | 28 | 39 | 38 | 40 | 42 | 38 | 43 | 37 | 38 |
| Child request | 26 | 7 | 36 | 31 | 39 | 19 | 11 | 34 | 32 | 23 | 24 |
| Archaeological interest | 26 | 26 | 17 | 25 | 30 | 45 | 37 | 29 | 17 | 25 | 23 |
| To take children | 24 | 10 | 39 | 28 | 32 | 18 | 13 | 22 | 32 | 20 | 24 |
| Brought relatives/friends | 18 | 19 | 27 | 23 | 19 | 21 | 15 | 10 | 10 | 10 | 16 |
| Visit area family origins | 6 | 3 | 4 | 7 | 7 | 8 | 7 | 5 | 5 | 10 | 7 |
| Revisit home area | 5 | 3 | 8 | 7 | 7 | 7 | 8 | 3 | 4 | 7 | 3 |

Source: Seren (1986a), Table 12, P. 54.

south dimension emerges. Higher percentages of visitors to the North Wales sites indicated 'general' and 'sightseeing' interests for their visits. This reached a high for Harlech Castle where 93% recorded 'general interest' and 85% 'sightseeing'. These figures were substantially greater than the 54% of visitors to Tintern Abbey indicating 'general interest' and the 53% at Castell Coch recording 'sightseeing'. These variations reflect differences in visitor types. The great majority of visitors to the North Wales sites are on holiday away from home (Harlech Castle, 93%), while the figures at Easter for the South Wales sites are substantially lower at around 50% (Seren, 1986a). Conversely, substantially more of the visitors to the South Wales sites are home-based day-trippers. The visitors to the North Wales sites are probably more prone to indicate a general interest and sightseeing as a reason for their visit since it is undertaken in the context of a staying-holiday. This is not necessarily the case for the day-tripper for whom the particular purpose of the trip is likely to loom larger.

Interestingly, the same north-south pattern is not apparent for the similarly ranked, but more specific reasons, associated with an interest in castles or history. Variations exist but they are of a lower order and probably reflect the impact of the particular attractions of the individual sites. The apparent domination of trip motivations by general recreational reasons in holiday areas like North Wales may well have more to do with the context of the trip than with the reasons for it.

Other noteworthy variations by site are apparent for both the child-related reasons. In general, children are more likely to be involved in the initiation of a visit to a castle than to either the Roman site or an abbey. As many as 30% of respondents at Kidwelly Castle indicated that the reason for their visit was at the request of a child. By contrast, as few as 7% at Tintern Abbey indicated this reason, while for Valle Crucis Abbey and the Roman site at Caerleon the equivalent figures were 11% and 19% respectively. In fact, visitor groups which include a child are more likely to visit a castle (ranging from 60%-33% across the eight sites) than an abbey (Tintern 28%, Valle Crucis 22%). (Seren, 1986a). Apparently, the appeal of a castle is a more potent influence on the trip motivations of family groups than are the other types of heritage sites.

Finally, it is interesting to note that an interest in archaeology is indicated by a disproportionately high percentage of visitors to the Roman baths, fort and amphitheatre at Caerleon (45%) and Valle Crucis Abbey (37%). Both these sites offer substantial elements of specifically archaeological interest. This is particularly marked at Caerleon where the Roman baths is presented as a sophisticated archaeological exhibition. This lends further support to the contention that a significant minority of visitors to heritage sites are motivated by a special interest in the particular characteristics of sites.

An analysis of the relationship between the social status of visitors and the reasons for their visits also proved

Table 3.9.
Reasons for visiting historic sites in Wales: Easter 1986: by social class

| | All respondents | A | B | C1 | C2 | D |
|---|---|---|---|---|---|---|
| N = | 2263 % | 568 % | 691 % | 304 % | 294 % | 96 % |
| **Reasons noted very important or important:** | | | | | | |
| General interest | 67 | 67 | 73 | 69 | 68 | 53 |
| Enjoy sightseeing | 66 | 69 | 68 | 70 | 65 | 60 |
| Interest in castles/abbeys | 62 | 66 | 69 | 63 | 60 | 61 |
| Historical interest | 61 | 65 | 70 | 60 | 54 | 49 |
| Educational interest | 46 | 50 | 54 | 45 | 42 | 36 |
| Ancient monuments interest | 46 | 52 | 53 | 48 | 37 | 31 |
| Day out in country | 43 | 43 | 41 | 46 | 49 | 53 |
| Change of scene | 39 | 38 | 41 | 41 | 40 | 45 |
| Architectural interest | 39 | 44 | 45 | 35 | 31 | 24 |
| Interest Welsh culture/history | 36 | 41 | 40 | 36 | 31 | 21 |
| Child request | 26 | 29 | 28 | 29 | 26 | 36 |
| Archaeological interest | 26 | 29 | 31 | 24 | 22 | 11 |
| To take children | 24 | 27 | 24 | 28 | 25 | 31 |

Source: Seren (1986a), (unpublished table).

Table 3.10.
Reasons for visiting historic sites in Wales, Easter 1986: by holiday status

| Reasons noted very important or important: | All respond-ents 2263 % | Holiday away from home 1474 % | Holiday at home 408 % | Not on holiday 361 % |
|---|---|---|---|---|
| General interest | 67 | 70 | 65 | 56 |
| Enjoy sightseeing | 66 | 71 | 60 | 52 |
| Interest in castles/abbeys | 62 | 65 | 62 | 55 |
| Historical interest | 61 | 65 | 60 | 48 |
| Educational interest | 46 | 50 | 45 | 34 |
| Ancient monuments interest | 46 | 50 | 47 | 30 |
| Day out in country | 43 | 41 | 47 | 46 |
| Change of scene | 39 | 38 | 44 | 41 |
| Architectural interest | 39 | 42 | 40 | 29 |
| Interest Welsh culture/history | 36 | 38 | 38 | 28 |
| Child request | 26 | 24 | 32 | 29 |
| Archaeological interest | 26 | 28 | 26 | 21 |
| To take children | 24 | 22 | 30 | 27 |

Source: Seren (1986a), (unpublished table).

82

instructive.    In   general,    the visits of the higher status
respondents   were   more   strongly related   to   the   specific
historical, heritage and educational reasons than were those
of the lower status groups (Table 3.9).   The extent to which
an   interest   in Welsh culture   and   history,   for   example,
influenced    the    visit   ranged   from   41%   for    class    A
(professional   occupations)   to only 21% for category D (semi
and   unskilled   occupations).    Equivalent   ranges   for    an
interest in ancient monuments were from 52% to 31%,   and for
an   architectural   interest from 44%   to   24%.    Conversely,
category   D   respondents recorded   the   highest   percentages
rating   a   'day   out' and a 'change of scene'   as   important
reasons for their visit,   although the differentials are not
as   great.    Apparently,   specific historical   and   heritage
interests were much more likely to attract visitors from the
upper   status groups,   while the recreational aspects of the
sites   has   a   slightly greater appeal for the   lower   status
groups.
Marked   variations   also   reflect   the   holiday   status   of
visitors (Table 3.10).   For all the more specific historical
and   heritage   reasons,   and for most   of   the   recreational
reasons,   those on holiday away from home are most likely to
signify   their   importance to the decision to visit a   site.
Home-based holiday-makers are rather less likely to indicate
the   importance of this wide array of reasons,   while   those
not   on   holiday recorded   even   lower   figures.    The
differentials   are of the order of 15%-20%.   This   probably
reflects the more 'purposeful' behaviour of those on holiday
compared   with the day-tripper,   amongst whom   the   'casual'
visitor is more likely to be represented.   The exceptions to
the   general pattern tend to confirm this   conclusion.    For
example,   those not on holiday are marginally more likely to
have been looking for a 'change of scene', a 'day out in the
country', or something to 'interest the children'.
The   reasons for visits do not vary markedly by the age of
visitor,   although   a number of exceptions   occur.    Teenage
visitors are less motivated by interests in castles,   abbeys
and history.    For example,   only 46% recorded an interest in
castles   and   abbeys compared with   the   average 62%.    A
similar,   but   less   marked tendency was also   apparent   for
interests in education and ancient monuments.   There is   no
obvious explanation for these findings.   Speculatively,   it
may   well be that this age-group is motivated by more active
leisure   pursuits than those currently offered   at   historic
sites.
Not   surprisingly,   the   30-49 year olds   recorded   higher
responses   for the two child related reasons.   This   simply
reflects   the   greater liklihood of their having a child   of
school   age.    Finally,   the   20-39   year olds   tend   to   be
motivated   marginally   more   by general   interests   and
sightseeing,   as well as by educational interests,   ancient
monuments   and   a day out in the country compared with   the
average visitor.   No obvious explanation,   however,   can be
offered for this finding.   It may well simply reflect a more
assertive manner by this age-group.
Supplementary   information   relating   to   the   reasons   for
visiting   Cadw   sites   is   available   from   three   surveys

83

Table 3.11.
Reasons for visiting historic sites in Wales, Summer 1986

| Reasons: | General Survey | Pricing Survey | Interpretation Survey |
|---|---|---|---|
| N = | 1811 | 961 | 913 |
| | % | % | % |
| Interest in castles/historic sites | 62 | 51 | 74 |
| Enjoy sightseeing/general interest | 48 | 49 | 54 |
| Brought children/wanted to come | 19 | 15 | 14 |
| Interest in Welsh culture | 18 | 18 | 26 |
| Day out in the country | 14 | 10 | 26 |
| Unable to go where originally planned | 6 | 4 | 1 |

Sources: Seren (1986c), p. 20; Seren (1986d), p. 12; Seren (1986e), p. 58.

Table 3.12.
Main purpose of visits to Cadw sites, 1986

| Reasons: | All sites | Tintern Abbey | Caerphilly Castle | Chepstow Castle | Caerleon sites | Caernarfon Castle | Conwy Castle |
|---|---|---|---|---|---|---|---|
| N = | 913 | 153 | 152 | 144 | 85 | 184 | 195 |
| | % | % | % | % | % | % | % |
| To relax | 20 | 19 | 24 | 31 | 11 | 13 | 20 |
| To be entertained | 14 | 10 | 18 | 11 | 11 | 17 | 15 |
| To be informed | 45 | 51 | 40 | 44 | 67 | 42 | 39 |
| To be educated | 17 | 18 | 16 | 13 | 9 | 19 | 19 |
| Don't know | 4 | 3 | 1 | 1 | 2 | 8 | 7 |

Source: Seren (1986e), Table 13, p. 58.

undertaken over the summer holiday period 1986. These comprise a general visitor survey broadly comparable with the Easter survey and undertaken at eight sites (Seren, 1986c). In addition, more specific surveys of Pricing Policy and Visitor Satisfaction were undertaken at six sites (Seren, 1986d), and of Interpretation facilities at six sites (Seren, 1986e). Each of these provides some additional insight into the reasons for visits at the height of the holiday season. The summer surveys, however, were not undertaken primarily to investigate the reasons for visits. A shortened checklist of six of the main motivational influences distilled from the Easter survey were, therefore, used for reasons of economy. Consequently, the results are not strictly comparable with the earlier survey, although a number of points of interest emerge (Table 3.11).

Again, two types of reasons dominated the decision-making process; an interest in castles or historic sites; and to enjoy sightseeing or a general interest. This situation is broadly consistent with the more detailed results from the Easter survey, except that the specific heritage interests are marginally of greater significance than the general recreational interests. The evidence on this point is, however, not entirely unambiguous, since the enjoyment of sightseeing and general interest (49%) was quoted as of similar importance to the heritage reasons (51%) by respondents in the Pricing and Visitor Satisfaction Survey (Table 3.12). The inconsistency may reflect an over-rigorous curtailment of the original checklist of reasons, combined with the prominent position given to an 'interest in castles and historic sites' on the questionnaire schedule. The evidence of the summer surveys are, consequently, best interpreted as confirming the dual importance of the general recreational and specific historical reasons for the decision to visit historic sites in Wales.

The array of secondary reasons are also broadly similar to those illustrated in the Easter survey and similarly incorporate the duality of the general recreational and specific heritage interests of the visitors. Similar prominence is given, for example, to those enjoying a 'day out' in the country and child centred resons as to those claiming an interest in Welsh culture and history (Table 3.11).

Finally, it is worthy of note that the variations in the importance of the reasons for visits expressed at the different sites and by the various social groups evident from the Easter survey were broadly confirmed by evidence provided in the General Survey of Summer Visitors (Seren, 1986c).


The functions of the visit

Other information available from the Cadw survey data allows the investigation of the reasons for visits to be pursued further. The survey of the impact of interpretative facilities included a question designed to assess the main purpose or function which the visit fulfilled. (Seren, 1986e). Respondents were asked which of four reasons they considered the most important feature of their visit (Table 3.12). Most support was provided for the statement which suggested that visitors came to be informed. This was consistent across all six survey sites and averaged 45%. A further 17% stated that they came 'to be educated'. Thus, 62% expressed more than a casual recreational attitude to their visit. This is consistent with the apparently increasing numbers who recorded specific heritage interests as reasons for their visits to historic monuments and suggests that visitors are demanding more from their experience then a casual walk around a pleasant site. The relaxation and entertainment facilities are clearly of secondary significance to visitors, although the caveat must be expressed that these functions are not necessarily as separate as is suggested by this type of analysis. The informational and educational facilities may well be part of, or contribute to, both relaxation and entertainment. Nevertheless, the importance of increasingly 'purposeful' visits to historic sites appears to be confirmed by these findings.

Additional support for this contention is provided by the particularly high percentage of visitors to Caerleon indicating that they had primarily come to be informed (67%). This is explained by the character of the site, the central feature of which is the archaeological exhibition at the Roman baths. The nature of the site has the effect of attracting a higher than average proportion of visitors seeking an educational experience. This also serves to underline the fact that from the visitor perspective not all historical monuments are perceived as offering the same experience.

Like the reasons expressed for visiting historic sites, the main experiences sought by visitors also varied according to their social characteristics. The most marked variations were again associated with social status (Table 3.13). The lower status C2 and D respondents were much more likely to have been attracted for relaxation and entertainment than to be informed, although this was partly compensated by higher percentages of these visitors claiming an educational purpose for their trip. By contrast, the professional AB and skilled non-manual respondents (C1) were significantly more likely to record an informational purpose for their visit.

Similar variations were also associated with the holiday status of respondents. In this case the home-based day-tripper was more likely to have been attracted by relaxation and less likely to have indicated an informational reason compared with the staying holiday-maker, the differential being 13% in each case.

Variations also reflected the age of visitors. The teenage group again demonstrated the greatest deviation form the norm. A far higher than average percentage were seeking entertainment, (40%), while information (23%) and education (10%) were of only secondary significance for this group.

Table 3.13.
Main purpose of visits to Cadw sites, 1986: by social class

|  | All respondents | A | B | C1 | C2 | D |
|---|---|---|---|---|---|---|
| N = | 913 | 146 | 319 | 91 | 198 | 63 |
|  | % | % | % | % | % | % |
| Reasons: |  |  |  |  |  |  |
| To relax | 20 | 17 | 19 | 21 | 23 | 27 |
| To be entertained | 14 | 10 | 12 | 13 | 20 | 16 |
| To be informed | 45 | 55 | 50 | 51 | 34 | 30 |
| To be educated | 17 | 13 | 17 | 13 | 21 | 22 |
| Don't know | 4 | 5 | 3 | 2 | 2 | 5 |

Source: Seren (1986e), (unpublished table).


Table 3.14
Reactions of visitors to Cadw sites, 1986

|  |  |
|---|---|
| N = | 2263 |
|  | % |
| Agree or strongly agree with statement: |  |
| Really enjoyed the visit | 89 |
| Information displays helpful | 67 |
| Probably visit another castle or abbey soon | 67 |
| Pay more if short guide booklet included | 56 |
| Enough to interest children | 34 |
| Entrance fee too high | 27 |
| Staff could be more helpful | 6 |
| Guided tour would increase enjoyment | 42 |
| Cafeteria - restaurant would increase enjoyment | 38 |
| Souvenir shop added to interest | 35 |

Source: Seren (1986a), Table 14, p. 56.

It is also interesting to note that the older the visitor the more likely were they to have been attracted by the informational function. This ranged from 23% for the 15-19 year olds to 59% for those over 60 years.

## The reactions to visits: visitor satisfaction

The reactions of respondents to the main elements of their visit provides a useful indication of the level of visitor satisfaction with the experience offered. Such information also provides insight into unfulfilled expectations of, or latent reasons for visits, both of which are likely to have an important bearing on management or developmental proposals designed to enhance visitor experience or increase visitor numbers.

Visitor responses to 10 attitude statements relating to the main aspects of the visit were included in the 1986 Easter Survey (Seren, 1986a) (Table 3.14). The vast majority of respondents agreed that they had 'really enjoyed the visit' (89%). Furthermore, a substantial majority found the information displayed at the sites added to the enjoyment of the visit (67%), while the same proportion expressed the view that they would probably visit another castle or abbey in the near future. Similarly positive attitudes to visits were reflected in a relatively high level of willingness to pay more if a short guide booklet were included in the entrance fee (56%), in the low level of agreement that the entrance fee was too high (27%), and in low level of dissatisfaction with the site staff (6%). Likewise, the similarity in the proportion of parties including a school-age child (41%) and those agreeing that there was enough to interest the children suggests that the youthful visitor is being adequately served. Taken together these facts suggest that the experiences offered at the 10 sites were broadly fulfilling current visitor expectations.

On a less positive note, however, a substantial minority of visitors (42%) expressed the view that a guided tour would have been a beneficial addition to the facilities offered. Similarly, 38% agreed that a cafeteria or restaurant would have added to their enjoyment, while only 35% considered that the souvenir shop contributed to their interest. At first sight it might be concluded from these facts that the addition of guided tours, catering facilities and improved souvenir shops would significantly enhance visitor satisfaction and strengthen the attraction of the sites. This, however, is not necessarily the case since comparable numbers of respondents disagreed with the need for improved facilities of these kinds on the grounds that they would detract from the historical authenticity of the sites. The division between visitors seeking an undeveloped heritage experience and those requiring enhanced recreational facilities constitutes a major problem for the formulation of strategies designed to increase visitor numbers. On the one hand there appears to be a need to offer more recreational facilities to increase the attractions of historic sites for one section of the community. Such demands will doubtless increase as visitors experience the wide range of recreational facilities offered at some of the more commercially orientated heritage sites. Alternatively, other visitors are primarily concerned with site conservation.

The conflict could be resolved in a number of different ways. New developments, for example, could be undertaken with due regard to the sensitivity of the characteristics of the site. On the other hand, recreational facilities might be channelled to a limited number of the least environmentally sensitive sites which also offer opportunities for commercial development. This issue is obviously of central concern for the development and marketing of heritage sites. Suffice it to say at this point that a significant element of visitor opinion is in favour of the provision of additional recreational facilities at historic sites.

Further analyses of the relationship between visitor characteristics and the pattern of responses noted above are also of interest since they tend to strengthen the conclusions of the equivalent analysis of the reasons for visits. Both the skilled manual (C2) and the semi-skilled and unskilled respondents (D), for example, expressed higher than average support for the provision of a short guide booklet (67% and 72% respectively), and for the provision of catering facilities (49% and 48%). This suggests the need to modify developmental policies in order to appeal more strongly to potential visitors from the lower status groups. On a similar issue, significantly higher percentages of the home-based visitors, and particularly day-trippers not on holiday, were in favour of the more recreational types of development such as catering facilities, guided tours, souvenir shops and facilities for children. The differentials were, however, of a relatively low order (circa 7%). Finally, the analysis of age variations revealed lower levels of satisfaction by teenage visitors. 78% agreed that they had really enjoyed the visit and a bare majority (53%) that they would visit another site soon. Again, those most likely to have a school-age child were most likely to agree that there was enough to interest the children.

Evidently, current visitor expectations appear to be largely fulfilled by the experiences offered at Cadw sites. There is, however, some evidence of a latent demand for enhanced recreational facilities if the sites are to attract a broader social spectrum of visitors. Dichotomous attitudes on this issue, however, suggest the need for caution if new developments are not to deter the current enthusiasts.


Conclusions

The evidence reviewed in this chapter suggests that the recreational and leisure activities of the great majority of people are dominated by informal pursuits undertaken in the context of trips to the countryside or to small country towns. the most common activities involve sightseeing, casual walks and picnics, all of which offer relaxation and the opportunity to enjoy the scenery and the outdoors in a leisurely and undemanding manner. Recent evidence, however, suggests that visits to particular attractions or 'managed sites' are becoming an increasingly important aspect of leisure behaviour. People appear to be becoming more 'purposeful' in the sense that they may be seeking to be informed or educated, even if in a rather general manner. Consequently, visits to historic and heritage sites rank high amongst the range of potential recreational destinations. They appear to serve the purpose of occasionally providing something of more specific interest to enhance a general leisure trip. For a significant minority, however, a visit to a historic site will form the basis of their leisure behaviour.

Early analyses of the reasons for visiting historic sites stressed the central importance of recreational motives. Recently, however, more detailed investigations conclude that interests in history and culture at the level of the informed layman are at least equally important determinants of the decision to visit a historic or heritage site. Furthermore, for a significant minority of visitors the pursuit of heritage information and education are primary motivating factors. When subject to detailed scrutiny the importance of 'purposeful' visits to historic sites compared with casual leisure motives becomes increasingly evident.

These generalisations, however, reflect current visitor profiles which are dominated by the higher status groups. The visitor survey data obtained from Cadw sites offered the opportunity to undertake additional analyses of visitor motivations relative to their social characteristics. This provided further insight into the reasons for visits, some of which have implications for development and marketing policies for historic sites.

It was, for example, evident that the particular historical and heritage characteristics of sites had greater appeal for the higher status visitors, while the lower status groups were motivated more by general recreational objectives. This feature was also reflected in the reactions of visitors to their experience. Overall, there was a high level of visitor satisfaction, but the lower status respondents were more likely to suggest the need for more recreational facilities such as cafeterias, souvenir shops and guided tours. Similar differences were noted between the staying holiday-makers whose interests were more likely to be historical, compared with the home-based day-tripper for whom the recreational aspects of the visit loomed larger. These findings suggest that site development policy should incorporate a stronger recreational dimension in those locations most likely to attract the lower status day-tripper. Caution, however, was suggested on this issue since it was equally evident that such policies might have a negative effect on the currently dominant visitor types.

Variations were also associated with the ages of visitors. Castles, for instance had a substantially greater appeal for family groups compared with abbeys and museums. This was related to the interests of the children and is indicative of the emotional appeal of the castle for the youngest visitors. For teenagers, however, there was less interest in the historical and heritage aspects of sites. Instead, they appeared to require a stronger 'entertainment' dimension to enhance their visit.

Together, these variations demonstrate that current and potential visitors to historic sites do not constitute an undifferentiated group. It follows that an awareness of market segmentation considerations should be incorporated into management, development and marketing policies for historic sites.


References

Bord Failte (Research Section) (1974). National monuments survey. Dublin: Bord Failte.

Bord Failte (1976). Report on a survey of Glendalough 1976. Dublin: Bord Failte.

British Tourist Authority and the Countryside Commission (1968). Historic houses survey. London: British Tourist Authority.

Countryside Commission for Scotland (1985). Patterns of countryside recreation trips. Scottish Leisure Survey Report No. 4. Perth: Countryside Commision for Scotland.

English Tourist Board Market Research Department and NOP Market Research Ltd (1982). Visitors to museums survey of 1982. Survey of 14 museums and galleries. London: English Tourist Board.

Fitton, M. (1979). Countryside recreation - the problems of opportunity. Local Government Studies, July/August 1979, 5, 4. pp. 61-89.

Gore, C. and Huggins, M. (1968). Landmark. A survey covering various aspects of interpretive centres. Edinburgh: Gore-Huggins Consultants.

Griggs, S. A., and Alt, M. B. (1982-83). Visitors to the British Museum (Natural History) in 1980 and 1981. Museums Journal, 82, pp. 149-155.

Kneale, P. E. and Turbridge, M. C. (1984). Creation and management of a heritage zone at Clonmacnoise, County Offaly, Ireland. A visitor survey report. Dublin: Environmental Sciences Unit, Trinity College.

Mackenzie, S. (1985). Recreation and holidays in the countryside. Scottish Leisure Survey report no. 1. Perth: Countryside Commission for Scotland.

Marplan Ltd. (1984). A survey of non-business visitors to Wales, 1984. (And 3 appendix volumes). London: Marplan.

Mears, W. (1976a). Survey of visitors to tourist attractions 1974. Report 6. Chepstow Castle. Cardiff: Wales Tourist Board.

Mears, W. (1976b). Surveys of visitors to tourist attractions 1974. Report 8. Penscynor Bird Gardens. Cardiff: Wales Tourist Board.

Mears, W. (1976c). Survey of visitors to tourist attractions 1974. Report 7. Dan yr Ogof Caves. Cardiff: Wales Tourist Board.

NOP Market Research Ltd. (1985). Survey of visitors to the Liverpool Garden Festival 1984. Final Report. (Prepared for the Department of the Environment). (NOP/3553). London: NOP Market Research Ltd.

Northern Ireland Tourist Board (1971). Caravan and camping holidays in Northern Ireland, 1970. Belfast: Northern Ireland Tourist Board.

Northern Ireland Tourist Board (1980). Holiday market in Northern Ireland 1979. Belfast: Northern Ireland Tourist Board.

Orkney Islands Council (1982). Orkney tourist survey, 1981. Kirkwall, Orkney: Department of Physical Planning and Development.

Owen, E. and Mears, W. (1974a). Survey of visitors to tourist attractions 1973. Report 3. Caernarfon Castle. Cardiff: Wales Tourist Board.

Owen, E. and Mears, W. (1974b). Surveys of visitors to tourist attractions 1973. Report 5. Welsh Folk Museum, St. Fagans. Cardiff: Wales Tourist Board.

Peat, Marwick, Mitchell and Co. (1984). Rhyl resort area tourism study. Revised July 1984. Cardiff, Wales Tourist Board.

Phillips, A. and Worth, J. (1985). Developing a strategy for leisure in the countryside. Proceedings of the Institute of Leisure and Amenity Management, Conference, 11 June 1985. Institute of Leisure and Amenity Management.

Public Attitude Surveys Research Ltd (1985). Historic buildings survey 1984. Volume 1 - questions (core) raised at all sites. (PAS 11195). (Prepared for English Heritage). High Wycombe, Bucks: Public Attitude Surveys Research Ltd.

Research Surveys of Ireland Ltd. (1983). Bord Failte - Fota Island study. Dublin: Research Surveys of Ireland Ltd.

Seren (1986a). Herbert, D. T., Prentice, R. C., Thomas, C. J., Edwards, J. A., Humphrys, G., Prentice, M. M.. Easter 1986 visitor survey. Final report. Swansea: Social Economic Research and Environment, Department of Geography, University College of Swansea.

Seren (1986b). Herbert, D. T., Thomas, C. J. Visitor survey report. Easter 1985. Swansea: Social Economic Research and Environment, Department of Geography, University College of Swansea.

Seren (1986c). Herbert, D. T., Prentice, R. C., Thomas, C. J., Prentice, M. M. General survey at Cadw sites. Summer 1986. Swansea: Social Economic Research and Environment, Department of Geography, University College of Swansea.

Seren (1986d). Herbert, D. T., Prentice, R. C., Thomas, C. J., Prentice, M. M. Pricing policy and visitor satisfaction at Cadw's sites. Swansea: Social Economic Research and Environment, Department of Geography, University College of Swansea.

Seren (1986e). Herbert, D. T., Thomas, C. J., Prentice, R. C., Prentice, M. M. Interpretation at Cadw's sites. Swansea: Social Economic Research and Environment, Department of Geography, University College of Swansea.

Wales Tourist Board (Strategic Planning and Research Unit) (1979). Resort advertising campaign 1979. Cardiff: Wales Tourist Board.
Wales Tourist Board (1984). Survey of visitors to the Big Pit mining museum, Blaenafon, 1983. Cardiff: Wales Tourist Board.

# 4 Marketing and advertising: the contribution and effectiveness of the media

COLIN J THOMAS

Marketing and consumer behaviour

A knowledge of the roles that historic sites play in leisure and recreational activities, as well as the more particular reasons for visits, is obviously essential information for those responsible for the development of sound strategies designed either to maintain or to enhance visitor numbers. Equally important, however, are the insights which can be obtained from the marketing literature generally, and more specifically from studies relating to advertising.

The extensive literature on marketing, consumer behaviour and the media is substantially orienated towards the choice and purchase of products in the commercial context. Only to a lesser extent does it cover consumption in the more general sense to include services such as leisure, and cultural and educational facilities. Also, the emphasis of the existing literature focuses upon the decision to purchase in an aspatial context rather than on decisions which concern the spatial behaviour (journeys) of individuals and groups to a limited number of specific sites.

For both these reasons much of the literature on marketing, consumer behaviour and the media has only oblique relevance to the marketing of historic sites. Nevertheless, some potentially useful insights can be obtained, the implications of which are at least of preliminary interest for marketing strategies for historic sites.

At the most general level a basic model of 'The Buying Process' (Consumption Process) is widely recognised (Foxall, 1977):

(i)     development and perception of a want or need;
(ii)    pre-purchase planning and decision-making;
(iii)   the purchase act;
(iv)    post-purchase reaction and evaluation;
(v)     repeat buying.

Promotional activities in the media are important at stages i-iii to initiate service utilisation behaviour, i.e. undertaking the leisure trip; while at stages iv-v investigations and analysis are vital to maintain and develop the initial impetus. In effect, the model stresses the importance of effective information at the early stages and the importance of a feedback mechanism to sustain or improve performance.


## Advertising effectiveness

Advertising in the U.K. appears to be generally acceptable to the public. An investigation of public attitudes to advertising by Wolfe (1983) reported that between 1968 and 1980 there was a positive shift from 68% to 77% of the population approving generally, while those who disapproved of advertising fell from 25% to 16%. More specific questions relating to newspapers and magazines and television were less approving with comparable figures of 41% to 47% and 33% to 50%, but again critics tended to be a minority of 10% and 15% respectively. On the question of advertising effectiveness a number of specific issues are of central importance. These include consumer sovereignty, selective perception, social status, unpredictability, learning cycle and reinforcement, emotional appeal, and cultural distinctiveness.
The issue of consumer sovereignty appears to achieve primary significance, i.e. the need to provide the consumer with a product which satisfies a demand, rather than to depend upon manipulative or persuasive advertising. Foxall (1977), for example, reports that 75% of food products fail at the stage of customer acceptance and for many other product ranges the figures for failures are even higher. The Nielsen Researcher (1973) reported that 67% of product failures related to the nature of the product and a further 30% to a combination of trade non-acceptance and pricing mistakes, irrespective of the volume of advertising. Similarly, Achenbaum's (1972) study of the effect on an advertising campaign concerned with hair sprays and denture cleaners reported that around 50% of the respondents changed their attitudes to the products but only a maximum of 13% actually changed brands. The implication if clear. Advertising may make people aware of a product, but its success depends upon a combination of the strength of its appeal and its associated price.

Evidence also exists that the effectiveness of advertising is reduced by the selective nature of perception. In effect, advertising which is interpreted as irrelevant to a consumer, the reasons for which are difficult to ascertain in detail, is to varying degrees ignored. Krugman (1965), for example, suggested that television advertising had a limited impact on the viewers' learning processes as a result of their having a low level of involvement in the general content of advertising. Similarly Steiner's (1966) study of audience behaviour in the U.S.A. reported a decrease from 75% to 50% of viewers paying full attention to the screen when commercials were shown. Similar findings were reported in the U. K. by Nuttall (1962).

On a related issue, Barwise, Ehrenberg and Goodhardt (1979) conducted an experiment on the relationship between levels of television audience appreciation and audience size. In general, the smaller audiences of informational programmes had higher levels of appreciation than the larger audiences of entertainment programmes. There was no evidence, however, to suggest that the quality rating of programmes were related to advertising effectiveness. Neither the 'Let's give the public the shows they like least so they'll watch the ads.' theory, nor the converse could be proven. Thus, the best measure of potential advertising effectiveness was considered to be the unrefined measure of 'audience size'.

Table 4.1.
General audience profile of I.T.V companies in 1981

| Ages: | % | Social status: | % |
|---|---|---|---|
| <35 | 24 | AB | 13 |
| 35-44 | 19 | C1 | 19 |
| 45-54 | 17 | C2 | 31 |
| >55 | 40 | DE | 37 |

Source: Sanctuary (1983).

Advertising effectiveness is also modified by its variable exposure to consumer groups defined by social class. Table 4.1, for example, indicates the general audience profile of I.T.V. companies in 1981 associated with the 8-10 million peak hour (7.30 - 10.30 p.m.) viewers (Sanctuary, 1983). This social status profile is the inverse of that of the current visitors to Cadw sites. Thus, if the intention of a television advertising campaign was to increase visitor numbers from the lower status groups, then television may well be an appropriate advertising medium. Conversely, if the intention was to increase numbers from existing visitor groups, this form of advertising is potentially less effective. (See also section on children

96

and advertising). Similarly, since it is the case that a substantial number of trips to ancient monuments are 'locally' based, then perhaps radio advertising should be seriously considered (Table 4.2).

Table 4.2.
Radio listening, spring 1982

%

Stations:

| | |
|---|---|
| Independent Local Radio | 33 |
| Radio 1 | 24 |
| Radio 2 | 21 |
| Radio 4 | 11 |
| B. B. C. Local | 6 |
| Radio 3 | 1 |
| Radio Luxembourg | 1 |
| Other | 1 |

Source: Coppen-Gardner (1983).


A similar situation exists for the printed media. Rich and Jain's (1968) early study of the effects of newspaper and magazine advertising on shopping behaviour in Cleveland, Ohio, indicated that a large percentage of all consumers obtained their pre-purchase information on fashion items from newspapers and magazines. However, this varied between 39% of low status respondents to 91% of high status shoppers. A similar study examining pre-purchases in Newcastle-Upon-Tyne (Foxall, 1975) produced consistent findings. Twelve per cent of middle class respondents obtained information from newspapers and magazines, while this fell to 7% for the low status group. Also 12% of the middle class respondents had referred to 'Which', while none of the low status sample had consulted this source. Clearly, the absolute figures varied considerably between the U.S.A. and the U.K. studies, a fact which Foxall attributes to the different products investigated and the substantially greater amount of advertising included in American periodicals. Nevertheless, the variability of exposure to printed advertising was consistently related to social class differentials in each case.

Similar findings emerge from readership surveys of national daily and Sunday newspapers. Carpenter (1983) presented information derived from the National Readership Survey and Audit Bureau of Circulations for 1981-82 which demonstrated pronounced social class differentials between the readers of the major British newspapers (Table 4.3). The significance of this for marketing activities associated with visits to historic sites is illustrated by a recent Scottish example. A press campaign designed to generate additional 'Friends (members) of Scottish Monuments' managed by the Scottish Development Department demonstrated

97

Table 4.3.
Circulation size and readerships of British national newspapers

| Title | Circulation (in millions) | GB adult readers (in millions) | Proportion of readers who were: | | |
|---|---|---|---|---|---|
| | | | Social group AB (%) | Age 15-34 (%) | Conservative (%) (a) |
| National Dailies: | | | | | |
| Daily Express | 2.1 | 6.0 | 19 | 34 | 42 |
| Daily Mail | 1.9 | 5.4 | 23 | 37 | 48 |
| Daily Mirror | 3.4 | 10.4 | 7 | 43 | 19 |
| Daily Record | 0.7 | 2.1 | 5 | 43 | na |
| Daily Star | 1.4 | 4.6 | 4 | 51 | 10 |
| Financial Times | 0.2 | 0.7 | 55 | 41 | 46 |
| The Daily Telegraph | 1.3 | 3.5 | 50 | 30 | 49 |
| The Guardian | 0.4 | 1.4 | 49 | 51 | 5 |
| The Sun | 4.1 | 12.2 | 6 | 46 | 16 |
| The Times | 0.3 | 0.9 | 57 | 47 | 45b |

a. National Opinion Polls 8-10 March 1982, commissioned by the Observer.
b. A small sample size.

continued .....

Table 4.3 continued...
Circulation size and readerships of British national newspapers

| Title | Circulation (in millions) | GB adult readers (in millions) | Proportion of readers who were: AB Social group (%) | Age 15-34 (%) | Conservative (a) (%) |
|---|---|---|---|---|---|
| National Sundays: | | | | | |
| Mail on Sunday | 1.3E | 3.5E | 27E | 45E | na |
| News of the World | 4.2 | 11.6 | 6 | 43 | 21 |
| Sunday Express | 3.0 | 7.7 | 27 | 32 | 54 |
| Sunday Mail | 0.8 | 2.4 | 8 | 47 | na |
| Sunday Mirror | 3.7 | 10.8 | 8 | 47 | 20 |
| Sunday People | 3.5 | 10.0 | 7 | 41 | 16 |
| Sunday Telegraph | 0.9 | 2.5 | 43 | 35 | 52 |
| The Observer | 0.9 | 2.8 | 44 | 49 | 23 |
| The Sunday Post | 1.4E | 4.3 | 9 | 33 | na |
| The Sunday Times | 1.3 | 3.9 | 45 | 48 | 33 |
| For Comparison: | No. of households | Total adults | | | |
| GB Adult Population | 21.5m | 43.2m | 16 | 38 | 27 |

a. National Opinion Polls 8-10 March 1982, commissioned by the Observer.

E = Estimate.

Source: JICNARS National Readership Survey and the ABC (Audit Bureau of Circulations) July 1981 to June 1982.

99

significant variations in sales performance (Lee, 1985).
The Scotsman, the Radio Times and the Sunday Post were
particularly effective both in terms of absolute recruitment
and per capita recruitment relative to other regional
publications (Table 4.4). Managerial care obviously has to
be exercised to maximize advertising effectiveness from
expenditure. This consideration is, of course, of lesser
relevance if the aim is to create a diffuse interest in a
publicly provided facility.

Table 4.4.
Friends of Scottish Monuments press advertising summaries to
30th September 1985

| | | Number of tickets sold: | | | |
|---|---|---|---|---|---|
| | Adult | Family | Reduced | Total | Media cost (pounds) |
| **Medium:** | | | | | |
| Scotsman | 25 | 65 | 64 | 154 | 990 |
| Press and Journal | 2 | 1 | 5 | 8 | 554 |
| Glasgow Herald | 16 | 25 | 9 | 50 | 960 |
| Dundee Courier | 4 | 7 | 16 | 27 | 561 |
| Radio Times Insert | 133 | 141 | 148 | 422 | *3,300 |
| Other Press | 9 | 5 | 18 | 32 | - |
| Sunday Post | 41 | 80 | 62 | 183 | 2,239 |
| **Mailers:** | | | | | |
| - Heritage | 11 | 38 | 16 | 65 | - |
| - SCO | 13 | 12 | 14 | 39 | - |
| - RIAS | 5 | 6 | 2 | 13 | - |
| Totals | 259 | 380 | 354 | 993 | |

NB. *excludes cost of production, which for Radio Times
insert was £2,000 for 200,000 leaflets.

Source: Historic Buildings and Monuments. Scottish Development. Letter G. M. Lee, 10-10-85.

The reaction of the consumer to advertising is considered
likely to incorporate an element of unpredictability, i.e.
the reaction to an advertisement need not necessarily be
that intended by the advertiser, or it may even be counter-
productive to the original intention. This idea emerges
intermittently as a cautionary note in the literature
reviewed, particularly when the need for monitoring studies
are stressed. However, while this is an intuitively
appealing notion, there appears to be no hard evidence to
support the contention.

Consumer reactions to advertising are characterised as conforming to a learning cycle (Foxall, 1977). The assimilation of information by individuals varies over time and incorporates an initial phase of rapid learning, after which a plateau is reached. If the plateau is to be maintained, intermittent reinforcement through additional advertising is required.

The aim of advertising is to increase the rate of learning about a product, but at the same time to reduce the rate of memory decay through reinforcement. This introduces the psychological 'law of effect' which suggests that actions which are enjoyed are repeated. Reinforcement is ' ... any event that strengthens the tendency for a response to be repeated'. (Howard, 1965). The general conclusion is reached that 'limited duration campaigns' of 2-3 months are the most effective advertising instruments, which can be supplemented by occasional reinforcement. In the context of visits to historic sites a number of speculative suggestions are offered. Firstly, any visit has to be interpreted as worthwhile or satisfying if the probability of a repeat visit is to be maximised. Secondly, information, readily available of an easily interpretable nature, should be available on alternative sites in the 'locality' to enhance the learning process and assist reinforcement. Thirdly, characteristics, attributes or experiences offered in any 'locality' might be developed with an element of variability consciously promoted.

A number of additional minor issues relating to the effectiveness of advertising are also worthy of note. There is, for example, a suggestion that advertising effectiveness can be enhanced if the content included an emotional dimension. A psychological experiment at the Saarland University Institute for Consumer and Behavioural Research suggested that the effectiveness of some 'eye-catching element or slogan' and that ' ... both rational information and emotional activation are necessary'. (Kroeber-Riel, 1977). Welsh Historic Monuments, 'Cadw' title and logo are broadly in accordance with this contention. In a recent comparative study of advertising in Canada, the United Kingdom and Turkey the cultural distinctiveness of advertising was stressed (Kaynak, Mitchell, 1981). In each country the same basic elements of a campaign were recognised: the message, the media and money; but the countries varied with respect to the number, quality and type of media available. Of more significance to the current review, however, was the suggested need to vary the details of the advertising content to accord with the way in which it was interpreted in different cultural and regional contexts.


Behavioural motivation

The preceding issues concerning advertising effectiveness were primarily concerned with consumer perception or cognition. However, an awareness of a phenomenon need not necessarily precipitate action i.e. purchase of a product or service (purchasing behaviour); or, more particularly in the current context, a visit or journey to an ancient monument (spatial behaviour). The decision to act requires something more. This can be defined as a motive, objective or goal designed to satisfy some particular need on the part of the individual or group (Foxall, 1977).

There is a substantial literature on the 'Theory of Human Motivation' initiated by Maslow (1943). This early work suggested that human motivation could be explained by a 'hierarchy' of needs" in man from a physiological level to satisfy hunger or thirst, to safety needs, affective needs (love), esteem needs, to the pinnacle of 'self actualization', or the use of an individual's capabilities to the full. Subsequently, the rigid hierarchical element of this scheme has been widely questioned and the debate had identified a whole array of influences considered to explain behaviour in a variety of contexts. These include social, cultural, socio-psychological and physiological needs; or more specific influences such as relaxation or leisure requirements. A comprehensive understanding of this literature would assist the design of questionnaire surveys undertaken to 'explain' the reasons for visits to ancient monuments. Such a review is not presented here for two related reasons. There is already some exploratory survey material concerning the reasons for visits to historic sites. This has already been presented in the previous chapter and will be discussed later in relation to the significance of the advertising media as motivating influences. In addition, a copious literature already exists which examines the theory of human motivation. This incorporates empirical investigations of consumer spatial behaviour in a variety of situations. Examples include shopping behaviour (Davies, 1973; Shepherd and Thomas, 1980; Penny, 1984), medical service utilization behaviour (Phillips, 1978) and leisure behaviour (Herbert and Aubrey, 1982). Standard procedures used include a variety of Likert and semantic differential scaling techniques via questionnaire surveys of sample populations.

There are, however, a number of additional factors included in the marketing literature on advertising which are relevant to an understanding of consumer motivation and spatial behaviour in the context of visits to historic sites. These are not elaborated clearly in the literature mentioned above. Regarding leisure behaviour Foxall (1977) suggests that family-group decision-making rather than individual decision-making might be significant for both choices of holidays and day trips. If this is so, it has market segmentation implications for directing advertising campaigns. Very little is actually known of this situation and of the related manner in which children influence family decision-making generally. There is, however, limited evidence to suggest that children exert a pervasive role on parental choice of holidays, cars and furniture, a process referred to as 'reverse socialisation' (Foxall, 1977).

A more recent study in West Germany (Gunter and Kleinert, 1978) which explored the need to regulate child directed advertising, indicated that 40-50% of 3 to 13 year olds watch 19 hours of television per week. Their consequent exposure to television advertising, particularly for the 5 to 7 year olds, encouraged early consumer socialisation and induced materialistic attitudes. This occurs prior to an understanding of the significance of commercials which is thought to develop at around 10-11 years of age. As a justification advertisers 'piously' suggest that such advertising is inherently harmless and, in any event, finances children's educational programmes.

Setting aside the ethical questions of such advertising for the moment, it might be concluded that given the apparent emotional appeal and potential educational value of visits to castles in particular, and to ancient monuments in general, the significance of both family-group decision-making and the influence of children on leisure behaviour and day trips is worthy of closer scrutiny. In fact, the evidence of visitor surveys at Cadw sites reviewed in the previous chapter indicated that child-related reasons contributed to the decision to visit in around one third of cases.

## Measuring advertising effectiveness

The preceding discussion concentrated on a number of issues drawn from the marketing literature relevant to the question of advertising effectiveness. There is, however, additional literature which assesses the techniques designed to measure advertising effectiveness. This, like the majority of the material already referred to, is primarily concerned with the sales effectiveness of advertising consumer products rather than leisure behaviour. A number of points raised in this work are, nevertheless, of value in the current context.

At the outset, a cautionary note is appropriate. Twyman (1979) reviews the general question of media audience measurement and concludes that it is difficult to compare the audience figures of one medium with another, and that measurement is in an event a problem throughout due to difficulties associated with both definitions and measurement devices. For example, in surveys such as the National Readership Survey of newspapers and magazines, is it the number of issues of a publication which is important or the number of readers? Similarly, how can the precise number of readers be gauged, and what level of exposure to a publication counts as readership? With regard to television, audience measurement is usually expressed in terms of units of time watched, which is not necessarily directly related to advertisement exposure time. A precise measure of the latter would require a detailed observational analysis which would be both difficult and costly to undertake effectively, and in any event would be unlikely to be able to gauge the level of attention given to the material. Measurement of radio audiences prove equally difficult, particularly since the medium is more portable and listening is frequently combined with other activities.

Thus, the apparent precision of media audience measurement should be viewed with an element of caution.

Corkindale (1984) provides a more direct review of the measurement of advertising effectiveness. The essence of the problem is to assess the contribution of advertising campaigns to sales figures; a problem central to the existence of a healthy advertising industry. A major project to examine this question was undertaken by the Marketing Communications Research Centre at the Cranfield School of Management in 1972-74 and a series of reports were subsequently published. The conclusions reached were that virtually none of the companies examined could demonstrate conclusively the sales effects of their media advertising. This is not to say, of course, that there was no effect. Rather, it was difficult to measure in detail and, therefore, to be in a strong managerial position to maximize the sales impact of advertising expenditure. The nature of the problem was indicated by Corkindale (1984) quoting Lord Leverhulme, ' ... 50% of my advertising is wasted but I don't know which 50%'. The reasons for this is that the techniques of measurement are insufficiently precise to produce a definitive result. However, the tone of Corkindale's article appears to be unnecessarily negative since the techniques which are widely used appear capable, at least, of producing indicative results, particularly if cautious interpretation is exercised on a number of points.

The simplest techinque is the MONITORING EXERCISE. In this case changes in sales performance are reviewed over time and related either to varying levels of advertising or to the use of different media. This can provide some indication, by inference, of advertising effectiveness. The problem in such cases is that the media effect cannot be isolated from the wider marketing environment. The influence of competitors' reactions, periodic high and low sales periods and salesmen supporting the advertising effort are all likely to have contributory effects (Broadbent, 1979).

In fact, these kinds of problems can be largely overcome by adopting a sounder social scientific experimental research design, otherwise known as advertising tracking studies. The aim is to isolate the effects of advertising on sales, and a combination of devices are usually used. Surveys can be undertaken of buyer behaviour before, during and after the campaign, while the amount of advertising can be varied over time, by media and by region. At the same time a 'control area', not subjected to any advertising can be maintained for purposes of comparison. Such tracking techniques are particularly effective for products which are known to be very responsive to advertising. These tend to be low-priced, frequently purchased convenience goods such as confectionery, toiletries and domestic cleansers. Colman and Brown (1983) report that Cadbury Ltd., extensively use this technique to maximize their advertising expenditure on a variety of products.

These techniques are, however, not without problems. Corkindale (1984) indicates that to be effective, experimental procedures require 'large scale' testing over

periods of up to two years. Such experiments are costly and
are likely to be cost effective only for firms with large
advertising budgets associated with low cost, high volume of
sales products. Even then the need to change advertising
content (copy) over time in accordance with the cognitive
learning cycle dimension of advertising effectiveness
introduces a 'confounding' influence into the assumed
relationship between advertising expenditure and sales
effects. Similarly, the need for a long term experimental
design is likely to prove too restrictive on wider issues of
company marketing policies, while regional variations in
competition and the the quality and efforts of the sales
force are also likely to prove problematic for a precise
research design.

To offset some of these problems Corkindale (1984)
suggests an alternative measurement technique; the ADLAB.
This involves a survey of samples of consumers who have been
subjected to varying exposure to advertising, preferably
without their knowledge by using cable television. This
procedure is currently illegal in the U.K.

The more precise experimental methods are unlikely to be
relevant to organisations with limited advertising budgets.
Most of the public authorities responsible for the
management of historic sites fall into this category. This
is particularly apparent when the nature of the 'product' is
considered. Historic sites are spatially diffuse and of an
extremely variable character. Also, visits to such 'leisure
facilities' necessitates a journey which requires stronger
motivation than that associated with the purchase of a
chocolate bar or washing detergent. In these circumstances,
the measurement of advertising effectiveness is inevitably
imprecise and is probably best undertaken via short term
monitoring studies, incorporating as much experimental
'control' as is feasible.


The marketing of services

The majority of the preceding discussion is derived from the
literature concerning the effects of advertising on the
marketing of consumed products in the commercial sector.
Before turning attention to the evidence of advertising
effectiveness with specific reference to the leisure
industry, two major considerations are worthy of note.
Firstly, many leisure, recreational and cultural activities,
with the major exception of commercial tourism, are public
services. Thus, the marketing considerations concerned with
the maximization of profit have limited or modified
applicability. Secondly, leisure, recreation and cultural
activities are services so that strategies designed to
promote products are not necessarily appropriate to their
marketing.

Throughout marketing since the early 1970s there has been
a clear recognition that with the increasing number of
products available to consumers, manufacturers have to be
much more market or consumer oriented in product development
if they are to remain competitive. The same consideration

has been recognised in the tourism industry (Burkart and Medlik, 1974) and in the context of non-profit making organisations generally (Kotler and Levy, 1969; Shapiro, 1973). With the growth of a 'leisure market' in the U.K. since 1973, resulting from a combination of the population having more spare time associated with shorter working hours, more early retirement and part-time employment; greater affluence; and less physically demanding occupations; as much as 23% of the household budget is spent on leisure activities (Yorke, 1984a). This expenditure has been directed to sporting activities, drinking, eating out, holidays and hobbies. Both local authorities and public bodies have been heavily involved in the provision and operation of such services, but competition from commercial operators has been intense so that Yorke (1984a) suggests the need for: ' ... a more customer or market oriented approach' for the success of publicly provided leisure services.

The literature relating to publicly provided services, however, indicates that due to the lack of both a strong market mechanism and commercial experience throughout management that a consumer orientation is the exception rather than the rule. The characteristics of the services provided tend to reflect a managerial or bureaucratic perspective, usually based upon only a limited knowledge of the requirements of potential clients (Beltramini, 1981; Ritchie and La Breque, 1975). Foxall (1984a) reports that this is particularly the case for sports and leisure centres where the range of facilities, prices locations and marketing strategies tend to be based upon centralised managerial decisions which pay scant attention to an examination of consumer demand. The implication is that if a public service provider wishes to achieve commercial success, then the public (or segment of the public) has to be provided with what it wants rather than what the organisation thinks it needs. Alternatively, even if commercial considerations are not paramount, it could be argued that for a public service to be most effective, it is incumbent upon the provider to research the public expectations of the service. The sorts of questions relevant for the management marketing and development of historic sites are as follows. Firstly, are there public expectations of the experience and facilities offered at historic sites? Secondly, do the public expectations indicate a segmented market? Thirdly, can public bodies cater for varying expectations by different development policies by site? Fourthly are the experiences and facilities provided at historic sites perceived as tourism, recreation, leisure, culture or education? Fifthly, what are the implications of this kind of information for management strategies?

Other specific characteristics of services have direct implications for marketing and advertising which are problematic, many of which have relevance for historic sites. Meyer and Tostmann (1978), for example, indicate that service provision lacks a specific product transfer. Services cannot be accumulated or transported. They are solely available at a point of supply as an opportunity which may or may not be taken. This locational inflexibility means that usage depends upon the consumer rather than the service provider. The need to induce the consumer to travel to the service is a significant obstacle to usage and requires particularly attractive or persuasive promotion, combined with high levels of satisfaction at the facility of repeat behaviour to the same or similar opportunites is to be undertaken.

The same authors suggest that the 'immaterial' or 'intangible' nature of most services hampers the development of a strong marketing image, particularly with regard to their differentiation from like competitor services. Thus, as far as possible, a service provider should aim to create a 'product' like image to maximize competitive impact. For international tourism the brochure is seen as the basic device to create a "tangible" sales identity (Greenley and Matcham, 1983).

On a closely related issue, Yorke (1984b) suggests that the requirement of public organisations to provide services in the 'public interest' or for the 'community' incorporates a fundamental marketing weakness. The usually limited development and promotional resources have to be used to satisfy all sections of the population. The advertising implication is that only a weak 'image' of the service is developed since it aims at too broad a customer base. This is of no great concern if the service is considered to be utilised sufficiently by all sections of the population. However, if the service is underutilised it can be argued that, in the first instance, the limited development and promotional resources would be best directed to encourage the use of the facility by those to whom the service is most likely to appeal. That is, market segmentation and target marketing based upon such criteria as age structure or socio-economic status should form an integral part of the promotional strategy. This might then provide a sounder base for the subsequent extension of the service to wider sections of the community.

Greenley and Matcham's (1983) study of international tourism provides a number of additional points of interest. Services are provided by individuals at the point of consumption (enjoyment) of the service. The performance of such individuals might have a significant bearing on consumer satisfaction, and of the liklihood of repeat behaviour. Yet the standardisation of this facet of service provision is extremely difficult to achieve, despite consistent recruitment strategies designed to minimize the potential problem. Similarly, fluctuations in the level of demand related to circumstances outside the control of the service provider, such as the weather, can also have a bearing on levels of enjoyment.

For Greenley and Matcham (1983) the inflexible nature of the 'product' offered to an incoming tourist was also considered a restriction for marketing strategies. This tends to be the situation for historic monuments as well, although in this case there is some scope for site development policies designed to modify or vary the nature of the experience offered.

In conclusion, a number of recurring themes relevant to the marketing and advertising of public, non-profit making services emerge. Firstly, clear objectives are rarely identified by such organisations. Secondly, these objectives tend to incorporate a weak consumer orientation. Thirdly, these facts create problems for the analysis of the 'market' and the associated development planning of service facilities. Fourthly, this has further implication for the imprecise identification of target segments and the efficiency with which they can be reached by promotional activities.

The key issue is that public service organisations providing leisure related facilities need to be more precise in establishing their objectives. They appear to be predisposed to react to external forces (usually stagnating or falling rates of usage). Only by the identification of positive objectives are they likely to prove more successful in a situation in which commercial competition has been developing rapidly in recent years.

## Advertising effectiveness and leisure activities

In addition to the general literature of marketing and advertising, investigations of advertising effectiveness in relation to leisure and recreational activities are becoming increasingly available. The greater part of this material concerns tourism and the activities of tourist boards some of which offers insights of potential value for the marketing of historic sites. The measurement of advertising effectiveness in the tourism industry focuses on a number of interrelated questions. Has the target market been adequately reached? Have the campaign messages been accurately received, perceived, recalled? Do the different media used demonstrate significantly variable results in terms of cost-effectiveness? Has the campaign resulted in demonstrable effects in terms of consumer decisions to purchase or to undertake particular activities? Finally, on balance, have the principal aims of the campaign been achieved?

The largest amount of information on this subject has been obtained by the Scottish Tourist Board. They embarked on a series of very positive advertising campaigns in the late 1970s. These aimed to increase general public awareness of Scotland as a potential tourist destination and to increase the overall level of British tourism to Scotland. The focus was, therefore, on information provision and persuasion. Central to the campaigns was the holiday brochure. This was distributed through travel agents, and from written and telephone requests generated in association with extensive press and television advertising. To a lesser extent exhibitions were mounted in selected English cities, while newsheets were distributed in targeted residential areas. The measurement of the effectiveness of these campaigns involved a series of monitoring exercises including directed small group discussions (debriefing exercises) and larger scale questionnaire surveys of respondents drawn from the travel trade, from brochure applicants, and from the general public. In most instances an experimental "control" group was maintained for comparison, while the investigations were undertaken before, during and after the campaigns.

These studies provided a profusion of detailed information, but a number of issues were consistently examined, which included, levels of distribution, levels of awareness of the advertising campaigns, content and quality of advertising copy and the persuasive effect of the campaigns. The consideration of levels of distribution focused primarily on levels of display, and the number and timing of the availability of brochures in travel agencies. Useful indications of the levels of brochure wastage resulted and the necessity to maximise distribution in the peak holiday decision-making period from January to March was demonstrated. Levels of awareness of the advertising campaigns was investigated through the press and television campaigns, although the awareness of travel agents of publicity material was also examined. The main monitoring device was the recall survey, both unprompted and prompted. Analysis of the content and quality of advertising copy was directed at brochure, press and television material and a general indication of the strengths and weaknesses of advertising copy as informational and sales devices was obtained. The degree to which brochures, the press and television advertising persuaded people to visit Scotland was also examined. Regarding the effectiveness of these campaigns, a number of conclusions relevant to the advertising of historic monuments emerged. For example, monitoring the uses of, and the attitudes of travel agents to, the brochures suggested that this resulted in significant improvements in their advertising effectiveness. Advice on the best timing for distribution and the development of a stronger sales orientation proved particularly valuable.

However, the positive promotional and associated sales effects of all aspects of advertising (the explicit persuasion function) was apparently very limited. Analysis was confined largely to respondents who had made postal or telephone requests for brochures after seeing advertising material in the press, on television, in newsletters or at exhibitions. Such respondents were at the outset strongly predisposed towards a Scottish holiday, hence their request for more information (Table 4.5). The effect of the promotional material was to 'convert' those who were probably going to take a holiday in Scotland into the 'definite' category. The initially 'undecided' category was only influenced to a limited degree. This suggests that the advertising effect was largely 'informational' in that it confirmed a strong tendency, rather than 'persuasive' in the sense that it generated higher levels of holiday interest in Scotland than would otherwise have been the case. This contention is supported by a similar monitoring exercise undertaken by the Wales Tourist Board (1979) following the 1978-79 advertising campaign.

Table 4.5.
Scottish holiday intentions - pre-brochure

|  | 1984 | 1983 | 1982 | 1980 | 1979 |
|---|---|---|---|---|---|
| No. seeing brochure (100%) | 370 | 540 | 686 | 655 | 850 |
|  | % | % | % | % | % |
| Definitely decided to holiday in Scotland | 38 | 35 | 33 | 40 | 43 |
| Probably decided to holiday in Scotland | 25 | 31 | 23 | 27 | 26 |
| Definitely/probably sub-total | 63 | 66 | 56 | 67 | 69 |
| Undecided | 33 | 31 | 38 | 26 | 26 |
| Decided probably not to holiday in Scotland | 3 | 2 | 5 | 5 | 2 |
| Decided definitely not to holiday in Scotland | 1 | 1 | 1 | 2 | 2 |

|  | T.V. | Press: | | |
|---|---|---|---|---|
|  | T.V. Times | Radio Times | Womens Mags. | News-papers |
| No. Seeing brochure (100%) | 193 | 99 | 40 | 14+ | 23+ |
|  | % | % | % | % | % |
| Definitely decided to holiday in Scotland | 33 | 38 | 58 | 71 | 52 |
| Probably decided to holiday in Scotland | 25 | 23 | 28 | 21 | 26 |
| Undecided | 38 | 33 | 13 | 7 | 22 |
| Decided probably not to holiday in Scotland | 3 | 4 | 3 | 0 | 0 |
| Decided definitely not to holiday in Scotland | 1 | 1 | 0 | 0 | 0 |

Note:  + Very small bases.

Source: Research Bureau Ltd., 1984.


In fact, the evidence of the analysis of group discussions
for the Scottish Tourist Board suggested that even as an
information device the brochure was ' ... weak as a positive
instrument for converting those not yet committed to a

Scottish holiday', and in the survey of brochure recipients only 12% indicated that it had positively influenced them (Travel and Tourism Research, 1979). Recent evidence from Wales points in the same direction. Marplan Ltd. (1984) reported that as few as 12% of staying visitors obtained the 'Wales Holiday '84' brochure prior to the trip, while Jones and Corr (1985) suggest that most people when planning a holiday in Great Britain do not consider getting brochures, or visiting a travel agent, at all.

It is, however, not really possible to judge from this kind of information whether advertising has a significant generative - persuasive effect on absolute levels of holiday visits to an area. The initial predispositions may or may not have been related to the advertising campaigns. Neither do such studies indicate whether the initial advertising generates visits from people who do not request information since they are never included in the monitoring analysis. To resolve this impasse a more detailed social survey investigation of the holiday decision-making processes of sections of the population would have to be undertaken; a much more difficult and costly task.

In the absence of such refined information a recent survey of brochure applicants undertaken by the Harris Research Centre (1984) provides some interesting additional insights into advertising effectiveness. On the evidence of the earlier discussion such respondents might be assumed to be both predisposed towards a holiday in Scotland and positive information seekers. Yet the major reason for deciding to holiday in Scotland by 65% of this group was previous experiences of holidays in Scotland. A significant 31% recorded 'tourist authority information', and 17% considered 'advertising' as an important contributory reason. Other more general reasons were, however, quoted at levels almost as important as advertising (Table 4.6). Apparently, a substantial inertia-conservative-risk minimisation dimension is entrenched in the holiday decision-making process, despite the operation of strong promotional activities by the Scottish Tourist Board over a relatively long period.

Evidence from Ireland is consistent with these findings. A recent study on the main influences on the choice of Ireland as a holiday destination demonstrated the marked significance of friends, relatives previous visits and ancestral ties relative to the promotional activities of the Tourist Board and the media (Bord Failte, 1985). Similarly, the Wales Tourist Board's investigation of their 1979 Resort Advertising Campaign highlighted the importance of 'personal recommendation' and indicated that brochures were usually obtained after the destination decision had 'more or less' been made (Wales Tourist Board, 1979).

The conclusion that such advertising campaigns have only limited promotional impact might, however, be premature. The activities of the Scottish Tourist Board were represented moderately strongly in the list of factors considered important to the holiday destination decision. Also, the previous 'experience of holidays in Scotland' and 'personal recommendation' are worthy of closer scrutiny. These reasons may well obscure the cumulative influence of a

111

Table 4.6.
Factors important in deciding to holiday in Scotland

Base: Phase 2 holidaying in Scotland

| | Total | Media: A Radio Times | B T.V. Times | C Readers Digest | D Television | E Womens Magazines | F Sunday Press | G Holiday ideas | H Scotlands for me |
|---|---|---|---|---|---|---|---|---|---|
| Unweighted Base | 385 | 43 | 33 | 48 | 51 | 38 | 29 | 59 | 84 |
| Weighted Base | 369 | 46 | 41 | 41 | 63 | 40 | 32 | 50 | 56 |
| | % | % | % | % | % | % | % | % | % |
| Very important sources: | | | | | | | | | |
| Experience of holidays in Scotland | 65 | 69 | 69 | 56 | 64 | 69 | 64 | 67 | 65 |
| Advertising about holidays in Scotland | 17 | 23 | 9 | 17 | 22 | 10 | 18 | 14 | 17 |
| Information/literature produced by tourist authorities | 31 | 37 | 20 | 30 | 36 | 26 | 28 | 36 | 30 |
| Things friends or relations have told me about scotland | 16 | 5 | 27 | 12 | 27 | 13 | 7 | 14 | 15 |

continued .....

112

Table 4.6 continued....
Factors important in deciding to holiday in Scotland

Base: Phase 2 holidaying in Scotland

| | Total % | Media: A Radio Times % | B T.V. Times % | C Readers Digest % | D Tele-vision % | E Womens Maga-zines % | F Sunday Press % | G Holi-day ideas % | H Scot-lands for me % |
|---|---|---|---|---|---|---|---|---|---|
| **Very important sources:** | | | | | | | | | |
| Films/TV programmes set in or about Scotland | 12 | 6 | 9 | 4 | 24 | 13 | 16 | 8 | 9 |
| Novels set in Scotland | 4 | 2 | – | 2 | 10 | 5 | 7 | 3 | 1 |
| Other books about Scotland | 6 | 9 | 11 | 2 | 5 | 8 | 3 | 2 | 7 |

Source: Harris Research Centre (1984), Phase 2 Tabulations, T20.

113

number of earlier advertising campaigns.  This point serves to underline the earlier suggested need for more detailed social survey analyses of the holiday decision-making process if the importance of advertising is to be clarified.


Table 4.7
Effectiveness of media for holiday advertising based upon prompted recall

|  | Recalling advertising for Scotland % |
| --- | --- |
| Medium: |  |
| T.V. | 85 |
| Newspapers | 22 |
| Magazines | 9 |
| Radio/T.V. Times | 7 |

Sources: Research (International) Bureau Ltd. (1983);
         Research (International) Bureau Ltd. (1984).


   Evidence is also available from Scotland on the relative effectiveness of the media for holiday advertising based upon prompted recall surveys of samples of the population at large. (Research (International) Bureau Ltd., 1983; 1984) (Table 4.7). Obviously, television emerges as by far the best medium to reach a mass audience.  However, despite the apparent effectiveness of television compared with the other media, recall levels are frequently low.  In 1978, for example, the Wales Tourist Board (1978) estimated that 88% of households in four I.T.V. areas saw their advertisements. An estimated 65% saw them at least four times.  Prompted recall levels, however, were only 37%, although this still compared favourably with the 18% achieved by the press. Similar results were recorded for the 1982 Scottish Tourist Board campaign.  Prompted recall levels for television advertising stood at only 40% at the height of the campaign, although this again compared favourably with the 13% recorded for the press. Notably, the unprompted equivalents were only 9% and 3% respectively (Travel and Tourism Research, 1982).
   Of particular interest, however, was the significantly higher level of recall for Thomson's Holidays (62%).  It is probable that the difference is explained by the more specific nature of such advertising compared with the more 'general' tone of tourist board campaigns.  If this is so, is implies that an advertising strategy for heritage attractions will need to be related to whether the aim is to promote an interest in ancient monuments in general or higher visitor numbers at particular sites.
   It is also worthy of note that although television advertising is comparatively the most effective medium for reaching a large audience, this is not reflected in the

114

origins of applications for brochures. The sources of applications for brochures is more or less equally divided between television and the press (Research Bureau Ltd., 1984). This probably reflects the more physically enduring nature of press advertising. A printed coupon is available for further action after it has first been noticed, while a response to television advertising requires immediate action to note an address or telephone number.

Finally, it is interesting to note that the social class characteristics of the population requesting brochures via television or the press is significantly different from those of the general population (Research Bureau Ltd., 1984). Over twice as many of the high status AB groups requested brochures compared to the general population, while the lower status C2 and DE respondents were similarly under-represented. It seems that mass media advertising is more effective in generating positive responses for additional information from the higher rather than the lower status groups. Thus, should an organisation wish to precipitate a positive response from the population at large, alternatives to television and the press will be necessary to generate levels of participation commensurate with the numerical significance of the lower status groups in the general population.

Investigations of the marketing and advertising effectiveness of individual recreational sites are likely to be of greatest relevance for the promotion of historic monuments. Before focusing on the issue of advertising effectiveness, some comments on the key characteristics of recreational visits to specific sites are necessary to provide preliminary insight into the context of advertising strategies.

Virtually all the studies reviewed in this section stress the importance of three major visitor types; those on holiday away from home; home-based holiday-makers; and home-based day-trippers. The significance of each at particular sites varies according to the location of the site and the time of the year, This was noted in an early study of visitors to historic houses (B.T.A. and Countryside Commission, 1968) and was clearly illustrated for recent visitors to Cadw sites (Table 4.8). In general, visitor profiles were dominated by holiday-makers, particularly those staying away from home. This was most evident for the North Wales resort areas where figures of 90% were recorded, and was slightly more apparent in the summer than at Easter for obvious reasons. A different situation was, however, recorded at both Castell Coch and Caerphilly Castle, where the two categories of home-based visitors were substantially more important at both times. This reflects their locations, central to the population concentrations of industrial South Wales, which provide a local market of home-based day-trippers. Castell Coch is particularly fortunate in this respect, located just beyond the northern edge of suburban Cardiff beside the M4 motorway.

This has implications for advertising since ' ... holiday visitors and day visitors are relatively discrete populations' in terms of the sources of information

Table 4.8.
Visitor types at Cadw sites, Easter and summer 1986

| | Tintern Abbey | | Castell Coch | | Caerphilly Castle | | Caernarfon Castle | |
|---|---|---|---|---|---|---|---|---|
| | E % | S % | E % | S % | E % | S % | E % | S % |
| **Visitor type:** | | | | | | | | |
| On holiday away from home | 64 | 78 | 38 | 49 | 48 | 64 | 88 | 95 |
| Home based holiday-maker | 23 | 10 | 22 | 20 | 23 | 9 | 7 | 1 |
| Home based day-tripper | 13 | 12 | 40 | 31 | 29 | 27 | 5 | 4 |

| | Conwy Castle | | Harlech Castle | | ALL SITES | |
|---|---|---|---|---|---|---|
| | E % | S % | E % | S % | E % | S % |
| **Visitor type:** | | | | | | |
| On holiday away from home | 78 | 86 | 93 | 93 | 66 | 77 |
| Home based holiday-maker | 21 | 2 | 6 | 2 | 18 | 8 |
| Home based day-tripper | 2 | 12 | 1 | 4 | 16 | 15 |

E = Easter 1986:  n = 1624.
S = Summer 1986:  n = 1347.

Source:  Seren (1986c.  Table 6, p.46).


associated with a particular trip (Mears, 1976). For example, day visitors to Dan-yr-Ogof caves in the Swansea Valley in 1974 relied heavily on 'informal, local' sources of information, while the holiday visitor was more likely to be directed via their accommodation and holiday guides (Table 4.9).

The great majority of all three groups travel relatively short distances to the sites. This was noted in the early study of English Historic Houses where 50 miles appeared to form a significant barrier (B. T. A. and Countryside

Table 4.9.
Information sources used by visitors to recreational sites

| | Caernarfon Castle % | Chepstow Castle % | St. Fagans % | Penscynor % | Dan-yr-Ogof % |
|---|---|---|---|---|---|
| Sources of Information: | | | | | |
| Mentioned by friends | 12 | 15 | 39 | 54 | 26 |
| Told at accommodation | 1 | 3 | 6 | 8 | 10 |
| Heard locally | 3 | 8 | 17 | 31 | 7 |
| WTB information pre-holiday | 2 | 1 | 3 | 4 | 6 |
| WTB information during holiday | 1 | 1 | 2 | 3 | 10 |
| Other guide/ brochure | 4 | 20 | 4 | 2 | 9 |
| Advert; magazine, newspaper | 2 | 1 | 5 | 16 | 8 |
| Investiture | 24 | - | - | - | - |
| TV, radio programme | 3 | - | 2 | 7 | 1 |
| Signpost | - | 3 | 2 | 11 | 4 |
| Tourist information centre | 1 | 2 | 2 | 1 | 5 |
| Found ourselves | 4 | 35 | 3 | 2 | 2 |
| Organised tour | 6 | 5 | 7 | 6 | 5 |
| Don't know | 23 | 5 | 4 | 1 | - |
| Other | 39 | 6 | 25 | 12 | 11 |
| At school | - | 7 | - | - | - |
| Been before | - | - | - | 22 | 17 |

Source: Mears (1976).

117

Commission, 1968). This does not appear to have changed substantially over time. N.O.P. (1985) reported that 75% of visitors to the nationally advertised Liverpool Garden Festival travelled less than 50 miles, while similar findings were recorded for visitors to Cadw sites (Chapter 2). Again the implication is that the promotion of particular recreational sites should be targeted 'locally' to maximise effectiveness.

The reasons for visits are also of interest. This topic has already been examined in the previous chapter, but the promotional implications of the findings are worthy of reiteration at this point. Leisure and recreational behaviour was dominated by informal activities, although visits to managed sites have increasingly achieved an important secondary status. Amongst such sites historic monuments ranked high. The motives for visits appeared to be divided almost equally between general recreational pursuits and more specific interests in history and culture. Visitors were anticipating a rather more 'purposeful' experience than a casual walk around an historic site. There was a marked expectation of a general educational interpretation of history and heritage from a substantial proportion of visitors. This implies that promotional and site development activities should stress a combination of the recreational and general educational opportunities offered by historic sites if the aim is to generate more visitors of the existing types.

There was, however, also evidence of a market segmentation of visitor types and expectations. A significant minority were, for example, motivated by 'specialist' interests in the sites. In addition, while the dominant high status visitors were attracted principally by historical and heritage interests, the appeal of the sites for the lower status groups focused more strongly on the recreational facilities offered. A similar difference existed between the expectations of the holiday-maker and the home-based day tripper. Finally, castles exhibited a stronger attraction for family groups with children compared with the other types of sites. This indicates that the promotional and site development strategies of public organisations responsible for a large number and variety of sites might vary their policies by site in an attempt to maximise visitor numbers across the whole market spectrum. With due regard to the sensitivity of the sites, the recreational facilities of those near to urban concentrations might be improved to appeal to the lower status or family day-tripper market. For example, the catering facilities offered at Stirling Castle might be developed elsewhere, or provisions like the adventure playground at Caldicot Castle with explicit historical themes could be provided for children. By contrast, sites of national historical significance might be enhanced to appeal to the specialist visitor. The Roman Baths development and museum at Caerleon is an obvious case in point.

The information sources used by visitors to recreational sites provides some insight into the effectiveness of advertising. The Wales Tourist Board's visitor surveys of the mid 1970s offer some early evidence on this issue (Table 4.9). 'Locally-based social interaction' emerged as the most important information medium at this time. By contrast, official tourism organisations and formal advertising were of minimal significance. Similar findings were repeated in circumstances where little promotional activity has been undertaken. A survey for the Countryside Commission for Scotland into recreational activities in the countryside indicated the minimal influence of formal advertising (Mackenzie, 1985), while Marplan's (1984) study of visitor's reasons for visiting gardens and waterfalls in Wales demonstrated a similar situation.

Even where substantial advertising effort is involved similar results occur. Cadw, for example, mounted a general advertising campaign in the periods up to and during the 1986 Easter and summer holidays, involving television, newspapers, magazines and brochures. Yet, the sources of information recorded by visitors at eleven sites at Easter were headed by the same kinds of local and social sources of information (Table 4.10), and these findings were broadly replicated in the summer survey (Seren, 1986c). Television was notably unimportant as a source of information, as were the other formal advertising media. Instead, the informal use of books and maps emerged as important secondary sources.

Table 4.10.
Information sources used by visitors to Cadw sites, Easter 1986

|  | % |  | % |
|---|---|---|---|
| **Sources of information:** | | | |
| Local knowledge | 31 | Holiday brochure | 5 |
| Friend or relative | 27 | T.V. programme | 4 |
| Book | 21 | T.V. advertisement | 4 |
| Saw it when passing | 19 | At accommodation | 3 |
| Map | 19 | Poster | 2 |
| Tourist board brochure | 13 | Newspaper advert. | 1 |
| Guidebook | 11 | Newspaper Article | 1 |
| Signposts | 9 | Radio | 1 |
| Cadw brochure | 6 | Other | 7 |

N = 2263

Source: Seren (1986a, p.18).


The results of these surveys were, however, not without promotional interest. Significant minorities simply 'saw the site when passing' (19%) or spontaneously responded to signposting (9%). The chance response to a visual stimulus was markedly more important for sites in elevated positions in proximity to main roads. At Easter, for example, just short of 40% responded to a chance sighting of Castell Coch and Valle Crucis Abbey. This increased to 56% for summer visitors to Castell Coch, while 45% and 33% respectively of those visiting Conwy and Raglan Castles indicated the importance of this source of information. These findings have two promotional implications; the 'visibility' of such sites can be enhanced by appropriate supplementary signposting; while these kinds of sites are likely to attract the highest proportion of 'casual' visitors, and might, where appropriate, be developed accordingly. It is also worthy of note that the various kinds of brochures, together constituted a significant additional source of visitor information.

Further analysis of the relationship between the social and holiday status of visitors and their sources of information also suggested promotional implications. For the Easter visitors, for example, the lower status C2 and D categories relied more heavily on local knowledge (39% and 41%) compared with the AB respondents (29% and 31%). Similarly, the lower status respondents were more likely to be 'just passing' (27%) compared with the professional groups (17%). By contrast, maps, books and guidebooks were most important for the higher status visitor. The influence of books was claimed by 27% and 24% of groups A and B respectively compared with only 14% and 15% of groups C2 and D.

Comparable variations were related to the holiday status of visitors. Not unexpectedly, local knowledge dominated the sources of information of the home-based holiday-makers and day-trippers. Just under two thirds of these groups indicated this source of information compared with 14% of the staying holiday-makers. Holiday-makers, however, also relied strongly on informal, but contrasting 'social' sources of information. Some 31% indicated friends or relatives as sources of information compared with 22% of home-based holiday-makers and 14% of day-trippers. Conversely, staying holiday-makers were more likely to use maps, books, guidebooks and brochures, although in no case were these sources quoted by more than 20% of respondents.

Evidently, a sounder knowledge of the antecedents of the local and social sources of information is necessary to encourage locally - based and lower status visitors. By contrast, the higher status groups and staying holiday-makers appear most likely to be responsive to the kinds of promotional material currently provided by tourist organisations.

However, the situation is probably more complex than it appears at first sight. The apparent domination of the decision-making process by 'local' and 'personal' sources of information may well be obscuring a more substantial advertising effect. For example, the 1968 B.T.A. and Countryside Commision visitor survey of historic houses recorded the importance of a similar array of information sources to those outlined above. Yet questions on the recollection of advertisements yielded far more positive results which closely reflected the advertising budgets between the media for three stately homes (Table 4.11). A more recent survey of visitors to the Ulster American Folk

Table 4.11.
Advertisements seen by visitors to historic houses

| | Ragley Hall | Castle Howard | Tatton Park |
|---|---|---|---|
| N = | 129 | 144 | 132 |
| | % | % | % |
| **Media:** | | | |
| No advertising seen | 35 | 19 | 30 |
| Television | 10 | 48 | 44 |
| Local press | 20 | 20 | 21 |
| National press | 4 | 3 | 9 |
| Newspapers (not stated where) | 1 | 2 | * |
| Magazines | 10 | 12 | 9 |
| Historic houses, castles and gardens' guidebook | 15 | 5 | 1 |
| AA/RAC guidebooks | 3 | 1 | 3 |
| Other guidebooks | 8 | 15 | 6 |
| Hotel posters and leaflets | 5 | 6 | 1 |
| Coach tour posters | 10 | 8 | 3 |
| Other posters | 6 | 3 | 2 |
| Other advertising | 2 | 2 | 3 |

N.B.  * less than 0.5%.

Note:  percentage total to more than 100 because some respondents mentioned more than one form of advertising.

Spending on advertising of historic houses.

| | Ragley Hall | Castle Howard | Tatton Park |
|---|---|---|---|
| Total advertising budget allocated in 1968 | % | % | % |
| **Media:** | | | |
| Television | – | 49 | 42 |
| Local press | 32 | 18 | 19 |
| National press | – | – | 8 |
| Magazines | 4 | 11 | 3 |
| Historic house, castles and gardens guidebook | 40 | 6 | 1 |
| AA/RAC guidebooks | – | – | – |
| Other guidebooks | – | 6 | 2 |
| Hotel posters and leaflets | 16 | 9 | 24* |
| Coach tour posters | – | – | – |
| Other posters | – | – | 1 |
| Other advertising | 8 | 1 | – |
| Total | 100 | 100 | 100 |

N.B.  * not all leaflets displayed in hotels.

Source: B.T.A. and Countryside Commision (1968).

Park suggested a similar paradox. Information sources were apparently dominated by local and personal contacts, yet awareness of advertising reached moderate levels of 30% for television, 23% for newspapers and 16% for radio (N.I.T.B., 1982).


Table 4.12.
Visitors recently seen a Cadw television advertisement, Easter 1986

| | % | | % |
|---|---|---|---|
| Tintern Abbey | 15 | Valle Crucis Abbey | 11 |
| Castell Coch | 44 | Conwy Castle | 20 |
| Caerphilly Castle | 33 | Harlech Castle | 15 |
| Kidwelly Castle | 32 | Criccieth Castle | 10 |
| Caerleon Roman Fort and Amphitheatre | 22 | Caernarfon Castle | 11 |

ALL Sites    23%

N = 2181

Source: Seren (1986a).


The experience of Cadw reveals a similar situation. While as few as 4% of visitors at Easter 1986 indicated a television advertisement as a source of information about a site, a significant minority of 23% stated that they had recently seen a Cadw television advertisement. Furthermore, substantial variations were recorded by site (Table 4.12). The figures were significantly higher for the South Wales sites, reaching a high of 44% in the case of Castell Coch. These variations reflect the difference between the preponderance of tourist visitors in the North and at Tintern Abbey, and the nearly even balance between tourists and home-based visitors in the south. Support for this contention is provided by the fact that only 11% of those on holiday away from home had seen a television advertisement, compared with 43% of home-based holiday-makers and 49% of those not on holiday. The exception of Caerleon reflects the fact that this site was not included in the television advertisements.
This evidence is indicative of a more important advertising effect than at first sight appears to be the case. Also, television is evidently less likely to attract tourists to sites than home-based visitors. This reflects the lower level of exposure to television advertising to those on holiday away from home.
The evidence suggests that surveys which simply present lists of sources of information for respondents to register as important to their trip decision-making are insufficiently subtle to test advertising effectiveness. The antecedents of the 'local' and 'personal' sources require closer scrutiny. In fact, the conclusion reached

with regard to the investigation of holiday decision-making
may be repeated here; there is a need for more detailed
social survey analysis of the day trip decision-making
process if the effectiveness of advertising is to be judged
accurately.
  In part, these findings probably refect the 'diffuse'
forms of advertising which characterised the promotion of
tourism and leisure until relatively recently, and may well
underestimate the potential effect of the promotion of
specific sites. Support for this contention is provided by
the fact that in cases where positive advertising has
occurred, at least a 'moderate' effect is suggested. Local
newspaper advertising was reflected in the Penscynor case
(16%), while the combination of the "free advertising" and
the strong 'emotional' significance of the investiture of
the Prince of Wales in 1969 was still reflected in the
Caernarfon Castle visitor survey of 1974 (24%) (Table 4.9).


Table 4.13.
How made aware of Fota Island - total mentions

Base: All respondents.

|  | Total | Cork City | Co. Cork/ Waterford | Rest of Ireland | Abroad |
|---|---|---|---|---|---|
| N = | 249 | 64 | 90 | 64 | 31 |
|  | % | % | % | % | % |
| Newspapers/ magazines/ television/radio | 59 | 77 | 66 | 53 | 19 |
| Friends/relatives/ word of mouth | 34 | 23 | 28 | 38 | 65 |
| Heard locally | 24 | 42 | 30 | 5 | 6 |
| Irish Tourist Board information | 5 | 2 | 2 | 3 | 26 |
| Sign posts | 4 | 5 | 4 | 3 | 3 |
| Guide books | 2 | 2 | - | 5 | 3 |
| Tourist office visit | 2 | 2 | - | 5 | 3 |
| Told at accommodation | 2 | 3 | 2 | 1 | - |
| Organised tour | 1 | - | 1 | 2 | - |
| Found it ourselves | 1 | - | 1 | 2 | - |
| Other | 5 | 3 | 6 | 8 | - |

Source: Research Surveys of Ireland Ltd. (1983).

The importance of active promotion and development was also suggested in the discussion of changing visitor numbers in Chapter 1. Development and promotion were considered the most likely reasons for the recent increases in visitor number at Bunratty Castle and Folk Park in County Clare and for many of the National Trust properties in Scotland. This stood in stark contrast with Welsh monuments which in 1984 barely retained the visitor numbers of the mid 1970s.

The potential importance of advertising is emphasised when the evidence of recent surveys is examined. In each of the following cases the effects of a positive advertising campaign was examined in greater depth than the cases previously note. The first of these concerns a visitor survey of the Fota Island Wildlife Park in Ireland (Research Surveys of Ireland Ltd., 1983). In this example the media influence was markedly more significant than the 'local' and 'personal' factors, which suggest the potential effectiveness of locally based advertising for the stimulation of day-trip activities (Table 4.13). A similar situation was noted for visitors to the Liverpool Garden Festival. (N.O.P., 1985). Local knowledge was still claimed as the primary source of information by the local (Merseyside) visitors. Yet, this probably subsumes the extensive publicity associated with the event, particularly in view of the importance of the media influence outside the immediate area (Table 4.14). It is interesting, however, to note that television programmes and news coverage appeared to be more potent influences than advertising as such.

Yorke (1984c) provides a third example concerned with the promotion a locally orientated facility. The effect of different marketing strategies adopted for two leisure centres was investigated using a home-based survey in their general 'trade-areas'. One centre (A) was not promoted strongly, while the second (B) instituted a strong local

Table 4.14.
Liverpool Garden Festival: sources of information

|  | All respond- | Mersey- side | N.W. | G. B. | Over- seas |
|---|---|---|---|---|---|
| N = | 3078 | 1316 | 570 | 1093 | 99 |
|  | % | % | % | % | % |
| T.V. programme | 29 | 14 | 44 | 45 | 10 |
| T.V. advertisement | 20 | 13 | 33 | 24 | 9 |
| Radio, national | 3 | 2 | 5 | 4 | 1 |
| Radio, local | 8 | 14 | 4 | 2 | 1 |
| National news | 11 | 5 | 21 | 18 | 7 |
| Local news | 14 | 22 | 9 | 5 | 5 |
| Garden magazine | 1 | 0 | 1 | 2 | 3 |
| Tourist brochure | 2 | 1 | 1 | 3 | 12 |
| Travel agent | 1 | 0 | 0 | 1 | 11 |
| Local knowledge | 30 | 57 | 12 | 2 | 0 |
| Friends, relatives | 11 | 7 | 11 | 17 | 25 |

Source: N.O.P. (1985).

Table 4.15.
Sources of information: urban leisure centres

|                      | Centre A<br>% | Centre B<br>% |
|----------------------|---------------|---------------|
| Local newspapers     | 17            | 38            |
| Promotional leaflets | 11            | 24            |
| Posters              | 10            | 29            |
| Word of mouth        | 50            | 37            |

Source: Yorke (1984c).


advertising campaign. The levels of awareness of the
facilities offered and the sources of information differed
markedly between the centres. A broader age-range had
significantly higher levels of awareness of a wider range of
facilities available at the actively promoted centre (B).
This was achieved by advertising in shopping centres,
schools, youth centres, by house to house pamphlet
distribution, and via the local press, including a free
community newspaper (Table 4.15). Centre B was consequently
used by more people, drawn from a wider age and social range
than its less-promoted counterpart. This had positive
implications for additional investment in both the range and
quality of services offered in centre B and is indicative of
the potential effectiveness of locally based advertising
campaigns.


## Local government services: marketing and advertising issues

In recent years, a stronger commercial dimension, involving
marketing and advertising considerations has increasingly
been introduced into the operation of public non-profit
orientated services. This reflects the development of
restrictions on public finance and an associated growth in
the degree of financial accountability required in the
provision of public services. This has occurred widely in
the management of theatres, museums, public libraries,
leisure and recreation centres, and local government
publications.
The development of active marketing and advertising
strategies for these services is still in a formative stage
compared with the leisure activities discussed in the
previous sections. The general problems associated with
their marketing and promotion were reviewed in an earlier
section. However, the issues raised in the literature on
local government service provision are worthy of
consideration in the current context since they are equally
apposite to the promotion of historic sites by public
bodies. A recurring theme is the need to specify CLEAR
OBJECTIVES. Nebulous concepts, such as to serve the 'public
interest' or the 'community' are insufficiently precise for
the development of strong promotional strategies
incorporating a meaningful 'product' image and effective

target marketing. This was considered essential by Cowell (1984) for the marketing of local government recreation and leisure services, and was seen as equally important for public library services (Coleman, 1984). Positive moves in this direction have been noted by Hardy (1981) for the grant-aided sector of the theatre. Objectives such as the dissemination of culture; the development of education and social awareness; to provide a platform for minority tastes; and, to create a community atmosphere in the urban population; have all been widely identified. However, even these are considered to be lacking in precision. For example, with regard to the 'dissemination of culture' the questions of what culture?; how should it be disseminated?; and to whom? are seen as requiring closer definition. The other objectives are also seen as somewhat lacking in precision. The clarification of these issues are seen as providing a necessary base for promotional activities and target marketing (Hardy, 1981).

An even more pervasive issue is the need to develop a stronger CONSUMER ORIENTATION. The integration of marketing with product development and the need to develop a product that people will want to buy has been widely recognised in the context of local authority publishing. The Hampshire Country Heritage Series of publications is seen as a particularly good example of this trend (Kerrington, 1984). Elsewhere, stronger positive moves in this direction are still considered necessary. A consumer orientation has been significantly lacking in the context of museum services. Historically, museum directors have regarded marketing and management techniques as having little to contribute. This has been combined with a minimum consumer orientation relative to the esoteric aims of promoting culture and conservation (Yorke and Jones, 1984). The objections to the development of a stronger market orientation have been that excessive demand may be stimulated which cannot be adequately met by existing resources. This might result in a large dissatisfied clientele rather than a satisfied minority. Yorke and Jones (1984) suggest that this is not necessarily the implication of a stronger market orientation. In the first instance, it may well be that some of the existing facilities are currently under-utilised, while larger audiences are capable of generating greater income, which, if managed carefully, could satisfy the specialist minority interest as well as a wider public without seriously disaffecting either group.

The potential conflict between a mass appeal-consumer orientation and the provision of traditionally minority cultural facilities was also apparent in the context of the marketing of theatrical productions. Characteristically, theatre audiences tend to be predominantly drawn from the higher status groups (AB) and students, categories which comprise only 17% of the population at large (Hardy, 1981). This reflects the 'high culture programmes' orientation of many artistic directors. It was considered that no amount of advertising will create a wider based popular appeal and associated higher levels of ticket sales. This is seen as requiring a modification of programme planning to appeal to a wider array of tastes.

A similar situation exists in the provision of public library services. Only 25% of the population are regular users of public libraries, while as few as 10% of the population is estimated to account for 98% of their use (Cronin, 1984). Again, it is recognised that there is a need to move away from the rather paternalistic stance of providing the 'best' of current literature towards a 'demand driven' service providing literature with a broader 'popular' appeal, if the service is to remain viable. Coleman (1984) suggested that the apparently alternative objectives need not necessarily be in conflict and that the public library service ' ... must engage in a constant process of monitoring use, whilst planning and introducing new services in order to retain present users and attract new ones'.

In conjunction with the development of a stronger consumer orientation, the literature also stresses the need to analyse and monitor the nature of the existing and future market (MARKET ANALYSIS AND SEGMENTATION), if the service is to be maximised. Moves in these directions have, however, varied significantly between the different services. Detailed investigations of this kind are still being urged to assist the management of local authority recreation and leisure services (Cowell, 1984). Similarly, for theatres the concentration of much 'market analysis' upon information derived from user surveys is recognised as having serious deficiencies since it says nothing of the non-theatre going public.

For museums the situation is more positive. Attendance figures and visitors surveys have been available for a long period of time. These have served a useful monitoring function in terms of the changing profiles of the museum-going population; the reasons for, and manner in which the services are being used; and the primary sources of information associated with visits. Many examples of such surveys are available (McWilliams and Hopgood, 1972; Greene, 1978). In addition, it seems that 'Museum workers have realised that effective surveys require the expertise of the social scientists if they are to be of any value' (Yorke and Jones, 1984). This is exemplified by Erwin's (1971) early study undertaken for the Ulster Museum in Belfast. It was not confined to an analysis of existing users but investigated a random sample of the general public and provided information on usage and awareness of the nature of the museum and related these to the social profiles of users and non-users throughout Belfast.

The situation is substantially similar in the case of public libraries. User surveys have been undertaken for some time and occasionally incorporate a significant degree of analytical sophistication. For example, Durcan's (1984) survey of the users of the central reference library in Derby provides some interesting insights into current patterns of usage. In addition, Cronin (1984) suggests that the need to incorporate the non-user as well as the user in

Table 4.16.
Information sources of people attending a discarded books sale

| | Customers attending sale |
|---|---|
| N = | 3273 |
| | N |
| Information: | |
| T.V. (3 by 7 secs. adverts) | 269 |
| Radio | 64 |
| Posters | 852 |
| Word of mouth | 553 |
| Newspaper feature | 129 |
| Newspaper advertisement | 1147 |
| Other (passers by) | 259 |

Source: Turner (1984).

marketing investigations of public library services is widely recognised in the profession.

As to ADVERTISING EFFECTIVENESS, there has been little investigation of the limited amounts of advertising undertaken to promote local government services. In essence, advertising strategies for these services are less well developed than for leisure and recreational activities. However, a survey of the information sources of people attending a sale of discarded library books in Falkirk is of interest (Table 4.16). This demonstrates the importance of the 'local' advertising media, particularly newspapers and posters, for the promotion of a local 'event'. This is broadly consistent with the advertising of particular recreation sites discussed earlier. However, in the absence of detailed information of the relative expenditure of the different media, no further conclusions can be drawn.

Also in the wider context of advertising, the use of various PROMOTIONAL ACTIVITES raises some additional issues. Promotion in this sense is defined by Cowell (1984) as the various devices designed to generate or heighten an interest in a facility among target market segments. These involve variable pricing mechanisms, such as discounts or group reductions; product devices such as 'image' or brand name promotions; and distribution devices such as game, charity event or visiting personality promotions. Essentially, these involve price manipulations or magnet attractions of various sorts.

Cowell suggests that such devices should not simply be judged in terms of the short term gains which might accrue from them, since they are likely to have longer term 'tactical' results in developing, maintaining or enhancing the image of the facility being promoted. In a similar fashion, some of the ancillary income generating activities increasingly associated with public service provision such as the sale of literary, craft and artistic materials in theatre shops (Hardy, 1981) or the commissioning of local history books, pamphlets, maps, postcards, pencils, tea towels and other trivia for sale in libraries or museums (Turner, 1984) is partly aimed at the same kind of effect. The advertising effectiveness, however, of such devices has yet to be investigated.

## Market segmentation and target marketing

A recurring theme in the literature on advertising effectiveness is the potential significance of market segmentation, i.e. the fact that goods and services are likely to appeal to, or be used by some sections of the community rather than others. This segmentation tends to occur, for example, by social status, age, stage in the life cycle and geographical location (national, regional or local); by particular interest groups; or by characteristics such as ethnicity or personality type. In particular, segmentation by social characteristics has been discussed in Chapter 2.

To be of value for marketing, Kotler (1980) suggests that such segments must exhibit a number of features. They must be measurable within the context of social survey methods at reasonable cost. They must be accessible via conventional advertising and promotional strategies, again at reasonable cost. They must be of a size sufficient to be worthy of commercial consideration. The specifics of these parameters will, of course, vary according to the nature of the product or service and the associated size of advertising budget.

The practical advantages of a knowledge of market segmentation is its use for target marketing (Yorke, 1984a). This involves three main issues. The first of these is the maximization of advertising effectiveness by aiming at the consumer segments defined as most likely to buy the product or use the service. These segments are derived from profiles of existing customers or users. However, the initial market analysis has the additional value of identifying gaps in the market for potential development, while also providing information on consumer attitudes which can be used to improve the customer appeal or consumer orientation of the product.

With respect to the marketing of historic sites a number of implications emerge from the earlier discussion. If the primary aim of advertising and promotion is to increase the use of a facility throughout the whole community, then the mass audience accessibility of television combined with a number of newspapers and magazines is likely to be the most effective strategy. Existing information relating to visitors to ancient monuments, however, suggests the potential value of market segmentation. The market is, for example, segmented geographically. Tourists are attracted to holiday areas in varying proportions from particular regions or countries. (see figures in Table 2.20). Likewise, visitors have been shown to travel relatively short distances to a historic site on the day of their visit (see figures in Table 2.14). Visitor profiles also exhibit a high incidence of the more mobile, higher status (AB) groups; many of whom fall into the 'family with young children' category; while those with particular historical interests constitute an additional sub-group. Similarly, the division between home-based visitors and staying holiday-makers have been demonstrated to be a strongly recurring feature of visitor surveys (Table 2.12). Such visitor profiles will be refined further as more information becomes available, but there is already little doubt of the importance of these sorts of market segmentation. These features can be incorporated in a marketing campaign by applying a range of target marketing strategies. In a television campaign the screening time has direct implications for the age-groups exposed to the advertisements. This is of particular significance if the aim is to generate interest amongst the younger age-groups. Similarly, the association of the advertisements with particular programmes can have social status implications for the audience reached. The content of the advertising can also be varied according to the target groups aimed at in order to achieve maximum attention. A fortuitous choice of particular national newspapers and magazines is likely to achieve the same kinds of result.

However, the short journeys (under 50 miles) undertaken by the great majority of visitors to historic sites suggests the value of spatially specific forms of promotional activity. At the same time, staying holiday-makers and home-based visitors are likely to respond to varying emphases in strategy. The earlier analysis of sources of information used by visitors suggested that the interest of staying holiday-makers is likely to be best generated via their accommodation, guide books, tourist information centres, local newspapers and improved signposting. The importance of providing effective publicity material at other major attractions was also indicated. The analysis of other sites visited and activities undertaken by visitors to Cadw sites in Chapter 3 is indicative of the kinds of locations at which such information might be disseminated most effectively. Similar information channels are likely to generate the interest of the home-based visitor. In this case, however, local newspapers, and posters in a variety of locations such as shopping centres, schools and leisure centres are likely to prove more important, while the greater potential effect of television advertising was also identified for this group.

In addition, the residential areas most or least likely to house potential visitors can be identified reasonably accurately using a combination of visitor survey information and census data. Visitor surveys can be used to establish a social profile of likely visitor and non-visitor types. The geographical distribution of the homes, or trip origins, of visitors can also be determined, either using conventional large scale maps and gazeteers, or, if postcode data is available, with the aid of the Central Postcode Directory (O.P.C.S., 1985) (1.6 million postcodes cover the whole country, one for approximately 10 households). This information can be matched with the Small Area Statistics data from the 1981 census at either the Enumeration District

level (130,000 for Great Britain) or at the larger scale
Ward level. By using standard target selection and
classification techniques via a main frame or micro computer
the areas to which target marketing or investigative surveys
should be directed can be identified (e.g. Edwards, 1985;
Yorke, and Meehan, 1986).

With regard to historic sites visitors are drawn strongly
from car-owning category AB families, primarily of the
middle age ranges (25-44). Using these criteria in
combination, Figure 4.1 has been compiled using the 1981
census ward data to illustrate the areas from which the
existing profile of visitors to Cadw sites from Wales are
most likely to come. Thus, if the aim of promotional
policies is to attract greater numbers of home-based day-
trippers similar to current visitor types, these are the
principal target marketing areas to which effort should be
directed. The areas are of two types. The higher status
suburban or rural margins of the larger towns of South Wales
are represented. Notable concentrations occur around
Cardiff extending west through the Vale of Glamorgan, as
well as to the west of Swansea and the adjoining parts of
the Gower Peninsula. In addition, a sporadic distribution
occurs widely throughout the sparsely populated parts of
rural Wales. This pattern, however, suggests a weak
promotional potential, since large parts of the urban
population concentrations of North East Wales, the three
large coastal towns of the South, and the coalfield valley
communities are not represented strongly amongst the target
areas. On a more positive note, however, if the absolute
numbers of persons in AB households are examined rather than
their relative concentration, a more encouraging situation
emerges (Figure 4.2). High status households are to be
found in significant numbers spread widely throughout
Cardiff, Swansea and Newport, amongst the valley
communities, and in restricted parts of North Wales.

Alternatively, should the aim be to extend the market by
promoting more visits from the skilled non-manual group
(C1), target marketing opportunities also exist. Figure 4.3
exhibits the relative concentration of this group which is
represented strongly throughout the urban population
concentrations of North and South Wales. The significance
of this pattern is confirmed by Figure 4.4 which identifies
the absolute concentrations of this group, largely in the
urban areas. At the other extreme, Figure 4.5 indicates the
distribution of the lower status households (C2 and D), few
of whom currently visit Cadw sites. In the short term,
these are the areas least likely to respond to promotional
efforts since the residents have relatively low levels of
car-ownership and are likely to require the enhancement of
the entertainment dimension of sites to attract a visit.

These findings are not intended as a definitive analysis
of target marketing for Cadw sites, but rather to indicate
the kinds of data and methods available to assist the
development of marketing initiatives. Such analyses can
also be undertaken at the smaller scale of the census
enumeration district to develop more detailed target
marketing strategies, either within cities or in the

Figure 4.1.
Cadw target marketing areas for home-based visitors

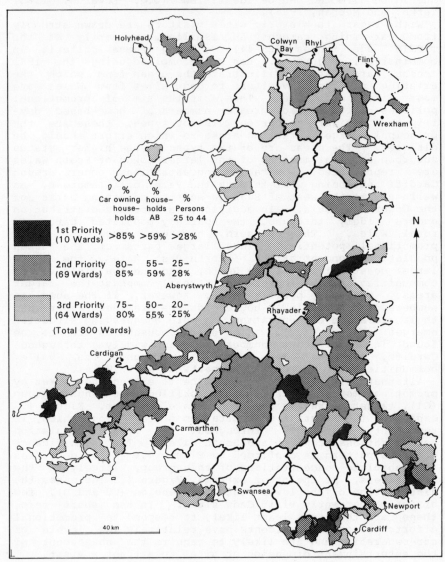

Figure 4.2.
Numbers of persons in households with economically active
head in Social Classes I and II (AB)

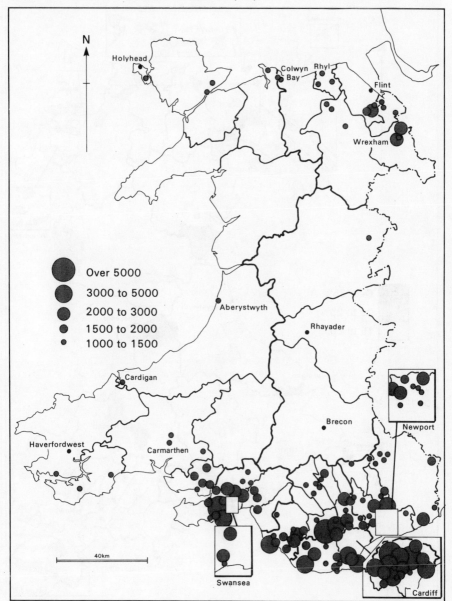

Figure 4.3.
Percentage of persons in households with economically active
head in Social Class III non manual (C1)

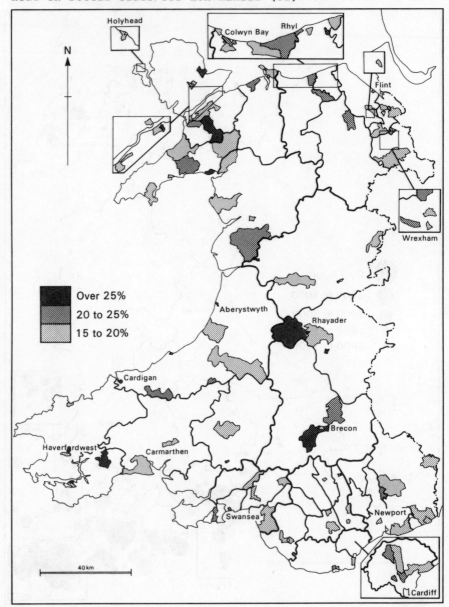

Over 25%
20 to 25%
15 to 20%

Holyhead
Colwyn Bay
Rhyl
Flint
Wrexham
Aberystwyth
Rhayader
Cardigan
Brecon
Haverfordwest
Carmarthen
Swansea
Newport
Cardiff

N

40 km

Figure 4.4.
Numbers of persons in households with economically active
head in Social Class III non-manual (Cl)

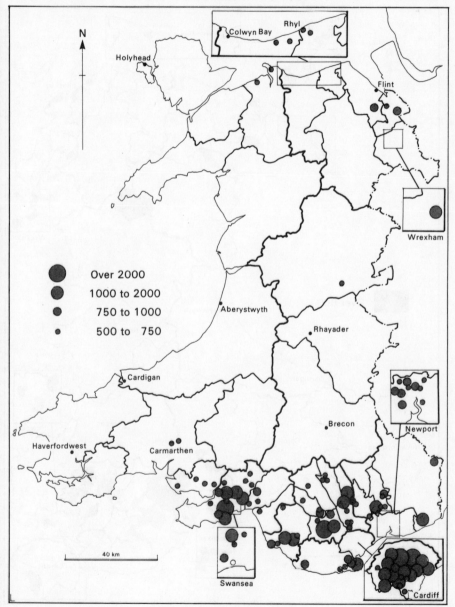

# Figure 4.5.
Percentage of persons in households with economically active head in Social Classes III manual, IV and V

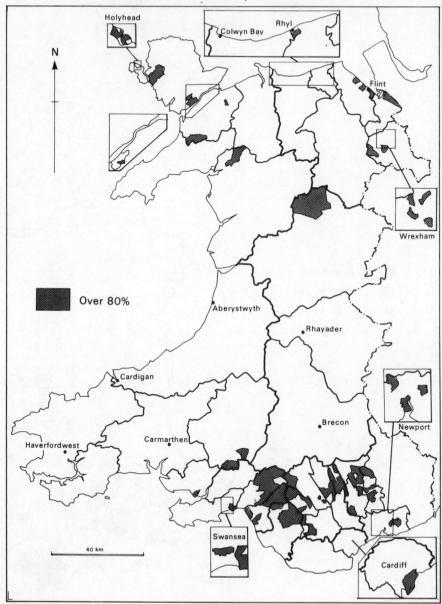

environs of a particular site. This kind of analysis is undertaken at most academic institutions, but is also offered as a commercial service by a number of specialist market research firms (O.P.C.S., 1985). Such investigations can incorporate the 'Target Group Index' developed by the British Market Research Bureau. This provides patterns of expenditure on goods and services defined by criteria such as age and social status (Rowley, 1984). Such techniques are also useful for the identification of lists of addressed most likely to elicit positive responses from postal promotional campaigns.

Conclusions

Marketing has recently emerged as an increasingly important issue for the management and development of historic sites. Specific studies of the promotion of historic and heritage sites are, however, not widely available. This chapter has, therefore, presented a broad review of the literature on marketing and advertising, potentially relevant to the promotion of ancient monuments in an increasingly competitive commercial environment.

Initially, a number of factors were identified which were considered central to the maximization of advertising effectiveness. This was followed by an assessment of the difficulty of measuring the effect of promotional initiatives, particularly in the context of leisure facilities. At best, it was suggested that short-term monitoring studies might provide a general indication of the impact of advertising campaigns on visitor numbers at historic sites.

The particular difficulties associated with marketing public services were also considered. The discussion identified the need for a stronger consumer orientation in developmental and marketing strategies, combined with clear policy objectives and a stronger "product-like" image for marketing leisure facilities. The achievement of these aims implied the need for stronger market research as a basis for policy formulation.

Advertising effectiveness was then examined more specifically in the context of leisure activities. The bulk of this literature, however, relates to the promotion of tourism rather than heritage sites. Nevertheless, some additional insights relevant to an assessment of promotional activities emerged. The relative efficiency of the different media for reaching mass audiences or specific target groups was suggested. Superficially, however, much of the evidence suggested the limited persuasional impact of advertising, although the evidence on this point was not unambiguous. In fact, the need for more precise forms of social survey analysis was proposed, if the promotional impact of advertising is to be judged more accurately.

Investigations of the marketing and advertising effectiveness of particular recreational sites were of more direct value to the heritage situation. Again, the limited positive value of various advertising strategies was initially suggested. The sources of information relevant to the trip decision-making process were apparently dominated by informal 'local' and 'social' channels of communication. The evidence of more detailed analyses, however, suggested far stronger advertising inputs of a variety of media than appeared at first sight. Evidently, there is a need for more sophisticated analyses of the trip decision-making process, if the effectiveness of advertising is to be adequately assessed.

The extension of the debate to the wider field of the marketing and advertising of local government services was also of value. Recent central government demands for economic accountability in the public sector have placed the providers of public recreational and cultural facilities in much the same position as the public bodies responsible for heritage sites. The local government experience served to reiterate the importance of clear policy objectives, a stronger consumer orientation, and the need for market research to maximize advertising and promotional activities.

The broad body of evidence reviewed in this chapter recurringly emphasise the need for effective market research to maximize the promotion of historic sites and to determine the significance of advertising amongst the various possible strategies. The concluding section stressed the importance of a precise knowledge of market segmentation and the potential value of target marketing techniques for the promotion of historic and heritage sites.

## References

Achenbaum, A. A. (1972). Advertising doesn't manipulate consumers. Journal of Advertising Research, 12, 2, 3-13.

Barwise, T. P., Ehrenberg A. S. C. and Goodhardt G. J. (1979). Audience appreciation and audiences size. Journal of the Market Research Society, 21, 4, 269-289.

Beltramini, R. F. (1981). Consumer - client orientation and public service marketing. European Journal of Marketing, 15, 4, 17-25.

Bord Failte (1985). We've been to Ireland! A report on a survey of visitor impressions. Dublin: Bord Failte.

British Tourist Authority and the Countryside Commision (1968). Historic houses survey. London: British Tourist Authority.

Broadbent, S. (1979). One way T.V. advertisements work. Journal of the Market Research Society, 21, 2, 139-165.

Burkart, A. J. and Medlik, S. (1974). Tourism. Past, present and future. London: Heinemann.

Carpenter, R. (1983). National daily and Sunday newspapers. In Bullmore and Waterson (Eds.). The Advertising Association handbook. pp. 35-57. London: Holt, Rinehart and Winston.

Coleman, P. (1984). Public libraries can and do make a difference: a case to be proved. European Journal of Marketing, 18, 2, 56-64.

Colman, S. and Brown, G. (1983). Advertising tracking studies and sales effects. *Journal of the Market Research Society*, 25, 2, 165-183.

Coppen-Gardner, B. (1983). Independent radio. In Bullmore and Waterson (Eds.). *The Advertising Association handbook*. pp. 100-114. London: Holt, Rinehart and Winston.

Corkindale, D. R. (1984). Measuring the sales effectiveness of advertising. The role of an ADLAB in the U.K.. *Journal of the Market Research Society*, 18, 2, 114-120.

Cowell, D. W. (1984). Sales promotions and the marketing of local government recreation and leisure services. *European Journal of Marketing*, 18, 2, 114-120.

Cronin, B. (1984). The marketing of public library services in the United Kingdom - The rationale for a marketing approach. The marketing of public library services in the U.K. - Practical applications. *European Journal of Marketing*, 18, 2, 33-44, 45-55.

Davies, R. L. (1973). *Patterns and profiles of consumer behaviour*. Newcastle Upon Tyne: Department of Geography, University of Newcastle Upon Tyne.

Durcan, A. (1984). A reference library talks to its users. *European Journal of Marketing*, 18, 2, 65-71.

Erwin, D. G. (1971). The Belfast public and the Ulster museum - a statistical survey. *Museum Journal*, 70, 4, 175-180.

Foxall, G. (1984a). The meaning of marketing and leisure: issues for research and devlopment. *European Journal of Marketing*, 18, 2, 23-32.

Foxall, G. R. (1975). Social factors in consumer choice: replication and extension. *Journal of Consumer Research*, 2, 1, 60-64.

Foxall, G. R. (1977). *Consumer behaviour: a practical guide*. Corbridge: Retail and Planning Associates.

Greene, J. P. (1978). A visitor survey at Norton Priory museum. *Museum Journal*, 78, 7-9.

Greenley, G. E. and Matcham, A. S. (1983). Problems in marketing services: the case of incoming tourism. *European Journal of Marketing*, 17, 6, 57-64.

Gunter, H. and Kleinert, H. (1978). The effects of advertising on children - some empirical research results, (abstracted from Jahrbuch der Absatz - und Verbrauchsforschung 1978, 4, 261-271). In Review of European Marketing, 8. *European Journal of Marketing*, 14, 9, 1980.

Hardy, L. W. (1981). Theatre objectives and marketing planning. *European Journal of Marketing*, 15, 4, 3-16.

Harris Research Centre (1984). *The effectiveness of ATB promotions; research report; and, phase 1 tabulations*. Richmond Upon Thames: Harris Research Centre.

Herbert, D. T. and Aubrey, P. (1982). *Work and leisure in a changing industrial region*. (A report for the Sports Council and SSRC Joint Panel on Leisure and Recreation Research). Swansea: Department of Geography, University College of Swansea.

Howard, J. A. (1965). *Marketing theory*. New York: Allyn and Bacon.

Jones, S. and Corr, P. (1985). A report of research findings to assist in a review of brochure policy. London: Schlackman Research.

Kaynak, E. and Mitchell, L. A. (1981). A comparative study of advertising in Canada, the United Kingdom and Turkey. European Journal of Marketing, 15, 1, 1-9.

Kennington, D. (1984). Local authority publishing in the United Kingdom. European Journal of Marketing, 18, 2, 121-128.

Kotler, P. (1980). Marketing management. 4th Edition. New York: Prentice Hall.

Kotler, P. and Levy, S. J. (1969). Broadening the concept of marketing. Journal of Marketing, 33, 1, 10-15.

Kroeber-Riel, W. (1977). Advertising through the emotions - for capital goods too, (abstracted from Rationalisierung 1977, 28, 10, 207-210). In Review of European Marketing Literature, 37. European Journal of Marketing, 14, 9.

Krugman, H. (1965). The impact of television advertising: learning without involvement. Public Opinion Quarterly, 29.

Lee, G. M. (1985). Personal communication from the Scottish Development Department, 10th October, 1985.

Mackenzie, S. (1985). Recreation and holidays in the countryside. Scottish leisure survey report no 1. Perth: Countryside Commision for Scotland.

Marplan Ltd., (1984). A survey of non-business visitors to Wales, 1984. (And 3 appendix volumes). London: Marplan Ltd.

McWilliams, B. and Hopgood, J. (1972). The public of Norwich Castle Museum 1971-72. Museum Journal, 72, 153-156.

Mears, W. (1976). Survey of visitors to tourist attractions 1974. Reports. Cardiff: Wales Tourist Board.

Meyer, P. and Tostmann, T. (1978). The marketing of services, (abstracted from Jahrbuch der Absatz - und Verbrauchsforschung, 1978, 4, 286 - 294). In Review of European Marketing Literature, 16. European Journal of Marketing, 14, 9.

Neilson Researcher (1973). Test marketing reduces risk, Jan/Feb, 1973, 10.

N.O.P. Market Research Ltd. (1985). Survey of visitors to the Liverpool Garden Festival, 1984. Final report. (Prepared for the Department of the Environment). (NOP/3553). London: NOP Market Research Ltd.

Northern Ireland Tourist Board (1982). Surveys of visitors to Ulster - American Folk Park. Belfast: Northern Ireland Tourist Board.

Nuttall, C. G. F. (1962). TV commercial audiences in the United Kingdom. Journal of Advertising Research, 2, 3, 19-28.

O.P.C.S. (1985). Census 1981. O.P.C,S. Monitor 20/8/85. Ref 85/2.

Penny, N. J. (1984). A geographical study of intra-urban shopping behaviour in Greater Swansea. Unpublished Ph.D thesis. Swansea: University of Wales, University College of Swansea.

Phillips, D. R. (1978). The utilisation of, and the attitudes of the public to general practitioner services: a geographical study in West Glamorgan. Unpublished PhD. thesis. Swansea: University of Wales, University College of Swansea.

Research Bureau Ltd. (1984). Scottish Tourist Board, marketing follow up study 1984, 'Scotland's for me' brochure recipients; postal survey stage 1; telephone follow up survey stage 2. (Prepared for the Scottish Tourist Board). London: Research Bureau Ltd.

Research (International) Bureau Ltd. (1983). Scottish Tourist Board marketing follow up study 1983, interim report. (RBL 33097). (Prepared for the Scottish Tourist Board). London: Research Bureau Ltd.

Research (International) Bureau Ltd. (1984). Scottish Tourist Board marketing follow up study, 1984. (Prepared for the Scottish Tourist Board). (Job 01147). London: Research Bureau Ltd.

Research Surveys of Ireland Ltd. (1983). Bord Failte - Fota Island study. (Written and tabular reports). Dublin: Research Surveys of Ireland Ltd.

Ritch, S. U. and Jain, S. C. (1968). Social class and life cycle as predictors of shopping behaviour. Journal of Marketing Research, 5, 41-49.

Ritchie, J. R. and La Breque, R. J. (1975). Marketing research and public policy: a functional perspective. Journal of Marketing, 69, 12-19.

Rowley, G. (1984). Data bases and their integration for retail geography: a British example. Transactions, Institute of British Geographers (New Series), 9, 4, 460-476.

Sanctuary, B. (1983). The ITV companies. In Bullmore and Waterson (Eds.). The Advertising Association handbook. pp. 90-91. London: Holt, Rindhart and Winston.

Seren (1986a). Herbert, D. T., Prentice, R. C., Thomas, C. J., Edwards, J. A., Humphrys, G., Prentice, M. M.. Easter 1986 visitor survey. Final report. Swansea: Social Economic Research and Environment, Department of Geography, University College of Swansea.

Seren (1986c). Herbert, D. T., Prentice, R. C., Thomas, C. J., Prentice, M. M. General survey at Cadw sites. Summer 1986. Swansea: Social Economic Research and Environment, Department of Geography, University College of Swansea.

Shapiro, B. P. (1973). Marketing for non-profit organisations. Harvard Business Review, Sept/Oct 1973, 123-132.

Shepherd, I. D. H. and Thomas, C. J. (1980). Urban consumer behaviour. In Dawson J. A. (Ed.) Retail geography. Chapter 1. pp. 18-94. London: Croom Helm.

Steiner, G. A. (1966). The people look at commercials: a study of audience behaviour. Journal of Business, 29, 272-304.

Travel and Tourism Research (1982). Marketing follow up study 1982. Final report. (Ref T144/final). London: Travel and Tourism Research; and Edinburgh: Scottish Tourist Board.

Travel and Tourism Research (Peter Hodgson & Associates) (1979). *Travel agents survey 1979. The effectiveness of 1979 marketing promotions: Travel Trade research 1, 2, 3 and Interim summary report.* London: Travel and Tourism Research.

Turner, N. (1984). Marketing the library service - sales and promotions. *European Journal of Marketing*, 18, 2, 72-81.

Twyman, T. (1979). The state of media research. *Journal of Market Research Society*, 21, 3, 221-227.

Wales Tourist Board (Strategic Planning and Research Unit) (1978). *Resort advertising campaign, 1978.* Cardiff: Wales Tourist Board.

Wales Tourist Board (Strategic Planning and Research Unit) (1979). *Resort advertising campaign, 1979.* Cardiff: Wales Tourist Board.

Wolfe, A. (1983). Public attitudes to advertising in the U.K. In Bullmore and Waterson (Eds.). *The Advertising Association handbook.* pp. 361-370

Yorke, D. (1984a). The marketing of local authority leisure services: introduction. *European Journal of Marketing*, 18, 2. 6-9.

Yorke, D. (1984b). Marketing and non-profit making organisations. *European Journal of Marketing*, 18, 2, 17-22.

Yorke, D. A. (1984). The definition of market segments for leisure centre services: theory and practice. *European Journal of Marketing*, 18, 2, 100-113.

Yorke, D. A. and Jones, R. R. (1984). Marketing and museums. *European Journal of Marketing*, 18, 2, 90-99.

Yorke, D. A., and Meehan, S. A. (1986). ACORN in the political marketplace. *European Journal of Marketing*, 20, 8, 63-76.

# 5 The heritage market of historic sites as educational resources

M MERLE PRENTICE AND
RICHARD C PRENTICE

## Introduction

In considering the potential of historic sites as
educational resources it is useful to consider the current
debate in the teaching of history under three headings.
Firstly, school education for children; secondly, historical
education for tourists; and thirdly, environmental education
and conservation of heritage. Each of these topics will be
discussed in turn, although in reality they are inter-
linked; for example, a child's experience as a young tourist
at Tintern Abbey may have important effects not only on the
child's understanding of that period of history at school
but also of the literature associated with the site, namely
Wordsworth's poetry: in addition, an appreciation of the
history and beauty of the Wye Valley may encourage the child
into a wider awareness of the environment, through which the
child will hopefully learn a greater respect for the
environment.

As a comparison with the discussion of current
developments in the teaching of history this chapter looks
at the present position in schools, concerning visits by
schools to heritage sites and their place in the curriculum.
The objectives of agencies promoting heritage education are
considered as an illustration of the varied interests of
agencies in heritage education. Evidence of the educational
interest of visitors, actual and potential, to sites is also
reviewed, as are the educational resources at sites.

Throughout the chapter reference will be made repeatedly
to the need to review the effectiveness of school visits

143

made to heritage sites. As site managers may not be familiar with the techniques of assessment available to school teachers a section is included to outline some of the more relevant techniques. It is the application of such techniques of assessment to visits to heritage sites which presents an exciting challenge into the 1990s.

## School education for children

Debates about the school curriculum over the past decade have produced a series of educational aims for primary and secondary schools. These aims have recently been summarised by the Schools Inspectorate and are:

  to help pupils to develop lively, enquiring minds, the ability to question and argue rationally and to apply themselves to tasks, and physical skills;

  to help pupils to acquire knowledge and skills relevant to adult life and employment in a fast changing world;

  to help pupils to use language and number effectively;

  to instil respect for religious and moral values, and tolerance of other races, religions and ways of life;

  to help pupils to understand the world in which they live, and the interdependence of individuals, groups and nations;

  to help pupils to appreciate human achievements and aspirations. (DES, 1985a, p. 3).

The contemporary teaching of history can concur with these aims. However, many site managers will recall the learning of history at school as the rote learning of dates and facts about political history. This was the traditional teaching of 'content', or a body of knowledge, rather than the understanding of 'concepts'. While the teaching of concepts cannot be divorced from the teaching of content the methods of teaching differ, particularly in that a text book may suffice for the teaching of content whereas field work is desirable in the teaching of concepts.

The Schools Inspectorate have made particular recommendations for the progressive development of historical skills in pupils aged 8-16 in the teaching of history through the primary and secondary schools. In the Inspectorates' summary view, history ' ... is concerned with explanations and origins ... it demands evidence to support statements ... and it depends on skills of reasoning, criticism and communications. History is concerned not with the conveying of accepted facts but with the making of informed judgements, and to the displaying of, the evidence on which those judgements are made' (DES, 1985b, p. 1). Specifically, the Inspectorate argue that history should be taught to enable the child's development towards an awareness of the nature of evidence; encouraging the asking of questions and the making of informed judgements; a sense of chronology; an empathy for historical situations and people; awareness of multiple causation; and an understanding of human environments.

In teaching an awareness of the nature of evidence the Inspectorate have suggested that the child should be encouraged not to generalise from premises based on inadequate evidence which may lead to an incorrect conclusion based on overgeneralisation or ignorance of the full circumstances. The Inspectorate recommend that ' ... pupils should be expected to collect evidence, judge its relevance to the present purpose, identify significant features or patterns in it, offer explanations for them, test the explanation by reference to other evidence, and arrive at a conclusion based on this process' (DES, 1985a, pp. 31-32).

Another ability to be developed is that of asking questions and making informed judgements. The Inspectorate termed this capability 'the key to historical knowledge' (DES, 1985b, p. 3). Questioning included the questioning of causation, function or technique; or past roles and behaviour, beliefs, opinions and attitudes. Furthermore, pupils should be helped to appreciate that the present world developed out of the past. The themes which are studied should allow the children to look for both similarities and differences between the past and the present, and to seek to explain why and how a change did or did not occur and thus to develop a sense of chronological sequence. An understanding of chronology can be developed either by reference to events from within the memory of the child and his or her family, or by reference ' ... to objects, places and pictures, so that stories and events are differentiated not only by dates but also, for example, by dress, weapons, forms of transport, or buildings' (DES, 1985b, p. 4). In asking what is different and what is the same between periods, children not only develop a sense of chronology but also a sense of continuity and change, and an awareness of anachronism.

Historical empathy is seen as the ability to enter into an informed appreciation of the points of view of people in the past, their predicaments and solutions to the problems they encounter in everyday life. This involves the child having the ability to see others as, and in the circumstances that, they saw themselves: this may be termed a Time Reflection Approach to Learning. Children should be taught that events may have more than one cause and because of this historical explanations are necessarily tentative, often qualified and liable to exceptions. Historical explanation seeks to link the occasion with the underlying trends or tensions: 'Pupils need to understand that human beings, in shaping their world, making their living, planning their futures, developing forms of government and law, are influenced to a greater or lesser degree by ideas and beliefs by their past, by the places and conditions in which they live and by the ways in which they need to relate to each other' (DES, 1985a, p. 19). In particular, pupils need to be aware that consecutive events do not necessarily have a causal relationship, but may be caused by other factors.

145

Finally, the Inspectorate see history as a part of environmental education seeking to develop an awareness, appreciation and understanding of surroundings both in the past and as they are related to the present. School based teaching of history can be either passive or active. Passive learning is where the child is taught in a didactic style by the teacher whereas active learning requires some involvement or input by the child, such as discussion, model making or a field study. Passive learning has often, in the past, been the learning of more and more historical facts with an emphasis placed on acquiring, remembering and recalling facts at competitive, high standards. The Schools Inspectorate have commented, 'Too often the difference measured between young people studying history at the age of 16 and those studying at the age of 9 or 10 is solely in terms of an increase of information, and this is a tradition that dies hard' (DES, 1985b, p. 1). This simple assimilation of facts does not meet the objectives set by the Inspectorate for school teaching in general nor for the teaching of history in particular. Furthermore, this assimilation of facts has often been described as boring, tedious and incomprehensible to children (e.g. Schurer, 1984). While it is not impossible to develop conceptual learning by passive learning, the development of conceptual understanding generally requires the pupil to employ a range of intellectual and physical skills. These skills may include not only intellectual and physical skills but also social skills (e.g. Nichol, 1984). Intellectual skills include the ability to find information from a variety of sources; social skills include the ability to participate in small groups and to exercise empathy; physical skills include the ability to manipulate equipment. Obviously, the development of such skills is more readily developed by active learning techniques than by passive learning techniques.

Active learning techniques include encouraging children to handle objects, to look at pictures, photographs and maps, to listen and to talk, to paint, to act, and to produce models. Techniques of this kind can readily be applied to the teaching of local history. Local history, and particularly the study of local population history is are now becoming increasingly popular in primary and early secondary school teaching (Schurer, 1984). Local history studies enable children to relate their work to the streets, houses and shops and often the families, which surround them: history is their inheritance.

In teaching historical empathy pupils can be encouraged, for example, to make domestic artefacts which were produced in the past by men and women in their homes. Artefacts of this kind include rug making and patchwork bedspreads both made from rags, and the production of vegetable dyes to colour clothes. Rug making and patchwork demonstrates the need of people in the past to recyle material whilst being both creative and productive. The production of vegetable dyes demonstrate that what we now term as weeds in the past include plants which were of everyday use and value. It should not be forgotten that the community includes

146

specialists, for example museum curators, who may be of assistance in active learning by bringing their expertise into the classroom along with artefacts and pictures which the children can be encouraged to handle, and discuss with him.

Active learning techniques extend beyond the school, and include both fieldwork and field visits. Fieldwork involves some project or task on site, outside the school, by the pupils; field visits are where pupils are simply shown sites outside the school. For site visits to enhance what children learn they need to have explicit objectives and not simply be a school excursion. To this end some institutions provide specialist packs for teachers to use pre and post visit. Field work takes various forms: the exploration of a village or a town; landscape studies; archaeological studies (including industrial archaeology); visits to ancient monuments and sites, castles, churches, abbeys, country houses, and heritage centres; and related work in industrial, folk, technology and science museums, as well as record offices. In this sense history and the historical resource are all around us. An appreciation of change and continuity can be well illustrated on a site visit. Children reading in a text book that Harlech Castle in North Wales, or Kidwelly Castle in South Wales, were serviced by sea may unquestionably accept the fact but their first reaction at being told this on a site visit would be disbelief for the sea is not close by: but, by questioning this on a field trip, involving active learning and observational skills, the chronological and geographical change since the castle was built may be realised. Continuity with the past may be demonstrated by children's visits to archaeological digs or museums, where successive eras of settlement are shown, in some cases from prehistoric to present times. By visiting a number of sites pupils can be introduced to questioning the reasons for the differences in their function or location. Furthermore, modern interpretative displays and facilities at sites and museums are in themselves, if properly designed, an educational resource. The advantage of such interpretation at sites is that if it is designed for children it can convey information in context, and particularly with a sense of place.

Disabled pupils, as well as able bodied pupils, can benefit from field studies; problems of access are generally the most restrictive (Croucher, 1981) and restrict in particular severely physically handicapped persons, generally in wheelchairs. In general, blind, partially sighted, deaf, mentally handicapped and moderately physically handicapped persons are not necessarily barred from benefiting from field studies simply by reason of their disability.

The combination of school based historical teaching along with fieldwork, if undertaken in such a way as to arouse an interest in history and historical environment, may enhance a person's historical interest and appreciation of sites for life. In this way education can be seen as being a background determinant to the leisure market for visits to historic sites.

## Historical education for tourists

The educational market for tourists is two fold: firstly, there is a formal education market whereby people attend educational courses which may involve historic site visits; and secondly, there is an informal educational market whereby tourists indirectly receive education from interpretative provision at historic sites. In their major review of tourism in Wales, the House of Commons Committee on Welsh Affairs concurred with the view that educational establishments and educational opportunities should be regarded as a tourism resource and recommended that 'the Welsh Office, the Wales Tourist Board, and the University of Wales should consider ways of attracting people to visit Wales through the fuller use of our educational assets' (House of Commons, 1987, p. liii). The Committee was advised that students educated in Wales may well, subsequently, retain their links with Wales and therefore may be potential future tourists to Wales. However, the extent of this effect was not estimated
The informal educational market for tourists is potentially much greater than the formal educational market as it can form a part of the total holiday experience. The interest of visitors in finding out about the historic sites they visit appears, from survey evidence, to have increased over the past twenty years: this has already been discussed under Chapter 3, 'The roles and reasons for visits to historic sites'. Many factors may have combined to promote this growth of the public's interest in their environment, including historic environments. For example, people are now more mobile, both in terms of moving homes from one region to another and in terms of accessibility to private transport which enables them to make day trips to other areas. Mobility can make people aware of differing regional histories. Furthermore, increased leisure time and holiday entitlement, give people the opportunity to pursue interests. In addition, increased levels of formal education may be assumed to have given people a broader awareness of their environments. Television may also have contributed to this broadening of interest in the environment. If people are to receive an informal education at historic sites then interpretation at these sites is needed. In this sense, interpretation at sites becomes an educational resource for both informal and, also, formal education. One objective of the Wales Tourist Board is 'To encourage the development and promotion of specific events designed for tourists and day visitors' (House of Commons, 1987, p. 362). These events include those which may be considered to be a formal or informal educational resource. The Board's marketing plan for 1986/87 included the introduction of a new support scheme for festivals and events. The main objectives of the new scheme were to improve the quality, professionalism and range of events, to

encourage new initiatives and to stimulate greater
cooperation between organisers. The House of Commons
Committee, however, emphasised that the ' ...Welsh tourist
attractions visited by in-coming tourists must reflect the
image [of Wales]' (House of Commons, 1987, p. xxxvii). The
development of this image, particularly through
interpretative provision, is implicitly an educational
resource. The elements which the Welsh Affairs Committee
considered important in developing this image of Wales
comprised: landscape, seascape and mountain in microcosm
together with maritime tradition; music, particularly
choirs and harps; written culture - both Welsh language and
English, e.g. Dylan Thomas; sport, particularly rugby and
climbing; historic monuments including industrial
archaeology; and famous people from Lloyd George, Aneurin
Bevan and Thomas Jefferson to contemporary personalities.
Elements of this list can be developed at different sites
and for different historical periods. The recognition by
the Welsh Affairs Committee of the need to develop this
image is, implicitly, a recognition of the changed leisure
and tourism market in terms of visitor interest and
expectations.

## Environmental education and conservation heritage

The heritage objective for environmental education includes
training potential managers to conserve historic sites; as
well as the education of the public about conservation.
Site education of visitors in conservation can involve
participation or information. Participation includes, for
example, rebuilding stone walls or cleaning up litter (it is
the doing of the task). Information is when visitors are
told about the problem, for example, information on footpath
erosion by visitors to a historic site such as Glastonbury
Tor. In particular, participation may act as a good
deterrent to vandalism by giving young persons
responsibility and involvement (Harrison, 1976). Cadw have
recently established two 'Carers' schemes for young people,
through school and community projects, as part of a campaign
to improve conservation education and to reduce vandalism.
Conservation education is also fundamental to
interpretative planning. In the Scottish 'Strategy for
Interpretation in Central Region' interpretation was
recognised generally as contibuting towards four objectives,
namely: creating an awareness and acceptance of the need for
conservation, and the need to provide resources for
conservation; creating recreational enjoyment in itself;
increasing visitor numbers and length of stay; and providing
primarily for informal recreation and education but also
contributing to new initiatives in formal education. The
Strategy linked education and interpretation largely in
terms of fieldwork and field visits (Central Regional
Council and Countryside Commission for Scotland, 1984). The
Strategy recognised that '... conservation is one of the
primary aims of interpretation' (ibid, p. 15). The aims of
the Strategy were defined as promoting conservation,

stimulating local interest, assisting formal education and developing tourism. In stimulating local interest and in assisting formal education the Strategy sought to complement the primary objective of conservation. In particular, interpretation was seen as making '... a positive contribution by providing interesting opportunities for people to utilise their leisure time and to become involved in environmental and conservation issues of concern to their communities' (ibid, p. 15).

A major Welsh conservation review, Cynefin, defined environmental conservation in the broad sense of ethics, heritage, arts, industry and employment, town and country, maritime, and education. It should be made clear that historic sites are only part of such a concept of conservation. The Cynefin Strategy included a seminar entitled, 'Towards a more intelligent use of the environment'. This seminar made a series of recommendations, of which, several apply to historic sites; these may be summarised as either encouraging outdoor education or facilitating outdoor education. The recommendations concerned both formal and informal education. In particular, the seminar recommended that the Wales Tourist Board attempt to attract and raise the awareness of tourists with the theme and logo 'Cynefin - our living environment'. The seminar recommended that interpretation of the logo should be included at all tourist information points (Cynefin Education and Training Working Group, 1982). Specific formal educational recommendations included: the encouragement of outdoor education developments for schools; greater emphasis on training teachers to use the outdoors by colleges; schools and other educational establishments should have the expertise of voluntary bodies available to them; local communities should be encouraged to use outdoor education resource centres; and there should be encouragement of more co-operation between individuals, local authorities, statutory authorities and voluntary bodies involved in outdoor education enterprises. The Cynefin seminar also produced recommendations for informal education, of which two are of particular relevance to the educational market of historic sites. Firstly, that the media implement a coherent approach to providing information and explanation about development, improvement and conservation schemes; and sites of historical, cultural and ecological significance. Secondly, that farmers letting cottages for holiday purposes be encouraged to provide information about farms. Such information can include historical buildings such as barns and relict landscapes with an ultimate conservation objective.

Not only the formal but also the informal education for conservation using historic sites relate to both the school curricula developments and the changing tourist markets. In view of the need to conserve historic sites and relict landscapes for future generations, the present generation should be educated to appreciate them. Increased environmental awareness may develop a market for visits to historic sites as well as being an educational objective of their managers.

## The present position in schools

Visits by schools (organised school parties) to historic sites and museums are not only common but also have long antecedents. This is not solely a British tradition; for example, by 1912 in Queensland with the agreement of the Department of Public Instruction a programme of talks was agreed with the Queensland Museum for organised school visits; thus, formalising school visits which were already common (Mather, 1986). More recently in 1986/87, 247,679 free admissions were recorded at Cadw's sites in Wales; most were school admissions. Furthermore, the Schools Inspectorate noted in their survey of the teaching of history in Swansea that most Swansea secondary schools organised visits to places of historical interest, both locally and further afield (H. M. Inspectors, 1986).

However, it should be noted that the extent of 'educational' visits might be overstated; several authorities have recently reported that such trips might be nothing more than days out for school children. 'Visits by school parties might be expected to cause fewer problems than other types of visit but there are complaints that some school parties suffer from a lack of adequate supervision and that a visit to the National Park is seen as a 'day out' rather than an educational experience for which preparation has been made' (Yorkshire Dales National Park, 1984, p. 106).

Despite the number of school visits which are made, there is very little published survey material recording the extent and the reasons for these visits in Britain. An exception to this was a survey of 284 schools in England which was undertaken by Cooper and Latham (1985). Cooper and Latham estimated that there were over eleven million educational visits in 1984 to attractions, including historical sites and museums. Most of these were undertaken in the months of April to July. The most popular attractions were historic buildings, theatres, museums and art galleries. The visits to the attractions varied in number by the age of the pupils (Table 5.1). Historic buildings, museums and art galleries were popular throughout the age range from 5 to 16 years. However, school visits for sixth formers showed a notably different pattern with nearly half of all the recorded sixth form visits being made to theatres.

Cooper and Latham have reported that the average distance travelled between the school and the attraction was just over forty miles, and the maximum distance varied between just under seventy-five miles for junior school pupils to over one hundred miles for sixth form pupils (Table 5.2). Most of the trips, other than for junior school pupils were around forty miles, or around eighty miles for a return trip. This distance, in many cases, would have included a range of attractions between which the teachers could have

Table 5.1
School visits in England

| Attraction: | Historic building % | Garden % | Museum; Art gallery % | Zoo; Wild-life park % | Theatre % | Other % | TOTAL N |
|---|---|---|---|---|---|---|---|
| School type: | | | | | | | |
| Junior/ first | 22 | 5 | 22 | 14 | 18 | 19 | 368 |
| Middle | 27 | 7 | 22 | 10 | 15 | 19 | 452 |
| Secondary/ upper | 25 | 3 | 18 | 9 | 24 | 21 | 546 |
| Sixth-form college | 15 | 2 | 20 | 2 | 46 | 14 | 294 |

Note: Percentages summate across the rows.

Source: Cooper and Latham (1985).


Table 5.2.
Average distance travelled on school visits in England

| | Mean one-way distance in miles | Maximum one-way distance in miles |
|---|---|---|
| School types: | | |
| Junior/first | 32.7 | 74.4 |
| Middle | 40.6 | 82.9 |
| Secondary/upper | 43.8 | 96.3 |
| Sixth-form college | 42.1 | 112.6 |
| ALL | 40.7 | - |

Source: Cooper and Latham (1985).


chosen (Table 5.2). Most of these trips involved a length of stay of under four hours at the attraction: and the majority of these trips were financed by either the pupils or their parents. In addition, the survey found that almost half of the schools which were surveyed could make as many visits as they wished, subject to timetabling and finance.

From the teachers' point of view, the teachers' educational packs and price discounts were the most common provisions sought in deciding which attraction to visit (Table 5.3). Educational packs for pupils and specialist

Table 5.3.
Provisions at attractions which are required by schools

Percentage of schools saying 'provision' is 'important', by type of school:

| Provision: | Junior/ first % | Middle % | Secondary/ upper % | Sixth- form college % |
|---|---|---|---|---|
| Teachers' education pack | 73 | 80 | 76 | 73 |
| Price discount | 68 | 65 | 68 | 68 |
| Pupils' educational pack | 55 | 59 | 60 | 54 |
| Specialist staff | 45 | 55 | 50 | 44 |
| Lecture rooms | 24 | 30 | 22 | 25 |
| Other | 10 | 16 | 12 | 5 |

Source: Cooper and Latham (1985).

staff available at the site were of only secondary importance: nevertheless they were, still, widely demanded. Sixth-form college visits were, again, exceptional compared to visits by younger pupils in that price discounts were disproportionately sought (presumably as sixth formers are generally old enough to be charged adult admission rates); and, neither teachers' educational packs nor specialist staff were so important. In that many sixth form visits were to theatres, rather than to historic sites, these different requirements are not surprising. There seems to be a substantial requirement for school parties to be provided with educational packs and discounted prices.

Other information on school visits and the place of history in the curriculum can be found in the Schools Inspectorate reports. The inspection undertaken in Swansea in 1985 has already been mentioned. The inspection showed that there were substantial variations between secondary schools in Swansea in not only the visits made in the teaching of history but also in the methods and techniques used in the teaching of the subject. The inspection recorded that only some schools were actually using their local environment as a resource in history teaching, while others were also making visits to castles in West Wales, to mining museums and to the Welsh Folk Museum (H. M. Inspectors, 1986). More distant visits of these kinds are within the general distance range which was found by Cooper and Latham for England. However, the Inspectors noted that ' ... some schools make disappointing use of the locality, planned integral visits occur infrequently' (H. M. Inspectors, 1986, p. 14).

The Inspectors also reported that some schools still needed to develop approaches to teaching which involved the pupils more in their learning, by placing greater emphasis on the study of evidence, fieldwork and empathy, and less emphasis on retention and recall, or copying, of a large body of factual information. Where audio visual rooms were available they were generally well used but inevitably restricted through heavy demand by other departments. Further variability between schools occurred in the use of art and craft as part of the work in history; the Inspectors noted that in some schools this was of 'good quality' but in others non existent. In some schools the Inspectors commented that notes were in a language too complex and removed from the children's own levels. The variability between schools in the teaching of history, shown by this one case example, is a reminder that the curricula developments outlined earlier are by no means universally applied in schools. In particular, active learning techniques, including fieldwork, are common but not universal.

## Objectives of agencies promoting heritage education

Site agencies promoting heritage education are to be found in both the public and the private sector. They include the major agencies caring for State monuments: in England, English Heritage; in Wales, Cadw; and in Scotland, the Historic Buildings and Monuments section of the Scottish Development Department. Both the Countryside Commission (in England and Wales) and the Countryside Commission for Scotland promote environmental education and interpretation largely as facilitators helping the site managers. The National Park Authorities, of which there are ten in England and Wales, variously promote heritage education, particularly that of landscape and built environment. The National Trust in England and Wales, the National Trust for Scotland and, in the Isle of Man, the Manx Museum and National Trust extensively promote site education and they have also developed off site educational resources. As the agencies responsible for many museums and country parks, local authorities have also, to greatly varying extents, aimed at promoting heritage education. Such developments are separate from the formal school provisions of the local authorities responsible for providing state education in Britain. It is not always the case that the same local authority which manages a historic site or museum is the one that provides the state education in the locality. Higher and further educational institutions, although they are not usually directly responsible for site management, can provide both formal courses and study holidays which involve heritage education and management. Other agencies can include regional development agencies, for example, the Shannon Free Airport Development Company; sub regional development agencies; agencies funded by the former Manpower Sevices Commission; various trusts; and a diverse range of private organisations. The aim of this section is ONLY to illustrate the educational role that some of the range of the agencies listed here have determined; it is NOT intended to be an exhaustive discussion of agencies.

English Heritage

English Heritage is the name by which the Historic Buildings and Monuments Commission for England is generally known; English Heritage was set up under the National Heritage Act 1983 and came into being in April 1984. Although funded by Government, English Heritage is an independent agency responsible for the conservation and presentation of England's historic monuments and buildings, most of which were formerly in the care of the Department of the Environment. English Heritage aims to increase popular understanding and enjoyment of heritage through presentation of its sites and educational facilities: 'One of the aims of English Heritage is to promote wider knowledge and enjoyment of England's heritage of ancient monuments and historic buildings' (English Heritage Education Service, 1986). Under the Act of 1983 which created English Heritage, it has a statutory duty to provide educational facilities, advice and information to the public. In fact English Heritage define their educational role more widely than specific site education and include heritage and conservation education of a wide scope. With regard to age range, English Heritage particularly target their educational work towards school children between the ages of ten and fourteen years. In order to assist teachers at all levels in education, English Heritage has set up an education service with regional education staff liaising with local authorities, teachers, and other individuals active in education. In addition, English Heritage seeks to arrange and teach courses run jointly with the Department of Education and Science. Other courses are of one day's duration on a variety of themes ranging from the use of the historic environment as a teaching resource to detailed studies of a particular site and planning school visits (English Heritage Education Service, 1986). Again to assist teachers, English Heritage has provided education facilities and services at certain sites, arranges for the secondment of teachers to sites, provides courses on interpreting historic sites, as well as producing publications, films and videos.

Cadw: Welsh Historic Monuments

Cadw, or Welsh Historic Monuments, is the equivalent agency in Wales to English Heritage in England. Cadw carries out the statutory responsibilities of the Secretary of State for Wales to protect, conserve and present monuments and historic buildings in Wales. Cadw's educational objectives are twofold. Firstly, 'Cadw ... seeks to broaden the awareness of all Welsh people wherever they may be, and the visitors to Wales, to help them learn, to understand, to enjoy the 6,000 years of history visible in the landscape' (Cadw, 1985). This first objective is furthered by site presentation and the 'Heritage in Wales' scheme whose membership in March 1987 stood at 12,305 members (individuals holding joint memberships are counted here as separate members). The second role of Cadw is more formally educational. Cadw has an education officer and a policy for education which was approved in principle by the Cadw Steering Committee in January 1986. Under the broad objective of presenting built heritage in an imaginative, interesting and attractive manner, Cadw seeks to provide educational bodies with assistance ' ... to create a greater interest in Welsh history, architecture and archaeology' (Cadw, 1986). Cadw furthermore seeks ' ... to identify the scope, content, tone of and target markets for 'educational' packs for sale to schools, universities, special interest societies, the general public' (Cadw, 1986). These educational materials are designed for use on and off site. Cadw is seeking to encourage educational visits to its sites by liaison with schools. As well as an educational officer, Cadw has established an Educational Consultative Committee as a means of developing school visits. The policy of increasing school visits to Cadw's sites has been successful, as educational visits have increased markedly in the period 1984/85 to 1986/87. In the first year, 1985/85, the number of educational free admissions at Cadw sites increased by 85% and in the second year, 1986/87, by a further 25%. Cadw reports that a high proportion of school visits are by pupils in the first two years of secondary schooling, but that a sizeable proportion are from the top junior sections of primary schools. This is the same age range as targeted by English Heritage. Cadw's policy for education includes the development of specific display material at sites for these age groups.

Cadw has identified three educational target groups. The first comprises eleven to thirteen year olds, top juniors and the first two years of secondary school. The second target group are thirteen to sixteen year olds studying exam syllabus work to G.C.S.E. level. The third target group is more diverse. It includes sixteen to eighteen year olds studying for 'A' levels. It also includes persons aged eighteen or over who are studying for higher education or who are generally interested being members of amateur and voluntary societies (Cadw, 1986). Cadw specifically seeks to promote an inter-disciplinary approach to the understanding of the built heritage, and for younger pupils, see the monuments as potential focal points of inter-disciplinary work encompassing interpretation, environmental studies (ecology, geography and geology), and the history of art. It is also Cadw's policy to assist in the fostering and spread of the Welsh language and to this end Welsh language as well as English language materials are being produced. Cadw is particularly concerned that where school groups visiting monuments are unprepared, pupils understanding and enjoyment of the monument is spoilt or even lost. To widen the knowledge of teachers and to assist in the training of student teachers, in 1987 Cadw had a display vehicle available for travelling exhibitions. These exhibitions were used at institutions of higher and further education, at teachers' centres, conferences and education resource days at monuments. Cadw is proposing to run lectures and courses for teachers and is exploring the possibility of holding monument holidays to give groups of children the opportunity to study in depth a historic monument, or group of monuments, at a distance from their school.

Countryside Commissions

Both the Countryside Commission, in England and Wales, and the Countryside Commission for Scotland are agencies promoting countryside recreation. As many historic sites are in the countryside, historic sites are part of the attractions for tourists and day trippers to the countryside. The Commissions do not themselves manage or own land or facilities, but rather, they work with other organisations. The Countryside Commission's educational programmes include the promotion of interpretation of sites and access to sites, and of the countryside generally, including relict landscapes. These objectives are achieved through both publications and courses. In addition to its role in assisting visitors to sites, the Countryside Commission is concerned with the awareness of visitors on site and their access on site. The Commission has noted that the aims of a programme of interpretation might include ' .. enhancing visitor enjoyment in the belief that an understanding of the countryside increases the pleasure derived from visiting it' and ' ... increasing the public's understanding and appreciation of the countryside leading to a respect for it and an awareness of the need for its conservation or development' (Countryside Commission, 1977). The Countryside Commission has drawn attention to '... what archaeological/ architectural/ landscape/ visual features exist?' and '... does the site have any social/ historical/ cultural significance?' (Countryside Commission, 1977). The Countryside Commission has also sought to promote the accessibility of countryside sites for disabled people (Countryside Commission, 1982). Furthermore, the Countryside Commission promotes residential courses for staff and volunteers employed in countryside conservation and recreation. Courses in 1986/87 included 'Education in the countryside', 'Interpreting historic sites', 'Disability and countryside recreation', 'Organisation of events', 'Design and graphics in interpretation' and 'Audio-visual aids in interpretation'. The course entitled 'Education in the countryside' was designed for staff or volunteers wishing to make closer contact with school groups. The course sought to advise on liaison with local education authorities and teachers, on assessing the potential of an environment or site for teaching, and how to approach the teaching of children of different ages and abilities. Courses such as these clearly seek to make staff involved in historic site management aware of teaching needs. Courses such as this also recognise that site managers may not necessarily be able to recognise or develop their site as an educational resource without guidance.

Table 5.4.
Interpretative themes in the Lake District National Park Centres, 1986

Centres:    Themes:

Bowness
Bay       -  Lake Windemere and the woodland industries of High Furness

Waterhead -  Landscape in Roman times, interest in the locality

Hawkshead -  Local landscape, Beatrix Potter

Coniston  -  Mining and quarrying, the former railway, steamers

Grasmere  -  Grasmere through the ages

Glen-
ridding   -  History of mining, steamers

Pooley
Bridge    -  Lowther Estates and the Yellow Earl, Dacre Castle, steamers

Keswick   -  Environs of Keswick, pencils, Hugh Walpole

Seatoller -  Craft demonstrations, Borrowdale Valley

Brockhole -  General exhibition: The National Park history;
                               land use;
                               conservation;
                               management

             Specialist display: Geology and lakes

             Talks and audio-visuals: conservation;
                                      rural economy;
                                      history;
                                      literature

             Special events and day courses: local crafts;
                                             photography;
                                             nature study;
                                             books.

Source: Lake District National Park Authority (1986).

Centres in the National Parks provide a range of interpretation for the general public which should be seen as an educational resource both generally and for secondary schools. For example, the range of interpretative themes as educational resources included in the Lake District National Park Authority's centres is shown in Table 5.4. These themes have a clear historical focus.

The ten National Parks offer either day visitor facilities or residential study centres from which countryside based activities, including educational visits to historic sites, can be arranged. There are also study bases, lecture rooms and information centres in the National Parks, with services varying from talks and video programmes to tutored courses. Most produce a range of publications relevant to school and youth groups and have a youth and schools liaison service offering advice on transport, accommodation, sites events, places to visit and (extremely important) safety. The National Parks have had a tradition of promoting active learning; and guided walks and special interest walks, for example, have long been a feature of the educational programmes offered by National Parks. The National Parks, however, have tended to see their individual educational role differently. The National Parks have recently reviewed their plans as required by statute. These reviews set out, amongst other things, the educational and information objectives of the individual National Park Authorities. For example, the Brecon Beacons National Park Authority states one of its objectives as follows: 'The N.P.A. (National Park Authority) recognises its opportunities and responsibilities towards the environmental education of the public in general and of school and college groups in particular' (Brecon Beacons National Park, 1986, para. 13.13). The Yorkshire Dales National Park implicitly define a much wider educational market with public understanding as one of six general aims (Yorkshire Dales National Park, 1984). In particular the Yorkshire Dales National Park seeks '... to promote a better understanding between town and country by giving the townsman a deeper comprehension of the significance of nature, an appreciation of country lore and an insight into the essential processes of primary production in which the countryman is engaged, and to associate local people with the purposes of the National Park and to enlist their goodwill' (ibid, p.13). The Yorkshire Dales National Park defines cultural heritage as one essential element of its statutory duty to preserve the natural beauty of the Park. In this context cultural heritage is seen as ' ... those man made attributes of the landscape which contribute to its beauty and its character and which in themselves have historic or cultural significance' (ibid, p. 10).

A major educational development of the National Parks has been youth and schools liaison. The work of this service can be summarised as, encouraging an awareness of the conservation needs of the Parks and promoting a high standard of group leadership. The Lake District National

Park Authority has defined four priorities for its youth and schools service. Firstly, responding to those groups which ask for assistance and acting as a clearing house for youth, school and educational requests. Secondly, providing a service to teachers, leaders and to the training institutions of teachers and leaders. Thirdly, increasing liaison with the owners, managers and booking secretaries of unstaffed outdoor centres; of day-visit centres; of camp sites and with sponsoring authorities. Fourthly, practical work with local schools is regarded as a priority especially at the primary school level (Lake District National Park Authority, 1986). Both the Lake District and Yorkshire Dales National Parks emphasise the importance of personal contact in their youth and schools services. This can range from visits to schools, clubs and teachers centres to meeting groups within the Park and spending time with parties in the field. The Yorkshire Dales National Park Committee, in particular, emphasises direct contact with visiting school groups preferring to structure the advice and help which it offers to meet the special needs of a particular groups, rather than to prepare general information packs for teachers. The Committee sees talks to groups of teachers as particularly cost effective in developing school pupils' environmental awareness throughout the academic year, and not solely on visits to the Park (Yorkshire Dales National Park Committee, 1984).

The National Trusts

The National Trusts are charities which hold countryside and buildings in the British Isles for the benefit of the public. The National Trust in England and Wales sees its role primarily to conserve its properties and ' ... the Trust feels it can only justify the allocation of a modest sum for its educational work' (National Trust, 1985). The Trust has taken the view as a charity that it should concentrate on what it considers is its primary role, namely the conservation of its properties for the benefit of present and future generations, rather than involving its staff directly in education. The Trust publicly justifies its educational work for its contribution towards the Trust's conservation objectives ' ... because an enjoyable experience may create an affection for historic and beautiful places which in turn is likely to lead to a desire to protect them' (National Trust, 1987a). The National Trust for Scotland explicitly recognises an educational potential in their properties which is perhaps more enthusiastically promoted than South of the Border. The Trust states ' ... there is a wealth of educational resource material which can in no way be disregarded and which the Trust must seek to develop and make available to an expanding market' (Ritchie, 1982, p. 3). The National Trust for Scotland defines its educational role as two fold: firstly, as assisting the formal educational system of schooling; and secondly, as part of a wider educational process of voluntary education on the part of visitors. The National Trust for Scotland believes 'the focus is the individual in response to the heritage, desiring to learn and to carry on learning. In these aspirations he makes great claims on the Trust' (ibid, p. 3). Both the National Trust and the National Trust for Scotland have officers responsible for educational developments. The Trust for Scotland was also involved in a three year cooperative venture with British Petroleum's Educational Service specifically to develop educational material for schools and colleges. In England, the National Trust is advised by a Panel of Youth which guides the Trust on all youth and educational activities. Represented on the Panel are various educational interests including local education authorities and youth organisations. The Trust has also developed a special project, 'The Young National Trust Theatre', wherein it seeks to centre its educational work on the arts; through this, schoolchildren are able to act out parts at sites to gain insights into events affecting the day-to-day lives of people in the past. The Trust has also produced educational publications, experimental projects and specialist courses for teachers and for the Trust's own staff.

The National Trust believes that as nature and beauty are vital to human well-being their educational emphasis at their sites is directed towards the makers and carers, the artists, craftsmen, husbandmen, naturalists and conservationists (National Trust, 1987a). The Trust emphasises active learning through personal involvement, particularly through drama, voluntary conservation work, looking for answers in a discovery sheet at a property, or researching a school project (National Trust, 1985). Both the Trust and the National Trust for Scotland emphasise involvement in conservation. The Junior Division of the Trust is responsible for the organisation of the Acorn Camps and Young National Trust Groups. The National Trust for Scotland likewise has its youth organisation, 'Youth in Trust'. Both Trusts organise working holidays, to undertake outdoor work which could not otherwise be afforded. The National Trust particularly targets school parties in the 9 to 13 years and 16 years and above age groups. This is clearly a wider age range than that targeted by English Heritage. To encourage school visits both the Trust and the National Trust for Scotland operate corporate schools membership. In Scotland a corporate membership admits up to twenty pupils and two teachers; in England and Wales up to sixty admissions are covered by the scheme. In the latter case the effective cost of membership per pupil for a year can be under sixty pence per head. Schools corporate members also receive free booklets and newsletters and special information for young people.

The National Trust for Scotland promotes its properties to teachers as ' ... accessible to you and your pupils as extensions to your classroom' (Ritchie, 1982). Specific subjects promoted are art, geography, history, plant and animal studies, literature, home economics, orienteering and hill-walking. The National Trust promotes four approaches to teachers. Firstly, research - finding out how and why; secondly, the subject approach, especially social or art history, geography, natural history, or art and architecture; thirdly, an integrated approach through environmental studies or a learning web, linking geography, history, social studies, natural history, conservation, ecology, leisure and the arts; and fourthly, the stimulation of creative response to the visit through the arts. Both the Trusts provide checklists for teachers to prepare for their visits, and the checklist produced by the National Trust for Scotland is included as Appendix 1. The checklist includes preparation, organisation at school, implementation at the property and evaluation of the visit back at school. The National Trust for Scotland emphasises the need to select an appropriate site for pupils in relation to the work done at school, and to prepare the pupils for the visit particularly in terms of what to look out for. Subsequently, teachers are advised to discuss with pupils what they have learnt from their visit in relation to their school work.

Both National Trusts have vigorously promoted membership schemes for the general public in the last ten years (Bouvaird et al, 1984). Members receive Trust magazines listing developments and events and explaining interpretative developments. The National Trust for Scotland produces a magazine named 'Heritage Scotland' and the National Trust produces one named 'National Trust Magazine'. The latter adopts a thematic approach for issues; and, recent issues have focused on small and vernacular buildings, water, country estates and the Spanish Armada. Both the increased opportunity to visit sites and the literature received by members can be regarded as part of a voluntary educational process. The Trusts also cater for disabled and handicapped visitors, for example, by producing facilities and special interpretation at certain sites. The National Trust also produces a guide of facilities to assist its disabled and visually handicapped visitors (National Trust, 1987b).

Local authorities

As well as their statutory educational responsibilities, local authorities have an educational role if they own historic sites, or manage museums and country parks. The educational role of these provisions is more often emphasised when the local authority is also an educational authority. For example, Wigan Metropolitan Borough Council has aptly combined tourism, leisure and educational objectives at the Wigan Pier Centre. The development includes a heritage centre, exhibitions and concert hall, a working mill engine, narrow boats and a water bus on the Leeds and Liverpool Canal, working machinery, a pub and restaurant, a gift and book shop, as well as an education and field study centre. Similarly, the Western Isles Council has developed the Western Isles Museum as an integrated educational, conservational and interpretative resource for the Hebrides. County-wide strategies for interpretation as an educational resource, however, are the exception rather than the rule. Central Regional Council in

Scotland produced such a strategy in conjunction with the Countryside Commission for Scotland (Central Regional Council and Countryside Commission for Scotland, 1984). In this Strategy the Education Department of Central Regional Council identified developments needed in interpretative provision if it is to be a useful educational resource. The Education Department of the Regional Council identified an essential problem with much existing site interpretation when used as an educational resource for schools and interest groups, ' ... most educational groups are likely to approach an interpretive facility with a fairly tightly prescribed thematic interest. In most instances their interest is likely to be more specific than, or tangential to, the theme of on-site interpretation which is likely to be directed more towards the needs of the general visitor' (ibid, p. 28). To overcome this problem the Council propose: firstly, to familiarise teachers with the opportunities for incorporating interpretative facilities into their work: secondly, pre-visit and follow-up material is being developed on a regional basis: thirdly, the Council seek a constructive dialogue with the providers of on-site interpretation as a means of overcoming the educational limitations of existing interpretative provision: fourthly, residential facilities are to be made available for short term residential visits: and, fifthly, information and materials are to be developed in both a professionally finished format and cost-effective manner.

Local authorities are a major provider of local museums. The traditional view of museums ' ... is that of a cabinet of curiosities, the closet of rarities where the precious and curious of the natural and the man made world vie with each other for prominence and space ... the association of overstuffed basements and dusty displays lingers on' (Stewart, 1984, p. 79). More usefully for education purposes local museums should be regarded as environmental record centres, and places where these records and their context are explained. Also, museums are vital links between the public and archaeologists. At a basic level, the role of museums as centres of information will depend on museums knowing the range and size of their collections. Local authority museums vary extensively in type and function. Whereas all can be regarded as having an educational function, this role has been variously developed. A good example of a local authority without formal educational responsibilities, who are nevertheless promoting a museum as an educational resource as well as a tourism resource, is Cotswold District Council. This District Council promotes the Cotswold Countryside Collection, a museum of rural life, at Northleach in Gloucestershire, as providing 'a rich and varied resource of use to school groups of all ages' (Cotswold District Council, 1987).

Some local authorities have been involved in heritage centre developments; that is, of centres seeking to explain the development of a whole community. Examples of centres developed by local authorities, both jointly and separately, are Beamish Open Air Museum in the North East of England,

163

and as already noted, Wigan Pier in the North West of England. At the Wigan Pier Centre, Wigan Metropolitan Borough Council has provided a schools centre, staffed by tutors seconded from local primary and secondary schools. Provisions include a lecture theatre as well as a collection of oral history tapes, transcripts, maps, objects and photographs. The Centre is promoted as an educational resource for local history, drama, creative writing, environmental science, geography, art, architectural studies, photography, tourism studies, leisure studies and business studies (Wigan Pier Schools' Centre, 1986). Wigan Heritage Centre's permanent exhibition, 'The way we were', seeks to depict life in Wigan around 1900. As an education authority, Wigan seeks to use the display as part of continuity and progression in schooling between primary and secondary levels, seeking to develop in pupils an awareness of similarities and differences, observational skills, recording skills, empathetic skills and interpretative skills. Development of skills of this kind concur with the recommendations of the Schools Inspectorate for the progressive development of historical skills in pupils throughout their primary and secondary years discussed earlier. The age range targeted at Wigan Pier is much wider than those targeted by the other agencies already discussed. In particular, at Wigan Pier the philosophy is embodied that the basis for the development of essential historical skills and concepts in secondary pupils can be forged in the primary schools.

Higher and further education institutions

Higher and further education institutions are part of the educational market for historic sites, both in terms of the formal courses that they provide and the less formal courses and study holidays which have been developed largely as means of gaining additional revenue. Formal courses may be divided into two sections. Firstly, where a historic site or similar resource is used for a field visit, as part of the course of study of a discipline such as geography or history. As the main agencies managing historic resources do not publish separate figures for higher and further education admissions to their sites, the extent of these visits is unknown. In the second type of formal course students are trained to manage resources, and British institutions provide courses on managing historic properties, museums and art galleries, interpretation and tourist guides (CRAC, 1987). Courses of the latter kind range from National Diplomas to Postgraduate qualifications. Educational institutions also provide less structured courses and study holidays. The Extramural Departments of Universities and the Workers' Educational Association have for many years offered courses of this kind. More recently, certain British Universities have promoted study tours and residential based study holidays. 'Academy Holidays', for example, provide study holidays on historical and other heritage themes at certain university sites throughout Britain. Holidays of this kind involve both lectures and field visits, and are part of the conference tourism developments by British universities seeking to use their buildings during the university vacations.

## Manpower Services Commission/ Training Agency

In an era of mass youth unemployment sucessive make-work schemes on the part of Governments have included projects with environmental and conservation objectives. A particular example of a Manpower Services Commission funded scheme which developed a historical resource was the 'Dundee Oral History Project'. This project had a dual purpose: firstly, to show that older people had a depth of experience invaluable to society; and secondly, to show that the long term unemployed can, with adequate funding, produce socially useful work (DOHP, 1987). The Project collated the historical reminiscences of the elderly and was advised by teachers and others working in education. One objective of the project was to produce learning packs for schools. As well as the Project's main aims, the educational aim was '... to encourage the pupils to take an interest in and discuss their local history' (ibid, p. 10). Other former Manpower Services Commission funded projects, such as the restoration of canals and reconstruction of tourist railways, have an indirect educational benefit by enabling the creation of a resource which can be used for educational purposes. More directly, the Commission jointly with the PICKUP Scheme have funded short courses on heritage management and training for small tourism businesses (Neave et al, 1988). Recently, the Training Agency has introduced the Enterprise in Higher Education Initiative to improve links between industry and higher education: tourism, as one industrial sector, can be expected to be included within this initiative.

## The Heritage Education Trust

In 1977 the Sandford Award was established to foster the educational use of historic properties by schools. One aim of the Award is to encourage owners and other agents responsible for administering such properties to develop educational services and facilities. Another aim is to ensure that such services and facilities are of a high standard and administered in such a way as to enable the visiting school to regard such visiting as a genuine part of its curriculum (Dyer, 1983). In particular, the Award seeks to encourage liaison between the managers of historic properties and schools both before the visit and as follow-up subsequently, as well as involvement with local education authorities. Prior to 1982, the Sandford Award was administered by the Council for Environmental Education. With the establishment of the Heritage Education Trust, in 1982, at St. Mary's College, Strawberry Hill, London, the administration of the Award was transferred to the new Trust. The Trust sees its role both as promoting the Award to properties and of spreading knowledge of it among schools.

Table 5.5.
The reasons given for visiting each museum: by gender

Key: M = Male
     F = Female

|  | Victoria and Albert Museum | | Science Museum | | National Railway Museum | |
|---|---|---|---|---|---|---|
|  | M | F | M | F | M | F |
| Weighted N = | 430 | 570 | 630 | 360 | 610 | 390 |
|  | % | % | % | % | % | % |
| **Reasons for visiting:** | | | | | | |
| To accompany someone else | 12 | 10 | 29 | 41 | 30 | 55 |
| General interest, reputation of the museum | 21 | 21 | 17 | 21 | 20 | 17 |
| Because the visitor liked the museum | 4 | 4 | 8 | 7 | 8 | 5 |
| Interest in the museum's contents | 25 | 25 | 32 | 17 | 44 | 26 |
| To see a special temporary exhibition | 24 | 28 | 11 | 9 | 0 | 0 |
| In conection with work or studies | 7 | 6 | 4 | 7 | 3 | 3 |
| To use information facilities | 4 | 5 | 1 | 1 | 0 | 1 |
| Casual or holiday visit | 10 | 7 | 14 | 10 | 21 | 20 |
| Other | 12 | 12 | 7 | 9 | 4 | 4 |

Note: (i)   The percentages add to over 100% as people could give more than one answer.
      (ii)  Source of table: weighted results from count-based samples of museum leavers.

Source: Heady (1984).

Evidence of educational interest at heritage sites

Several surveys have included specific questioning on visitors' educational interest at heritage sites. The questions asked have ranged from the importance of education in the decision to visit, to those about the visitors' views on the importance of education to their visit. Surprisingly, perhaps, the vast majority of visitors to the major British museums do not visit in connection with their work or studies, nor to use the museums' information facilities (Heady, 1984). Visitors came instead, for

166

leisure interests; either having a particular interest in the museum's contents , or, a more general interest (Table 5.5). Despite the comparative unimportance of education as a reason for visiting, many visitors considered that it was important to have learnt something from their visit (Table 5.6). This was particularly the case for adults, between half and two-thirds of whom thought that learning was important. The importance of an educational emphasis in

Table 5.6.
Percentages of visitors who thought learning was important: by age

|  | Victoria and Albert Museum (a) % | Science Museum (b) % | National Railway Museum (c) % | N (a) | N (b) | N (c) |
|---|---|---|---|---|---|---|
| Age (years): |  |  |  |  |  |  |
| 11-20 | 43 | 47 | 36 | 255 | 337 | 187 |
| 21-30 | 54 | 57 | 41 | 262 | 320 | 198 |
| 31-40 | 60 | 64 | 44 | 131 | 167 | 82 |
| 41 and over | 62 | 69 | 60 | 355 | 221 | 129 |

Note: Quota samples of museum leavers

Percentages of visitors who thought learning was important by age at which full-time education was completed.

|  | Victoria and Albert Museum (a) % | Science Museum (b) % | National Railway Museum (c) % | N (a) | N (b) | N (c) |
|---|---|---|---|---|---|---|
| Age at which education was completed: |  |  |  |  |  |  |
| 16 or less | 50 | 53 | 44 | 172 | 271 | 258 |
| 17-20 | 55 | 57 | 48 | 246 | 313 | 135 |
| 21 or over | 63 | 65 | 54 | 318 | 245 | 77 |

Note: (i) Visitors still in full-time education are excluded from this table.
(ii) Quota samples of museum leavers.

Source: Heady (1984).

167

Table 5.7.
Further information wanted by visitors to the Victoria and Albert Museum galleries

| | Art of China and Japan | British Sculpture | Tudor Art | Continental 17th Century Art |
|---|---|---|---|---|
| N = | 98 | 75 | 75 | 95 |
| | % | % | % | % |
| **Information wanted:** | | | | |
| More detail, technical information | 9 | 11 | 15 | 8 |
| How things work | Ø | Ø | 1 | Ø |
| How things were made, materials used | 29 | 12 | 24 | 19 |
| Uses, purpose | 22 | 21 | 19 | 26 |
| Who made things | 5 | 33 | 8 | 24 |
| Origins, history of things | 41 | 31 | 28 | 39 |
| Historical background | 32 | 24 | 35 | 18 |
| Information about the subject depicted | 1 | 23 | 8 | 5 |
| Better presented information | 26 | 16 | 37 | 28 |
| Don't know | 1 | Ø | 3 | 3 |
| Other | 19 | 12 | 13 | 14 |

Note: (i)   The percentages add to over 100% as people could give more than one answer.
      (ii)  Quota samples interviewed as they left selected galleries.

Source: Heady (1984).

interpretative provision can also be seen in the types of further information sought by visitors at the Victoria and Albert Museum. Historical background, and in particular how things were made and used, were of extensive interest (Table 5.7).

In contrast to the visitors at National Museums, visitors at Cadw's sites in the mid 1980s more commonly gave education as the main purpose of their visit. Substantial numbers also gave 'to be informed' as their main reason, and

Table 5.8.
Main purpose of visit to Cadw's sites, summer 1986

|  | Tintern Abbey % | Caerphilly Castle % | Chepstow Castle % | Caerleon Baths and Fort % |
|---|---|---|---|---|
| Main purpose of visit: |  |  |  |  |
| To relax | 19 | 24 | 31 | 11 |
| To be entertained | 10 | 18 | 11 | 11 |
| To be informed | 51 | 40 | 44 | 67 |
| To be educated | 18 | 16 | 13 | 9 |
| Don't know | 3 | 1 | 1 | 2 |

|  | Caernarfon Castle % | Conwy Castle % | ALL sites % |
|---|---|---|---|
| Main purpose of visit: |  |  |  |
| To relax | 13 | 20 | 20 |
| To be entertained | 17 | 15 | 14 |
| To be informed | 42 | 39 | 45 |
| To be educated | 19 | 19 | 17 |
| Don't know | 8 | 7 | 4 |

Source: Seren (1986a).

taken together these two reasons accounted for a majority of summer visitors (Table 5.8). In general, forty-five per cent of summer visitors to Cadw's sites gave 'to be informed' as the main purpose of their visit and approximately one in six visitors gave 'to be educated' as the main purpose of their visit. The findings for Cadw's sites suggest the importance of information as sources of general education for visitors.

Members of Cadw's club, 'Heritage in Wales', should not be assumed to be representative of visitors generally to Cadw's sites. However, the reasons given for joining 'Heritage in Wales' are indicative, at least, of one market segment of visitors, presumably enthusiasts for heritage. Members joining in both 1985 and 1986 were surveyed for their reasons for joining 'Heritage in Wales' (Tables 5.9 and 5.10). In both years the preservation of heritage and the opportunity to learn about Welsh history were of dominant importance as reasons for joining. The opportunity to enjoy special lectures and tours was generally unimportant as a reason for joining, once again emphasising the importance of general and informal education as reasons for visiting historic sites. It should also be noted that the

Table 5.9.
Reasons important on joining Heritage in Wales in 1985

Proportions of the sample indicating the importance or unimportance of the following statements.

| Statements: | Important % | Unimportant % | Uncertain % | N |
|---|---|---|---|---|
| 'Joining Heritage in Wales was an opportunity for me to learn more about the history of Wales' | 82 | 10 | 8 | 1,062 |
| 'I hoped that by becoming a member I would be able to preserve heritage in Wales' | 84 | 6 | 10 | 1,063 |
| 'On joining Heritage in Wales I hoped that membership would enable me to save money when visiting several historic sites' | 72 | 22 | 6 | 1,061 |
| 'I wanted to save money on Cadw gifts and souvenirs by joining Heritage in Wales' | 8 | 83 | 10 | 1,056 |
| 'I joined Heritage in Wales to enjoy special lectures and tours' | 20 | 52 | 28 | 1,051 |
| 'I liked the idea of receiving a copy of the Heritage in Wales newspaper direct to my home' | 59 | 26 | 15 | 1,062 |

Source: Seren (1986b).

Table 5.10.
Reasons for joining Heritage in Wales in 1986

| Statements: | Very important % | Quite important % | Unimportant % | Uncertain % | N % |
|---|---|---|---|---|---|
| 'I hoped that by becoming a member I would be able to preserve Heritage in Wales' | 46 | 43 | 8 | 3 | 1,002 |
| 'On joining Heritage in Wales I hoped that membership would enable me to save money when visiting several historic sites in Wales' | 49 | 39 | 13 | 0 | 1,010 |
| 'Joining Heritage in Wales was an opportunity for me to learn more about the history of Wales' | 33 | 56 | 9 | 2 | 999 |
| 'I liked the idea of receiving a copy of the Heritage in Wales newspaper direct to my home' | 12 | 48 | 34 | 7 | 998 |
| 'On joining Heritage in Wales I hoped that membership would enable me to save money when visiting several historic sites in England or Scotland' | 19 | 37 | 39 | 5 | 1,004 |
| 'I joined Heritage in Wales to enjoy special events, lectures or tours' | 5 | 24 | 60 | 11 | 1,002 |
| 'I wanted to save money on Cadw gifts and souvenirs by joining Heritage in Wales' | 2 | 11 | 84 | 3 | 1,003 |

Source: Seren (1987).

171

opportunity to save money when visiting several sites was also a frequent reason for joining in both years. The survey of members who joined in 1986 showed that the opportunity to preserve heritage and to learn about heritage was most important for the minority of members who were manual workers. Whereas members aged under twenty-five disproportionately gave the 'opportunity to learn about history' as a reason for joining, members aged over fifty-five years disproportionately gave 'preservation of heritage' as a reason.

Surveys of perceptions of natural heritage on the Isle of Man suggest that wildlife parks are seen as educational resources, as well as having conservation roles and being places to visit simply for the pleasure of seeing animals. Nearly half of the Island's residents interviewed thought education to be the main function of such a site, as did a third of visitors to the Island (Prentice, 1988a; 1988b). For residents, education was the most commonly perceived role but for visitors to the Island education was placed a substantial second to conservation.

It should also be noted that specifically educational programmes for schools may not be seen by teachers as primarily educational in the sense of enhancing specific understanding of a site. The Scottish Social Education Project found that headteachers rated outdoor educational programmes primarily as assisting the social development of pupils and preparing them for leisure (Orr and MacBeath, 1983). Cognitive development, character development and environmental awareness formed a second order of importance in the judgement of headteachers. Fewer than one in five headteachers, who thought that outdoor education positively influenced the atmosphere of the school, considered that this influence was educational. In contrast, half of the headteachers thought that this improvement was social or emotional. These findings tend to confirm the criticisms made concerning school visits which were discussed earlier.

## Educational resources at heritage sites

It is impossible to include all types of resources here without producing a catalogue. The full range not only includes the site itself but the specifically educational interpretative provision at or for the site. Main media groups include: copy, graphics, photographic prints, projected still photographs, projected moving photographs, optical and lighting effects, sound effects, artefacts, models and replicas, reconstructions, live exhibits and viewing devices (Aldridge, 1975; Pennyfather, 1975). In selecting educational resources it is important to recognise the differences between active and passive learning, the different educational markets, and the different ages and abilities of visitors.

School visits should be set within the context of preparation, organization, implementation and evaluation (Ritchie, 1982). This model, for example, was followed in a series of field studies for Lanarkshire (Johnstone, 1969), which represents an early example of active learning in the context of historic sites, places and museums. A critical element is preparation prior to the fieldwork and many agencies recognise this in their youth and schools work. For example, the Lake District National Park organises half day or whole day activity study sessions on land use conflicts and environmental activities for which background information is supplied, and then reinforced in the activity session. The programme is known as 'Learning through experience', with the modules targeted to different age ranges. The Forestry Commission have also produced a series of teaching packs for the natural heritage that they manage which can be obtained by the teacher in advance of the visit and used in preparation for the visit (e.g. Forestry Commission, undated).

Literature for schoolchildren to use on site has been increasingly produced and generally takes the form of a series of questions, the answers to which pupils seek from the interpretation on site. Because of this, literature can range from historical detail to historical and geographical context. Shannon Development has produced particularly clear 'Young visitors guide booklets' which take the visitor around the site, explain the period context and ask the young person to answer a series of questions and quizes based upon what they see, and the context in which it is set. Shannon Development produces these guides for both its reconstructed crannog and its castles (Shannon Development, undated). The North of England Open Air Museum at Beamish has produced an extensive series of booklets for children to complete as they tour the Museum. The booklets are in two series, 'Explore Beamish' and 'Discover Beamish'; the latter is for young childen. Each booklet takes a topic from the Museum's collection. These include: the railway station, the transport collection, the home farm, the pit cottages, the town houses, the co-op store and outside the town. The booklets take the form of a series of questions about the items on display and the children are encouraged to answer the questions by filling in their answers in the booklet. The 'Discover Beamish' series directs the child's attention to things by suggesting that they look at specific items. The importance of recognising the different cognitive levels of age groups is best illustrated by comparing two texts from the Beamish booklets on the same subject; both encourage active learning through observation and fieldwork. In the 'Discover' series rolling stock is described with pictures as:

> Go on to the platform. From here you can see wagons, coaches and steam engines. They all have wheels and run on rails, so they are called rolling stock. Draw the steam coming out of the engine. Write wagon, engine or coach on the correct picture.
> (North of England Open Air Museum, 1987a, p. 8).

In the 'Explore' series the questioning is more extensive:

> On the track you will see several types of rolling
> stock. Spot the steam locomotive which served Lambton,
> Hetton and Joicey Collieries. Find a stock of coal on
> top of the engine, near the cab. What would this be
> used for? Where would the waste from this process
> escape? ... Look at the ends of the locomotive. When it
> moved coaches or waggons could it: push/ pull/ do
> either ....
>                (North of England Open Air Museum, 1987b, p. 4).

The Cotswold Countryside Collection also produces quiz
sheets as do Cadw, for example; these again are usually
available to teachers in advance of pupils visiting a site.
Some commercial publishers also produce site guides suitable
for secondary school children; the Frank Graham guides to
'Hadrian's Wall in the days of the Romans' are a case in
point (Embleton, 1978; 1981; 1983). Longman also produce
activity guides for heritage sites (e.g. Birt, 1984). More
recently cartoons have been used to encourage young persons'
interest, questionning and understanding in the context and
function of sites; and Cadw, for example, are currently
producing a cartoon series for young people (White and Owen,
1987a, 1987b, 1988).

Recent approaches to on site education have also included
attempts to re-create the period. For example, the National
Trust for Scotland has produced 'Companion Guides' to their
domestic properties in Edinburgh in which people supposedly
tell their own tales at different periods. The Trust gives
'teachers' hints' on how the children may wish to compare
the properties on their visit with that of their own home
environment. In its Georgian House in Edinburgh, the Trust
informs its visitors with a film portraying daily life in
the house when it was newly built. The visitor can then
relate what he or she subsequently sees to the function
shown in the film (Graham et al, 1980). At Beamish Open Air
Museum the skill of empathy can be developed through active
learning in the field where craft demonstrations, for
example rag rug making, can be observed. In addition the
Museum produces for sale a step by step guide leaflet on how
the visitor can practise the craft. This craft could then
be attempted on the visitor's return to school or home.

The re-construction of the past can, of course, be taken a
stage further. Both English Heritage and Cadw have
developed events in which children 'dress up' to act out a
day set in one of their properties. For example, events of
this kind have been run at Neath Abbey and at Heveningham
Hall (Fairclough and Redsell, 1985). Cadw have organised a
series of monastic days at Neath Abbey for primary school
children from the locality: the children were told that they
were to be monks for the whole time that they were at the
Abbey and were given habits to increase their sense of role.
The children learnt a Latin monastic chant and were served
with a monastic meal of vegetable broth and brown bread.
They were also shown ceramic tile making and made their own
decorations on the tiles. Similarly, the pupils were shown

the functions of herbs and ground herbs themselves and were
encouraged to compare the smells of herbs. A professional
calligrapher demonstrated basic skills of calligraphy and
the children were encouraged to write letters of the
alphabet holding the pens correctly. Furthermore, the
children also received basic tuition in the use of the drop
spindle for spinning and had the opportunity to use the
spindle themselves. These monastic days were held for a
week in October 1987. In December 1987 Cadw also held
events for older children to demonstrate 'A Victorian Hall
Christmas' at Caerphilly Castle for which a booklet on
Christmas traditions in Wales was produced (Cadw, 1987).
Like English Heritage and Cadw, The National Trust also
encourages active learning and the skill of empathy through
drama and the dressing up of its young visitors.

The theme of living history has also been developed in
other ways. For example, the Dundee Oral History Project
recorded the oral reminisences of elderly people and
produced learning packs for schools based on this archive.
The learning packs included transcripts of the interviews in
original dialect, period photographs and newspaper
clippings, and a cassette tape of the reminiscences included
in the transcript (Dundee Oral History Project, 1987). In
contrast, at Wigan Pier actors portraying family events from
the turn of the century appear on the scene acting out an
episode next to the visitors who are treated as unobtrusive,
observant ghosts. Visiting school children themselves
become actors, as pupils, in the museum school room. The
Wigan Pier exhibition 'The way we were' is an unusual
educational resource in that it stimulates the five senses:
smell - coal burning in the pub and being mined; sound -
cooing pigeons and street noises; sight - the darkness of
the pit, dim lighting in the schoolroom, period dress and
period furnishings; touch - sitting on wooden schoolroom
benches at wooden desks with slate writing board in hand,
and operating peep machines on the pier; taste - coal in
the atmosphere.

Of equal importance in planning school trips is the
production of guides for teachers which the major agencies
produce (e.g. English Heritage, 1986; National Trust, 1987);
also, guide books to available sites also abound (e.g.
Cumbria Association for Environmental Education, 1982;
Countryside Commission for Scotland, 1983; Northumberland
County Council National Park and Countryside Committee,
1987). Field guides are also increasingly available for
teachers; for example those produced by Northumberland
County Council National Park and Countryside Committee
(Hopkins, 1982; 1983; 1985).

Educational resources for adult education and general
visiting are largely those which are provided as general
interpretative media at sites. As well as site
interpretation (which is discussed in detail in Chapter 6 of
this book), educational material includes walks, trails and
field guides. Walks can be organised or self guided and
there is now an abundance of literature promoting 'town
trails' and 'historic walks' (e.g. Eden District Council,
1984; Mid Western Regional Tourism Organisation, undated).

The Yorkshire Dales National Park is unusual amongst the National Parks for having produced a series of guide cards for walkers in the Dales. These include walks to built heritage as well as landscape heritage. In recognising the potential for joint visiting by at least one market segment of the visitors to the Glasgow Garden Festival, in 1988, the Scottish Office promoted 'a Govan trail' around historic buildings in the vicinity of the Festival gardens (Watson, 1988).

However, it must be re-iterated that the resources for most adult education are generally available as site interpretation available at sites, or for sites, or as published literature.

## Measuring the educational effectiveness of field visits

Site managers can benefit from an understanding of how school teachers can assess what children have learnt on school visits, the feedback from which enables managers to modify their product for schools. The importance of evaluating what has been learnt from school visits to heritage sites has already been emphasised as essential to making such visits an integral part of the curriculum. The reader is again referred to Appendix 1, and particularly to the section on evaluation. In the present section the techniques appropriate to assessing what the pupils have learnt from their visit are outlined for the benefit of site managers who may be unfamiliar with techniques of this kind. Managers can encourage the use of these techniques to measure the effectiveness of their interpretative provisions for schoolchildren. The more general evaluation of interpretative displays for adults at sites is to be found in Chapter 6. The terms 'assessment' and 'evaluation' should not be confused. Assessment is the process of gathering information, both by teachers about their pupils and about their teaching, whereas evaluation involves making judgements based upon the information provided by assessment. Whilst there is an extensive literature on the assessment and evaluation of learning in the classroom, the application of these techniques to learning from school visits to heritage sites is by no means universal. Sometimes, it is assumed implicitly that the educational resources which are being developed at sites are effective learning aids, rather than this effectiveness being demonstrated. The measurement of effectiveness is the measurement of how far the visit has achieved, if at all, the learning objectives which should be expected of it. A failure to measure the effectiveness of school visits results both from the recognition of the variation within how groups of supposedly like individuals learn, and from the manner in which school visits have often been regarded in the past by school teachers; that is as days out, largely unrelated to the school curriculum. It should be noted that the recognition of the variation between individuals in their cognitive styles, personality and background, and in how they learn (Whitehead, 1975; Wolfson, 1976) has not stopped the development of techniques for assessment in the classroom and the beginnings of assessment-led curriculum development (Duncan and Dunn, 1988).

Means of assessment can be differentiated into objective and subjective techniques. Managers will be familiar with subjective techniques in which the correctness of the answer is determined by the teacher's judgement. For example, as school children, many of us will recall having to write essays entitled 'My trip to ...', or something similar, after a school trip. Essays are a subjective means of assessment, and cannot be regarded as objective tests of learning for they are not a standardised task and so cannot be objectively scored. Instead, essays can be regarded as tests of expression, grammar and command of English, as well as of learning. Such an essay could relate an excellent story of the coach journey, snacks and comradeship, but with little reference to what knowledge had been gained about the site which had been visited. However, asking a child to write allows the child to organise knowledge and concepts, and for originality and imagination. If essays are used for the assessment of visits, the teacher usually has a clear idea of the answer which is expected and should design a title which is tight enough to give this. General titles which give no guidance to the child are difficult to assess in terms of particular knowledge. Other kinds of subjective techniques include structured observation, listening and informal assessments (the latter in other than formal situations) (Duncan and Dunn, 1988).

Objective techniques are those which yield answers which in assessment are independent of the teacher's judgement. When questions are specific, and if marking schemes are used, objectivity in assessment is increased. In particular, objective assessment avoids the 'halo' effect, where assessment is subject to personal likes and admiration (or the converse). Objective techniques include alternate response items, multiple choice items, matching items, and restricted response tests. When designing tests of this kind certain preliminary questions need to be answered (Thorndike and Hagan, 1977). These include the following. What function is this assessment intended to serve? What objectives is the teacher trying to achieve? How much emphasis has been given in the visit to the topics to be tested? What relative emphasis should each of the content areas, and each of the process objectives, receive in the test? What type, or types, of items would be most appropriately used in the test? How long should the test be? What should the difficulty of the items be to achieve adequately the purpose of the test? Questions of this kind are essential to any test plan and to the scientific evaluation of the effectiveness of educational resources generally. As such, site managers need to be aware of questions such as these in the design of their schools packs and like educational material.

In writing objective tests certain rules need to be followed. The reading difficulty and vocabulary should be a suitable match in terms of simplicity to the abilities of the class. The items must have a correct answer on which experts would agree, and should deal with important aspects of the content area. The questions set must be clear and unambiguous, avoiding such things as double negatives.

Alternate response items are those in which a pupil is given two choices from which to select an answer. The most widely used variant of this technique is to present a statement requiring the pupil to indicate whether it is true or false. The true-false variant of the technique is most suited to assessing the knowledge of facts which are unequivocally true or false, and is particularly well suited to situations where only two contrasting options exist. The latter is rarely the case, particularly when knowledge of the context of 'place' and 'period' is being assessed, and the use of these statements when more than two options are appropriate can be misleading. The alternate response technique is limited in its usefulness also because pupils can guess when answering, and can expect to get half marks randomly. Standard statistical corrections exist to counter the effects of guessing, including the formula (Lovell, 1973):

$$Score = R - 0.5 W$$

where, R = the number of answers correct; and
W = the number of answers incorrect.

Multiple choice questions are structured so that the pupil choses one answer from a given menu of options. At least three options are necessary, but to minimise the effect of guessing four or five choices are commonly given. Multiple choice questions are particularly useful in assessing pupils' learning or understanding of context, as well as facts, from site visits. Figure 5.1 shows some multiple choice questions applicable to fifth form geography students visiting Cregneash village on the Isle of Man. These questions have been developed from the official guide books and the on-site interpretative provisions, in particular the audio-visual presentation and the exhibition, which form educational resources for schools. The questions presented in Figure 5.1 are designed to assess how far the pupils understand some of the main elements of Manx crofting life, principally its subsistence and cooperative nature, its reliance on farming and fishing, and some elements of its technology. Standard formulae may be applied to multiple response questions to counter the effect of guessing, and are particularly desirable when fewer than five alternatives are given. A standard formula is:

$$Score = R - \frac{W}{n - 1}$$

where: R = number of answers correct;
W = number of answers incorrect; and
n = number of alternative responses for each question.

Figure 5.1.
Multiple choice questions to measure the effectiveness of
site visits: an example pertaining to Cregneash, Isle of
Man

Did the community's livelihood at Cregneash depend on:

   - mainly farming?
   - mainly fishing?
   - manufacturing goods for sale to other communities?
   - farming and seasonal fishing?
   - smuggling goods to England?

Was the organisation of agriculture at Cregneash:

   - hierarchical under a landlord's agent?
   - cooperative between families?
   - reliant on the individual efforts of farmers?
   - dependent on temporary workers coming from outside?
   - run as a single farm?

How was the grain traditionally threshed at Cregneash:

   - in the mill?
   - by stacking into haggards?
   - with grinders?
   - by putting into thurrans?
   - with flails?

What was the focal point of a Manx cottage:

   - the kitchen?
   - the haggard?
   - the open hearth?
   - the cuillee?
   - the loft?

What is thought to be the age of Harry Kelly's cottage:

   - 19th century?
   - 18th century?
   - modern reconstruction?
   - 16th century?
   - 14th century?

Traditionally the cottages at Cregneash were roofed with:

   - reeds?
   - slates and tiles?
   - marram grass?
   - straw?
   - top sod and wheatstraw?

(Correct answers in terms of the Manx Museum and National
Trust's interpretation are underlined).

In using all objective tests pupils should be advised not to guess answers and, furthermore, that they should not answer any question for which they genuinely do not know the answer. In designing multiple choice questions the options should be meaningful, and individually should be kept as short as possible. The statements should be clear and for younger pupils should avoid negatives. Clues as to the correct answer should not be included in the statement, and overall the easy items should be placed first in the test in order to assist the less able children or those lacking in confidence. In addition, the correct answer should vary in its place amongst the options.

Matching item tests are where there are several problems whose answers may be drawn from a single list of possible answers. For example, the pupil could be given a list of occupations usually found in a castle and also a list of rooms, and the pupil has to match the occupations and the rooms on the basis of where these persons would generally have worked. Restricted response tests are where the pupil has to produce an answer in response to a question for which no possible answers have been offered as part of the test, but where only one answer will be deemed to be correct. For example, a pupil could be asked, 'What was a Cregneash cottage traditionally roofed with, in addition to wheatstraw?' The correct answer would be top sod. However, although a pupil may know how a Manx cottage was traditionally roofed, he or she might be unable instantly to recall the words 'top sod', which is on the 'tip of his or her tongue'. Restricted response questions of this kind may not, because of the 'tip of the tongue' recall problem, adequately measure knowledge. Of the objective tests discussed in this section that of multiple response using five response options is recommended: critically, the five options must be valid options and chosen to be meaningful, so as to ensure a wide range of sensible choice. Critical also is the opportunity to use multiple response questions not only to assess the knowledge of facts but also of context, that is, the experience of both 'place' and 'period' which site visits can achieve.

The more general advantages and disadvantages of objective tests should also be considered in any test plan for evaluating the effectiveness of school visits to heritage sites. The advantages of objective tests compared to subjective tests include both ease of marking, and ease and quickness of answer. This often means that as more questions can be asked in a given time, more can be accomplished (Oppenheim, 1976). The pupil spends his or her time thinking and not writing, and as long as the questions asked cover all levels of difficulty, the mark distribution can easily be converted into other scales used in educational assessment (Lovell, 1973). Objective tests also enable the teacher to spot consistent misunderstandings and to correct them in subsequent teaching. As such, techniques of this kind act as a spur to enhancing the effectiveness of teaching, as well as of learning. However, techniques of this kind are not without their disadvantages. Their design is a skilled job and the teacher's views enter into the content of the test. The tests take no account of lucidity of expression and can be artificial in their phrasing. Pupils are also 'forced' to chose between options which they might not either have thought of themselves, or consider to be valid. Because of the skills necessary in designing tests of this kind, the designers of educational resources at heritage sites, and not the teachers alone, should seek to produce standard tests to supplement their school packs. Without appropriate developments and assessment the effectiveness of school visits is likely to be minimal in terms of learning and visits to heritage sites are likely to remain largely as outings.


Conclusions

Heritage sites can be invaluable resources both for active learning by school children and for the general education of the segment of adult visitors coming for non-specific reasons, but expecting to learn something from their visit. A smaller and more specialist market is also to be found in adult study holidays and like organised activities. Heritage sites have to be developed and managed in such a way as to achieve this role as an appropriate resource. The contribution of heritage sites both to active learning by school children and to the general education of visitors is, in part, a managerial decision.

Recent curriculum developments have emphasised active learning, particularly in subjects to which heritage sites can be readily seen as a potential resource. The teaching of history is a case in point. Contemporary curriculum developments in the teaching of history emphasise the skill of asking questions and making informed judgements. Pupils' questions should include the issues of causation, function or technique and past roles. Field studies and other active learning techniques can contribute to this critical ability. The teaching of history is moving away from the rote learning of 'facts', and the managers of heritage sites should continue to respond to this change by developing appropriate educational resources. In particular, the development of heritage museums and centres in the 1980s can be seen, in part, as a response to this change in the objectives of primary and secondary education. Centres of this kind describe how people lived in the past, and enable children to compare their contemporary world with that of people in the past who lived in their town or region. Learning of this kind by pupils may be termed a Time Reflection Approach to Learning.

An increasing proportion of visitors to heritage sites seek to learn something, however general, from their visit; they seek to be informed. Site interpretation can contribute to this general educational need, and represents a contribution to the main adult market for education. More specific requirements are made by the minority market for formal adult education; as these are varied, general provision is difficult.

Underlying much heritage education is a further educational objective to that of developing a critical ability. It concerns the promotion of environmental conservation, and particularly of heritage conservation, through education. In this sense, education is seen as a facilitator of conservation. Conservation objectives include the creation of an awareness and acceptance of the need for conservation, and of the need to provide resources for conservation. In particular, the Cynefin Strategy for Wales has promoted conservation objectives through education, and particularly through the education of school children.

Despite the curriculum developments in schools the pattern of change in school teaching practices in history has been varied, even locally within areas. Visits to heritage sites by school children are substantial, yet it would be incorrect to assume that all schools make visits of this sort, or that all visits of this kind foster learning. Nor is is correct to assume that teachers always expect such visits to contribute to active learning of subject matter: the learning of social skills may be more important as teaching objectives. To be successful in teaching subject matter, the visit needs to be integrated with the curriculum, and in particular to involve preparation and review. Pupils need to be told the purpose of the visit and what to look for on site, and subsequently to apply what they have learnt from the visit to their school work. The National Trust for Scotland has been particularly active in the organisation of active learning of this kind, as have several of the National Parks.

Despite the number of school visits made, there is little published material recording the reasons for these visits. From the limited material available we have some idea of the age range of pupils and their trip distances. Most visits are made within forty to fifty miles of the school, and historic sites appear to be popular throughout the age range of compulsory schooling. In order to develop sites to meet the needs of school visits managers may wish in future to find out why their sites are being visited. Indeed, the whole market segment represented by schools visits is under-researched in terms both of school activites and of the specific benefits teachers perceive their pupils gain by visits, other than in the general terms of active learning.

The present educational contribution of the major agencies responsible for heritage sites varies substantially. The positive role of the National Trust for Scotland, in particular, has already been mentioned. Both English Heritage and Cadw are developing 'living history' programmes for schools, and targeting their efforts to specific age ranges. The Countryside Commissions have encouraged interpretative developments, both generally and specifically, the latter by short courses. The National Parks have a long tradition of active learning in their walks programmes and like activities; the informational role of the Parks having been variously developed into interpretative and educational provisions. Diversity is, however, to be found amongst other public bodies, for example, local authorities. In particular, museums vary in their developments as educational resources. Best practice can be instanced from Wigan Pier and Beamish Open Air Museum, and other like sites. But many museums remain cabinets of curiosities rather than educational resources.

Specifically educational resources at heritage sites have been variously developed, and examples of good practice have been reviewed. In terms of both active learning and literature it is essential to remember that children are not one market segment alone, but that they are differentiated, in particular, by ability and age. Resources have to be designed with these differences in mind. However, it is equally important to realise that most existing on-site interpretation is implicitly designed for adults, and as a consequence is of limited value, if any, for school children, other than at G.C.S.E. level. The more general point is that the educational effectiveness of recent developments at heritage sites has not often been assessed. Rather, these resources have been assumed to be effective in assisting learning by school pupils. The assessment of the effectiveness of both school visits and educational resources designed for these visits is a major research requirement for the 1990s.

Heritage sites can both respond to and develop educational markets, particularly those of school education and general information for adults. In the one sense they are 'demand-led', in the other, they create demand, and demand is 'supply-led'. The expansion of active learning in schools presents a broad context of demand, but equally the best forms of display stimulate thoughts of how teaching can be improved by utilising the resources available. It is a fair conclusion that the educational market for heritage sites has the potential for continued expansion and substantial product differentiation into the 1990s. It is equally apt to conclude that this market will likely become both competitive and discerning as teachers find themselves able to choose between the alternative products offered by site managers.


Appendix 1.
Visiting a National Trust for Scotland Property
Suggested check-list for teachers

Preparation

Consider appropriateness of a visit for pupils in relation to work done in school.

Select property to visit.

Make preparatory visit to property. NB Free admission for teacher.

Survey to test suitability for organized visit, e.g. size of property.

Note teaching points with help of Guide Book.

Time length of visit.  NB Pupils' span of attention.

Discuss with NTS staff arrangements for visit, e.g. best time for school visit (avoid, if possible, busy tourist season), maximum numbers; pupil - teacher ratio, respective roles of teacher and NTS staff, how to use property, length of booking time needed, needs of other visitors, facilities for disabled.

Check for special facilities for school parties, e.g. availability of study/exhibition area, audio-visual displays supply of worksheets, clipboards.

Consider access for buses; parking; toilets; recreational facilities; e.g. picnic area, cafeteria, shop for souvenirs, postcards, adventure playground, local recreation, shops, post office, early closing.

Think of additional places of interest to include in visit (For extended visit consider arrangements for accommodation, e.g. Youth Hostel, guest house, school).


Organization
At school

Consult with Head Teacher and other staff in school, e.g. local requirements for safety, other school activites.

Consider methods of paying for visit, for transport.  NB Special terms for Group Membership of NTS.

Make booking for visit well in advance
- at least 2 weeks, the earlier the better;
- write to or telephone NTS reprepresentative (consult Educational Guide for details) giving details of visit, e.g. intended date and time of visit (with alternatives), number in party, services required;
- inform NTS staff of context of visit and age and ability of pupils.

Wait for confirmation of booking.

Notify parents - give details of visit, ask for permission, perhaps request help as escorts.

Consider need for additional help from staff/students.

Clarify main aims and objectives of visit and what pupils are to see and do on the visit and afterwards.

Prepare pupils for visit
- relevant work in school, explain purpose, time and place
  of visit;
- tell what to look out for on visit; perhaps show
  slides/postcards;
- emphasise need for responsible behaviour on visit.

Indicate appropriate clothing needed

Consider arrangements for refreshment - packed lunch:
brought by pupils, supplied by school/host school.

Discuss how much money needed, e.g. for snacks, souvenirs,
postcards.

Encourage pupils to bring cameras to record evidence for
later use.

Prepare worksheets, if desirable - refer to Guide Book and
perhaps additional background material.

Have at hand, for emergencies, spare cash, first aid.

Inform NTS representative of any change of plans or
cancellation.


Implementation
At the property

Meet NTS staff: pay for admission/ show school's corporate
membership card.

Escort pupils round the property. NB Pupils are still in
YOUR charge.

Help pupils to gain most from visit, e.g. by relating to
classroom work.

Allow time for pupils to study points of particular interest
and recording what has been learnt.

Consider needs of other visitors.

Provide opportunity for supervised recreation.

Ensure opportunity for supervised recreation.

Ensure pupils use litter receptacles.

Abide by appropriate codes of conduct.

Know where and when to meet for return journey.

Get back safely to school.

**Evaluation**
Assess the value of the visit back at school.

Discuss with pupils what they have learnt from the visit relating to their school work.

Apply what the pupils have learnt from their visit to their school work, e.g. reporting back, presenting their findings.

Evaluate the success of the visit, e.g. did the pupils enjoy themselves? Would they go back? Were the arrangements satisfactory? Would you go back? Was it 'cost effective'?

Consider informing the NTS staff of the value of the visit; consider getting pupils to write about their visit to NTS staff.

NB NTS staff appreciate evaluation of visits.

Source: Ritchie (1982).

**References**

Aldridge, D. (1975). Guide to countryside interpretation. Part 1. Principles of countryside interpretation and interpretive planning. Edinburgh: Her Majesty's Stationery Office.

Birt, D. (1984). Beamish North of England Open Air Museum activity guide. London: Longman.

Bouvaird, A. G., Tricker, M. J. and Stoakes, R. (1984). Recreation management and pricing. The effect of charging policy on demand at countryside recreation sites. Aldershot: Gower.

Brecon Beacons National Park (1986). Draft Plan, First Review. Brecon: Brecon Beacons National Park.

Cadw (1985). Heritage in Wales. Membership scheme leaflet. Cardiff: Cadw.

Cadw (1986). A policy for education. Cardiff: Cadw.

Cadw (1987). Caerphilly Castle. A Victorian Hall Christmas. Cardiff: Cadw.

Central Regional Council and the Countryside Commission for Scotland (1984). Strategy for interpretation in Central Region. Perth: Countryside Commission for Scotland; and Stirling: Central Regional Council.

Cooper and Latham (1985). The market for educational visits to tourist attractions. Dorset: Department of Tourism and Field Sciences, Dorset Institute of Higher Education.

Cotswold District Council (1987). Educational and party visits. Pamphlet. Cirencester: Cotswold District Council.

Countryside Commission (1977). Interpretive planning. Advisory Series Number 2. Cheltenham: Countryside Commission.

Countryside Commission (1982). Informal countryside recreation for disabled people. Advisory Series Number 15. Revised edition. Cheltenham: Countryside Commission.

CRAC (1987). The handbook of tourism and leisure 1988. London: English Tourist Board.

Croucher, N. (1981). Outdoor pursuits for disabled people. Cambridge: Woodhead-Faulkner.

Cumbria Association for Environmental Education (1982). Field studies in Cumbria. A resources guide for teachers. Whitehaven: Cumbria Association for Environmental Education.

Cynefin Education and Training Working Group (1982). 'Towards a more intelligent use of the environment'. pp. 333-339. In Cynefin: a Welsh conservation strategy. Cardiff: Nature Conservancy Council Headquarters for Wales.

Department of Education and Science (1985a). The curriculum from 5 to 16. Curriculum matters 2. A H.M.I. Series. London: Her Majesty's Stationery Office.

Department of Education and Science (1985b). History in the primary and secondary years: A HMI view. London: Her Majesty's Stationery Office.

Duncan, A. and Dunn, W. (1988). What primary teachers should know about assessment. Sevenoaks: Hodder and Stoughton.

Dundee Oral History Project (D.O.H.P.) (1987). The world's ill- divided. Booklet accompanying B.B.C.2 Open Space Film. Dundee: (D.O.H.P.) Dundee Oral History Project.

Dyer, M. (1983). 'The Sandford Award and heritage education'. Interpretation, 24, p. 9.

Eden District Council (1984). Walking East of Eden, Alston Moor walks 1 to 5. Penrith: Eden District Council, East Fellside and Alston Moor Project.

Embleton, R. (1988). Housesteads in the days of the Romans. Newcastle upon Tyne: Frank Graham.

Embleton, R. (1981). The Stonegate. Corbridge, Vindolanda and Carvoran in the days of the Romans. Newcastle upon Tyne: Frank Graham.

Embleton, R. (1983). The outpost forts of Hadrian's Wall in the days of the Romans. Newcastle upon Tyne: Frank Graham.

English Heritage Education Service (1986). Information for teachers. Folder. London: Historic Buildings and Monuments Commission for England (English Heritage).

Fairclough, J. and Redsell, P. (1985). Living history. Reconstructing the past with children. London: Historic Buildings and Monuments Commission for England (English Heritage).

Forestry Commission (undated). Grizedale Forest, field studies guide. Edinburgh: Forestry Commission.

Forestry Commission (undated). Thornthwaite Forest, Whinlatter, teacher's pack. Edinburgh: Forestry Commission.

Graham, I., MacSween, K. and Watt, J. S. K. (1980). A companion to Gladstone's land. Edinburgh: National Trust for Scotland.

Harrison, A. (1976). 'Problems: vandalism and depreciative behaviour'. Chapter 24. In Sharpe, G. W. (Ed.). Interpreting the environment. London: John Wiley and Sons Inc.

Heady, P. (1984). Visiting museums. Office of Population Censuses and Surveys, Social Survey Division. SS1147. London: Her Majesty's Stationery Office.

Her Majesty's Inspectors (1986). Report by H. M. Inspectors on a survey of history in the secondary schools of Swansea, West Glamorgan. Inspected during Autumn Term 1985. WSS 6/86. Cardiff: Welsh Office.

Hopkins, T. (Ed.) (1982). A fieldguide to the Hadrian's Wall area. Hexham: Northumberland County Council.

Hopkins, T. (1983). A fieldguide to Plessey Woods Country Park. Hexham: Northumberland County Council.

Hopkins, T. (Ed.) (1985). A fieldguide to the Cheviot Hills. Hexham: Northumberland County Council.

House of Commons (1987). Tourism in Wales. Volumes 1 and 2. House of Commons Paper 256-I and 256-II. London: Her Majesty's Stationery Office

Johnstone, J. S. (Ed.) (1969). Field studies in Lanarkshire. Hamilton: Hamilton College of Education.

Lake District National Park Authority (1986). The Lake District National Park Plan. Reviewed 1986. Kendal: Lake District National Park Authority.

Lovell, K. (1973). Educational psychology and children. Eleventh edition. Sevenoaks: Hodder and Stoughton.

Mather, P. (1986). A time for a museum: the history of the Queensland Museum, 1862-1986. Queensland, Australia: Board of Trustees of the Queensland Museum.

Mid Western Tourism Organisation (undated). A walking tour of historic Ennis. Limerick: Shannonside, Mid Western Regional Tourism Organisation.

National Trust (1985). The National Trust and education. Revised edition. London: The National Trust.

National Trust (1987a). Advice to teachers. Revised edition. Bromley, London: The National Trust.

National Trust (1987b). Facilities for disabled and visually handicapped visitors in 1987. London: The National Trust.

Neave, D. Moorhouse, J. and Millar, S. (1988). 'Profits from the past in heritage studies'. Pickup, Spring 1988, 23-24.

Nichol, J. (1984). Teaching history: a teaching skills workbook. London: Macmillan Education.

North of England Open Air Museum (1987a). Discover Beamish railway station. Beamish: North of England Open Air Museum.

North of England Open Air Museum (1987b). Explore Beamish railway station. Beamish: North of England Open Air Museum.

Northumberland County Council National Park and Countryside Committee (1987). Visit planning guide to the Northumberland countryside. Hexham: Northumberland County Council.

Oppenheim, A. N. (1966). Questionnaire design and attitude measurement. London: Heinemann.

Orr, D. and MacBeath, J. (1983). Social education though outdoor activities. Glasgow: Jordan Hill, College of Education.

Pennyfather, K. (1975). Guide to countryside interpretation. Part 2. Interpretive media and facilities. Edinburgh: Her Majesty's Stationery Office.

Prentice, R. C. (1988a). The domestic market for the Curraghs Wildlife Park. St Johns: Isle of Man Department of Agriculture, Fisheries and Forestry.

Prentice, R.C. (1988b). Amenity resources and tourism: the present role of the National Glens and the Wildlife Park as summer tourist attractions. St Johns: Isle of Man Department of Agriculture, Fisheries and Forestry.

Ritchie, W. K. (1982). Educational guide to the National Trust for Scotland. Edinburgh: British Petroleum and National Trust for Scotland.

Seren (1986a). Herbert, D. T., Thomas, C. J., Prentice, R. C., and Prentice, M. M. Interpretation at Cadw's sites. Swansea: Social Economic Research and Environment, Department of Geography, University College of Swansea.

Seren (1986b). Prentice, R. C. Heritage in Wales membership. Survey of members who joined in 1985. Swansea: Social Economic Research and Environment, Department of Geography, University College of Swansea.

Seren (1987). Herbert, D. T., Prentice, R. C., Thomas, C. J. and Prentice, M. M. Survey of Heritage in Wales members who joined in 1986. Swansea: Social Economic Research and Environment, Department of Geography, University College of Swansea.

Schurer, K. (1984). 'Population history, microcomputers and education'. Economic and Social Research Council Newsletter, 52, pp.24-26.

Shannon Development (undated). Craggaunowen. A young visitor's guide. Shannon Airport: Shannon Free Airport Development Co.

Shannon Development (undated). Bunratty Castle. A young visitor's guide. Shannon Airport: Shannon Free Airport Development Co.

Stewart, J. (1984). 'Museums - 'Cabinets of curiosities' or centres of information?' pp. 77-89. In Martlew, R. Information systems in archaeology. Gloucester: Alan Sutton.

Thorndike, R. L. and Hagen, E. P. (1977). Measurement and evaluation in psychology and education. New York: John Wiley.

Watson, M. (1988). 'A Govan trail'. In Welcome (News for Friends of the Scottish Monuments), 10. Edinburgh: Scottish Office.

White, R. and Owen, D. (1987a). Conwy Castle. Cardiff: Cadw.

White, R. and Owen, D. (1987b). Caerleon Roman Fortress. Cardiff: Cadw.

White, R. and Owen, D. (1988). Gerald's Wales, a twelth century journey. Cardiff: Cadw.

Whitehead, J. M. (Ed.) (1975). Personality and learning, volume 1. London: Hodder and Stoughton.

Wigan Pier Schools' Centre (1986). A handbook for teachers. Wigan: Wigan Metropolitan Borough Council.

Wolfson, J. (Ed.) (1976). Personality and learning, volume 2. London: Hodder and Stoughton.

Yorkshire Dales National Park Committee (1984). <u>National Park Plan: first review</u>. Leyburn: North Yorkshire County Council, Yorkshire Dales National Park Committee.

# 6 Does interpretation help?

DAVID T HERBERT

## Introduction

The United States National Park Service has been using
countryside interpretation since 1916 and when Freeman
Tilden sought to explain the term 'interpretation', he spoke
of the work of those concerned with revealing to visitors to
national parks, monuments, historic sites and other such
places, something of the beauty and wonder, the inspiration
and spiritual meaning that lie behind what the visitor can
with his senses perceive. He invokes the idea of the genius
of the revealer 'the man or woman who uncovers something
universal in the world that has always been here and that
men have not known. This person's greatness is not so much
in himself as in what he unveils' (Tilden, 1977, p. 5).
Interpretation has these broad aims. Its role is to make
people more aware of the places they visit, to provide
knowledge which increases their understanding and to promote
interest which leads to greater enjoyment and perhaps
responsibility. Interpretation is now applied to many forms
of heritage. It is present in national parks and nature
reserves, in country houses and castles, in historic sites
and places. It has the dual purposes of serving the best
interests of the visitors who come to see and experience a
site and also those of the place itself. Good
interpretation will raise the value of a site in the eyes of
those who come to visit; greater value will lead to greater
conviction of the need to preserve and protect. This
duality of purposes is admirably expressed in an American
Park Services manual (Tilden, 1977, p. 37): 'Through

Figure 6.1.
Stages of interpretation: a schema

| Principles: | relate to 'experience' | seek to 'reveal' | view as an 'art' | seek to 'stimulate' | aim for 'wholeness' |
|---|---|---|---|---|---|
| Aims: | to educate | to inform | to enhance | to entertain | to manage |

| Methods: | spoken word | written word | visual display. | performance |
|---|---|---|---|---|
| examples: | guide, recording, listening posts, live sound effects. | signs, notices, texts, murals, panels, wall charts, posters, publications, guide books. | artefacts, videos, graphics, maps, photographs, prints, replicas, models, projected images, reconstructions, viewing devices, lighting sequences. | events, tableaux, use of costumes. |

Outcomes:

for interpreter: greater sympathy, better 'managed' visitors, greater number of visitors.

for visitor: greater awareness, better understanding, self-fulfilment, enhancement, (and enjoyment.
interpreter)

interpretation, understanding; through understanding, appreciation; through appreciation, protection'.

This chapter examines the key features of an interpretative approach to heritage sites, it is concerned with aims and objectives and basically with the question of 'What we are seeking to achieve through interpretation'. Once interpretation is used, the question of its effectiveness becomes relevant. Interpretation involves both broad strategies and more specific techniques and media appropriate to the particular circumstances of a site. Aldridge (1975) makes the useful distinctions between interpretation for historic sites, natural sites and conservation education. At historic sites interpretation is defined as the art of explaining the past, in relation to environmental and social conditions, to casual visitors by bringing it to life, usually in thematic or story form. At natural sites, interpretation is the art of revealing the relationships between people and environments and of explaining the character of an area. The target groups and basic method are the same; in both situations the purpose is the increase visitor awareness and desire to conserve. Conservation education is more explicitly the art of teaching with more in-depth methods to more committed students of heritage.

In this chapter the various approaches to interpretation at historic sites will be examined and the effectiveness of methods used will be assessed. There is a general aim of understanding the principles of interpretation and the issues raised both for policy-makers and practitioners. Figure 6.1 provides a useful structure for at least the early part of the chapter. In addition to indicating the initial sequence of principles, aims and methods, it provides summary indicators of each of these.


## Tilden's principles of interpretation

Although it was primarily aimed at the countryside and national parks, the definitive statement on the 'philosophy' of interpretation remains that enunciated by Tilden initially in 1957 (Tilden, 1977). He wrote as a practitioner working within the National Park Service of the United States of America but in the words of his foreword written for the 3rd edition of 1977: 'Freeman Tilden wrote about fundamentals - the guiding principles and underlying philosophy of the interpreter's art and craft', (Tilden, 1977, p. xi). Hammitt (1981) described Tilden as the provider of a philosophical base for environmental interpretation and argued that a conceptual base for his principles could be found in cognitive psychology.

It is worth restating Tilden's six principles in order to set some conceptual framework for the discussion of interpretation. The first of these states: 'Any interpretation which does not somehow relate to what is being displayed or described to something within the personality or experience of the visitor will be sterile' (Tilden, 1977). The contention here is that a visitor will, in a sense, 'interpret' the interpretation, see things through his or her own eyes, and will relate the words or images used to a personal knowledge and experience (This of all the principles relates most strongly to cognitive theory). Interpretation must therefore be meaningful, legible and capable of being understood in various frames of reference. Tilden's second principle concerned information: 'Information as such, is not interpretation. Interpretation is revelation based on information. They are different things but not all interpretation includes information' (Tilden, 1977). Interpretation is the art of conveying information, it has a teaching and an illuminating role which reaches out to the visitor. It conveys not simply facts but also meanings and values; it seeks to enrich the senses from being in a specific place.

Tilden's third principle concerned subjectivity: 'Interpretation is an art, which combines many arts, whether the materials presented are scientific, historical or architectural'. (Tilden, 1977). The messages which interpretation seeks to convey are often subjective and qualitative, they reach out to the emotions and affective properties. Those who interpret should rely on the arts of creativity and imagination. This leads on to the fourth principle: 'The chief aim of interpretation is not instruction but provocation' (Tilden, 1977). This principle has the aim of stimulation and an awakening of interest; of increasing the visitor's awareness of what is being seen or experienced. Good interpretation will leave the visitor with the urge to delve further, to widen horizons or to seek for new knowledge.

The argument of Tilden's fifth principle concerned the familiar one of gestalt or wholeness; it is better to leave visitors with one or two complete pictures rather than with a mixture of information: 'Interpretation should aim to present the whole rather than a part, and must address itself to the whole person rather than to any phase' (Tilden, 1977). Finally, Tilden emphasised that children have fewer experiences to draw upon and interpretation must be aware that it is providing new knowledge; the process of communication has different qualities. This sixth principle states: 'Interpretation addressed to children (up to the age of 12 years) should not be a dilution of the presentation to adults, but should follow a fundamentally different path' (Tilden, 1977).

Those concerned with the provision of interpretation must eventually become involved in detailed planning of displays; there are questions of balance between written texts, photographic, illustrative or cartographic materials, audio-visual displays and others. Tilden does not provide direct guidance on these issues, important though they are, what he does provide is a set of more basic principles on the art of interpretation. If these principles are followed, the interpreter has moved a long way towards the attainment of his aims and objectives.

Aims

Putting the principles of interpretation into practice is a
sensitive and demanding task. Whereas principles can be
regarded as having a generality which should normally be
applied to all interpretative strategies, aims and
objectives are more likely to vary with the specific policy
of the agency involved or with the special characteristics
of a site. Historic sites have many common features with
natural sites but there are significant points of difference
which are likely to emerge when aims and objectives are
specified. Features of human occupance for example are much
more likely to become foci in the interpretation of historic
sites: a castle or an abbey is the stage upon which
communities were formed and people lived their lives.
Whereas, for example, the aim in a nature reserve may be to
demonstrate the wonders of nature and to press the
conservation message, in a castle or abbey it may be to use
the relict building as a vehicle to re-construct past
events. Much of interpretative practice flows from
objectives. These influence the form of media, the content
of messages and the level at which they are pitched. Any
eventual evaluation must relate to objectives; as Putney and
Wagar (1973) argued, you cannot say how well you are doing
unless you specify what it is you are trying to do. Aims
and objectives may vary, therefore, but there are a number
which are typical of most forms of interpretation.
One typical aim is that of achieving a sense of respect
for the qualities of the site and recognition of a
conservation role. Prince (1983), particularly in the
context of national parks and nature reserves, argued that
facilities should always be subservient to the nature of the
location, putting place first and interpretation second. As
a practical guideline this suggests that any form of
interpretation should fit the setting as closely as
possible, the less 'visible' the better in some senses.
Given the duality of the interpretative role, there is
almost inevitably a tension between the aim of enhancing the
visitor's experience and that of least disturbance to the
site. Uzzell (1985) discusses the useful idea of
interpreter as broker or intermediary between the visitors
and the environments which they wish to understand or at
least experience. Several writers have stressed the dual
roles of interpretation. English Heritage, in its statutory
role, is required to promote public enjoyment of ancient
monuments and historic buildings but also to advance
knowledge and a sympathy for preservation. Mahaffey (1970)
stated the purposes of interpretation in historic sites as
to widen horizons of knowledge, to create empathy towards
cultural and natural surroundings and to promote
appreciation of heritage. The 'hidden agenda' in the aims
of interpretation seeks to convert the unaware and to
strengthen the beliefs of those partially committed to the
cause of preservation.
Beyond the task of nurturing a sense of sympathy for the
preservation of sites, interpretation has a number of
established aims (Figure 6.1). By and large these serve

the purposes of both the visitors and the interpreters though the balance of interest may swing one way or another. Light (1987) identified eight aims of interpretation and although most of these can be related to the summary headings indicated in Figure 6.1, there are other aims designed to advance the purposes of the interpreter which can be briefly discussed. Firstly, it could be argued that interpretation forms part of a general strategy to promote tourism and therefore to contribute to more general economic development in particular areas. Tourism has an economic impact and good interpretation through attracting more visitors to a site may aid this process and help satisfy a more general demand for countryside recreation. Secondly, interpretation can be used as a form of propaganda, not strictly tied to preservation, in order to support the purposes of a specific lobby such as the agricultural community (Uzzell, 1985), regional interests or organizations such as Friends of the Earth.

One central aim of interpretation is clearly educational and Tilden wrote his principles with this central idea. This aim is most specific for high interest groups such as local historians or archaeologists and is more general for children who may visit historic sites as part of their learning process. At one level, interpretation serves to convey basic facts: for whom a castle was built, when it was built and for what reasons. At another level the interpreter needs to use information as a means of achieving a wider understanding of a site in its temporal, spatial and cultural contexts. To the extent that the interpreter is an educator, he or she needs to assume the best qualities of pedagogic practice and to relate to the kind of audience being taught. To educate in some formal sense is one aim, to inform 'informally' is another. Most visitors do not come to be educated but they are willing to pick up bits of information in an informal way. Visitors are using their leisure time and are in a leisure frame of mind, they are sporadic in their visits and are certainly not a committed or captive audience. Planning of the Jorvik Centre at York recognized these facts. The sequence has been designed to build up comprehension cumulatively with a limited number of clear take-home messages. Those with limited background knowledge or a modest capacity to learn receive them at one level, but the more experienced and insightful can derive much more (Addyman and Gaynor, 1984).

Evidence shows that different types of people respond differently to interpretation. Prince (1983) showed that whereas professional groups saw interpretation as an integral part of a countryside visit, manual workers regarded it as far from essential. Evidence from the Cadw surveys showed that whereas there was a strong level of general support for interpretation, 94% thought that all sites needed displays of some kind, there were differences by social class, age, length of visit and some other sources of visitor variation (Seren, 1986). The nature of the visitor group is clearly important and a significant feature of the Cadw survey of interpretation was that three-quarters of those interviewed expressed an interest in castles and historic sites. If these two facts are taken together, there is a significant group of visitors likely to be amenable to the educational roles of interpretation and a much larger group who are willing to be informed, despite the fact that they are for the most part leisure-oriented. There is a general acceptance that the need for self-fulfilment is an important motivation for recreational activity (Iso-Ahola, 1983) and interpretative facilities which help a visitor to develop a critical insight and appreciation of historic buildings provides a boost to self-esteem (Light, 1987).

The aim of enhancing the enjoyment of a visit more directly addresses the leisure context. Interpretation can enhance enjoyment in basic ways. It can make the visit easier and more comfortable by, for example, directing people to the most spectacular views, along the easiest most manageable routes and towards any facilities (though admittedly this moves from interpretation to facilitation). Visual displays may not have much effect in terms of educating or informing many visitors but they create impressions, leave images and provide the kind of awareness which makes a visit more memorable. Interpretation can add to the enjoyment of a visit because it stirs the imagination and affects the emotions; a visitor may leave a site with a sense of well-being and if that is so, enjoyment has been enhanced through interpretative displays.

Entertainment as an aim is more purely leisure, it is most evident in the growth of visitor centres, heritage centres, theme displays, staging of events or re-enactments and elaborate models with light and sound effects. At York's Jorvik Centre, visitors can travel by time cars via time tunnels to tenth century Coppergate where visual displays, old Norse recordings and 'balanced olefactory experiences', allow them the experience of the former Viking settlement. At Kentwell Hall each year, two hundred volunteers re-enact everyday Tudor domestic life for visitors to this centre in Suffolk. Events and displays of this kind are capable of attracting large numbers of visitors. There is a need to be mindful of the historical significance of a site which should remain different from the kinds of theme parks which are developed for purely entertainment purposes. Harrison (1985) argues that interpretation should remain uncompromising in its authenticity and not lapse into pure entertainment.

Finally, as an aim of interpretation, there is an increasing tendency to use it for management purposes. Movement of visitors can be controlled by signs or barriers to avoid congestion, to keep people away from sensitive areas and to bring visitors towards significant points of interest which they might otherwise miss. Facilities, such as toilets, washrooms, catering and rest areas, can be strategically placed so that they draw people away from parts of the site most in need of protection. Interpretation as a management tool can also be used to convey any 'messages' which the managers wish visitors to receive. Messages on the need for preservation, on the need for more funds, or on other nearby sites of interest may

Table 6.1.
Main purpose of visit

|  | South Wales: | | | |
|  | Tintern Abbey | Caerphilly Castle | Chepstow Castle | Caerleon Roman Baths and Fort |
|  | % | % | % | % |
| To relax | 19 | 24 | 31 | 11 |
| To be entertained | 10 | 18 | 11 | 11 |
| To be informed | 51 | 40 | 44 | 67 |
| To be educated | 18 | 16 | 13 | 9 |
| Don't know | 3 | 1 | 1 | 2 |

|  | North Wales: | | |
|  | Caernarfon Castle | Conwy Castle | ALL sites |
|  | % | % | % |
| To relax | 13 | 20 | 20 |
| To be entertained | 17 | 15 | 14 |
| To be informed | 42 | 39 | 45 |
| To be educated | 19 | 19 | 17 |
| Don't know | 8 | 7 | 4 |

Source: Seren, 1986.

form part of this strategy. There may be different kinds of messages for tourists and for local visitors. For tourists the aim is promotional with encouragement to visit historic sites, for locals it is more concerned with fostering a sense of common responsibility for part of the regional heritage. This last comment stresses the need for the forms which interpretation takes to follow the set objectives. Interpreters can think of target audiences for specific forms of display, especially where children are involved. An interpretation survey was conducted at six Cadw sites and will be discussed more fully in the next section; it is of interest here, however, to record the main purposes and reasons for visit given by those interviewed (Tables 6.1 and 6.2). At all sites the most common response to the question of main purpose of visit was 'to be informed'. This ranged from 39% at Conwy to 67% at Caerleon with an average for all sites of 45%. Far fewer had come to be educated and for significant minorities the main purpose of the visit was to relax or to be entertained. This finding tends to re-inforce some of the prevalent beliefs about visitors. Whereas a small minority seek to be 'taught' about a site in any formal sense, there is a large group which is interested in acquiring some knowledge. The desire to be able to relax or to be entertained is strongest in those South Wales sites, Caerphilly and Chepstow where day trips from local people are more common. A high

Table 6.2.
Reasons important in decision to visit site

|  | Percentages % |
|---|---|
| Reasons important: | |
| Interest in castles/ historic sites | 74 |
| Interest in Welsh culture/history | 26 |
| Special 'event' on | 2 |
| Enjoy sightseeing/general interest | 54 |
| Part of day out in country | 26 |
| Brought children/children wanted to come | 14 |
| Unable to go where planned | 1 |

Source:   Seren, 1986.


proportion of visitors declared an interest in castles or other historic sites as constituting an important reason for their visit; this was balanced by high season sightseeing and general interest. The former suggests that large numbers of people have a sufficient level of interest to be amenable to interpretation but also that the leisure mood of many will set limits to what can be attempted.


Methods of interpretation

Having identified the broad principles behind interpretation and the general aims which interpreters follow, the next step involves implementation and the form which interpretative facilities take. Figure 6.1 indicates the main forms which are available and will provide some structure for the discussion. The range and variety is of course considerable and other authors have provided much more detailed lists (See, for example, Aldridge, 1975 who classified interpetative devices under the three headings of two-dimensional, sound effects and three-dimensional: summarised in Figure 6.2). As the tables show, the interpreter has a considerable range of choices from which to select. There are decisions on the medium to be used, whether it is for example a written text or a sound recording, on the content of the message, whether it is long or short, detailed or simplified, and on the way in which it is put across, theatrically or factually. Although a variety of media may be used at any one site, the notion of achieving a unity of theme needs to be adhered to. A general strategy which integrates and leaves the visitor with a whole picture is always a key desideratum. This notion of unity of theme requires a logical sequencing of messages, each component should be compatible with its neighbours.
    Aldridge (1975) provided a useful set of guidelines on the selection of media within an overall strategy; he basically identifies the conditions which a medium must satisfy; i.e.

Figure 6.2.
Main media groups (after Aldridge, 1975)

1.  Two dimensional

Copy:  written word, text

Graphics:  drawings, artwork

Photographic prints:  opaque still prints
all on
signs,  murals, panels,  wall charts,
posters, publications

Projected still photographs: black and white or colour,
projected  by front or  back
projection,
as still or slide sequences

Projected moving photographs:  black and white or colour

Special optical and lighting effects:  mirrors and lenses,
Pepper's ghost box,
Claude glass,
camera obscura,
microscope, filters,
automatic lighted
sequences,
son et lumiere,
stereo viewing


2.  Sound effects

Commentaries,  natural sounds,  music,  choral,  historic
recordings, sound archive
on
message repeaters, listening posts, tapes, sound tracks


3.  Three dimensional

Artefacts:  rocks, minerals, fossils, dried plants, animal
bones, clothing, tools, arts, ornaments

Models:  casts of footprints,
model reconstructions,
scale models, dioramas, working models

Full-scale reconstructions:  skeletons, animals,
tableaux, costumed figures,
buildings, machinery.

Figure 6.3.
Guidelines for media presentations

General objectives

to attract attention, to give information,
to stimulate interest, to encourage participation


Essential general qualities

visibility, accessibility, brevity, clarity, legibility,
stimulating ease of comprehension


Specific qualities

signs:      cheerful, colourful, decorative, artistic,
            bold print, use of pictograms

wall panels:    text kept to minimum, focus on objects,
                bold legible print, right level of vocabulary,
                durable material, controlled frequency

guide-cards:    controlled length of text,
                clear legible print,
                right level of vocabulary,
                relate to objects or viewpoints,
                essential features, some use of graphics,
                laminated

guide books:    designed mainly as souvenirs, reference books,
                extend detail, use graphics

maps:   simplify, orientate, identify routes,
        provide regional context,
        laminate

sound/audio equipment:    good working order, well maintained,
                          vandal-proof, easy to use,
                          controlled length, right voice,
                          visual effects comprehensible

models:   to scale, good quality, not over elaborate,
          some animation, use of sound/light

indoor exhibitions:   good sequencing, build up story,
                      parts relate to whole,
                      panels with cartoon sequence,
                      devices  which  allow
                      visitor    participation,
                      films, talks, lectures, bookshop

facilities:   toilets, shelter, refreshments, sales.

it must: be capable of communicating the message effectively; be compatible with other media being used; aid the overall presentation of the message; convey the message at the right level and pace; be designed to the highest possible standards; allow the visitor to feel at ease and involved; answer questions which visitors are most likely to have; and allow participation in some circumstances. Guidelines of this kind clearly make demands on the interpreters. They are required both to set the overall theme, to consider the specific objectives at any one site and to satisfy the conditions whereby individual media can contribute to that theme. Interpreters need to be well trained, to be able to co-ordinate with other staff and to be concerned with the effectiveness of their efforts. Guidelines on the media to some extent overlap with those on the message but there are some basic points to be rehearsed. Nothing in excess is one general notion. A message, however conveyed, must be concise, pithy, capable of catching the eye and perhaps stirring the imagination but not over-taxing the intellect. Most writers urge interpreters to avoid long sentences, clumsy style or layout and to make good use of provocative titles and captions. Research in museums (Aldridge, 1975) has stressed the importance of having type-size which can be easily read in given lighting conditions, of layout and lighting which is capable of gaining attention and of choosing vocabulary and language of an appropriate level. There are a number of basic rules for the content of messages: they must be visible, accessible, clear, legible and able to stimulate interest. Beyond these the content requires detailed planning which is often site-specific but Figure 6.3 summarises some of the most common guidelines.

Table 6.3.
Quality of displays

| Displays | % | Print size | % |
|---|---|---|---|
| Easy to miss | 13 | Easy to read | 89 |
| Visible | 19 | Readable | 6 |
| Well placed | 64 | Difficult | 3 |
| Don't know | 4 | Don't know | 2 |

| Photographs | % | Maps | % |
|---|---|---|---|
| Clear | 77 | Easy to follow | 70 |
| Not too clear | 2 | Just follow | 10 |
| Very clear | 0 | Difficult | 3 |
| Don't know | 20 | Don't know | 17 |

Source: Seren, 1986.

Visitor reaction to quality of presentation can of course be measured and Table 6.3 summarises four sets of responses at Cadw sites. These were concerned with the visibility of displays in general, the print-size of texts, the clarity of photographs and prints and with whether maps, diagrams and sound commentaries were easy to follow. Generally, as the tables show, Cadw sites performed well on these tests of quality with at least 64% giving 'strong' positive responses and large majorities giving generally favourable responses (95%, for example, found the print-size on notices readable). For operators concerned with quality, these tests need to be site-specific or even facility-specific and can provide crucial monitoring of items of interpretation.

As this section begins to make more extensive use of Cadw data, the particular set of surveys which focused on interpretation can be described at this point. As John Carr shows in his concluding chapter, interpretation has become one policy thrust for Cadw since its formation in 1984. Prior to that date, sites had basic guidebooks but apart from a small number of monuments with quite elaborate displays, most had little more than simple Ministry of Works labels to help visitors understand something of the site. Since 1984 a range of interpretative displays have been introduced and basic ingredients of guide books and signs have been substantially upgraded in quality. In the summer of 1986, a survey of interpretation was conducted at six sites. This survey was concerned with ways in which visitors reacted to interpretation in its various forms, it was also concerned with questions of effectiveness and with policy implications. Forms of interpretation available at the six sites ranged from simple signs to elaborate exhibitions (Figure 6.4). Of the six sites, Caernarfon Castle provided the widest array of facilities which included an audio-visual theatre, a tape-slide presentation and a comprehensive bookshop. Caerphilly Castle and Caerleon Roman Fort and Baths are well equipped with interpretative material and the fully enclosed Baths is in effect a display in its own right. Tintern Abbey has an exhibition area though elsewhere on the site there is only limited interpretation; only basic materials were present at Conwy and Chepstow Castles.

A sample size of 913 visitors was obtained from these six sites with 85 visitors interviewed at Caerleon (combined Fort and Baths) and 195 at Conwy. None of the other sites had less than 144 interviews. The visitor profile was similar to that of other reported surveys and only a few salient details will be recorded here. Higher social class groups were strongly over-represented in the sample with 54% in the AB (managerial and professional) groups. 79% of visitor groups were composed of two to four persons, over three-quarters were on holiday away from home, over half had travelled less than 20 miles and 57% had spent between 30 and 90 minutes at the site. South Wales sites, especially Caerleon and Chepstow, attracted more local visitors; Conwy in particular had fewer visitors of high social class and this reflects the more general holiday-making role of North Wales.

Figure 6.4.
Availability of displays and aids: by survey site

| | South Wales: | | | | North Wales: | |
| --- | --- | --- | --- | --- | --- | --- |
| | Tintern Abbey | Caerphilly Castle | Chepstow Castle | Caerleon Roman Baths and Fort | Caernarfon Castle | Conwy Castle |
| | % | % | % | % | % | % |
| Directional signs | * | * | * | * | * | * |
| Outdoor information plaques | * | * | * | * | * | * |
| Introductory exhibition | * | * | | * | * | * |
| Prints/photographs | * | * | * | * | * | * |
| Maps/plans | * | * | | * | * | |
| Display items | * | * | | * | * | |
| Models | * | * | | | * | |
| Sound commentaries | | | | | * | |
| Audio-visuals | | | | | | |
| Live performances | | + | + | + | + | + |
| People in period dress | | + | + | + | + | + |
| Guide book | * | * | * | * | * | * |
| Educational activity folder | | | | | | |
| Guided tours | + | + | + | + | + | + |

* Display or aid available
+ Occasional activity

Source: List provided by Cadw, 1986.

204

Table 6.4.
Numbers of visitors having seen interpetative displays or facilities

| | South Wales: | | | | North Wales: | | ALL sites | N |
|---|---|---|---|---|---|---|---|---|
| | Tintern Abbey | Caerphilly Castle | Chepstow Castle | Caerleon Roman Baths and Fort | Caernarfon Castle | Conwy Castle | | |
| Interpretative displays/facilities: | % | % | % | % | % | % | % | |
| Sound commentary | 27 | 53 | * | 74 | 39 | * | 45 | 574^ |
| Directional signs | 33 | 57 | 21 | 44 | 79 | 83 | 56 | 913^ |
| Plaques/wall panels | 78 | 68 | 92 | 34 | 61 | 98 | 75 | 913^ |
| Guide books | 44 | 33 | 31 | 24 | 33 | 28 | 33 | 913^ |
| Prints/photos | 62 | 95 | * | 77 | 72 | 70 | 75 | 769^ |
| Maps/plans | 79 | 75 | 58 | 98 | 51 | 84 | 72 | 913^ |
| Models | * | 66 | * | * | 52 | * | 58 | 336^ |
| Display items | 48 | 32 | * | 65 | 22 | * | 38 | 574^ |
| Audio-visual | * | 8 | * | 84 | 33 | * | 49 | 269^ |
| Exhibitions | 84 | 85 | * | 8 | 32 | 54 | 56 | 769^ |

^ indicates the absolute numbers over all sites.

All figures, with the exception of the last column, are percentages.

Percentages for 'all sites' excludes those where no display of this type is available.

* shows sites without display item.

Source: Seren, 1986.

Table 6.5.
Numbers of visitors who examined a display feature carefully

| Feature: | South Wales: | | | | North Wales: | | |
| --- | --- | --- | --- | --- | --- | --- | --- |
| | Tintern Abbey | Caerphilly Castle | Chepstow Castle | Caerleon Roman Baths and Fort | Caernarfon Castle | Conwy Castle | ALL sites |
| | % | % | % | % | % | % | % |
| Sound commentary | 30 | 61 | – | – | 47 | – | 40 |
| Directional signs | 32 | 33 | 67 | 57 | 46 | 20 | 36 |
| Plaques/wall panels | 51 | 29 | 89 | 45 | 61 | 85 | 66 |
| Guide book | 40 | 20 | 30 | – | 39 | 78 | 41 |
| Prints/photos | 71 | 77 | 55 | 87 | 76 | 79 | 77 |
| Maps/plans | 69 | 60 | 79 | 88 | 56 | 84 | 73 |
| Models | – | 75 | – | – | 46 | – | 55 |
| Display items | 62 | 47 | – | 79 | 62 | – | 59 |
| Audio-visual | – | – | – | 31 | 78 | – | 46 |
| Exhibitions | 77 | 78 | – | – | 78 | 71 | 77 |

Percentages are of the numbers of visitors stating that they had seen a display item at the site.

Where less than 20 visitors responded to the question, the percentage is not recorded.

Source: Seren, 1986.

Table 6.6.
Numbers of visitors regarding the display as containing about the right amount of information

|  | South Wales: | | | | North Wales: | | |
|  | Tintern Abbey | Caerphilly Castle | Chepstow Castle | Caerleon Roman Baths and Fort | Caernarfon Castle | Conwy Castle | ALL sites |
|---|---|---|---|---|---|---|---|
|  | % | % | % | % | % | % | % |
| Feature: | | | | | | | |
| Sound commentary | - | 80 | - | - | 95 | - | 86 |
| Directional signs | 55 | 69 | 100 | 84 | 91 | 98 | 86 |
| Plaques/wall panels | 50 | 65 | 71 | 76 | 84 | 88 | 73 |
| Guide book | 90 | 86 | 100 | - | 71 | 94 | 94 |
| Prints/photos | 89 | 89 | - | 89 | 95 | 93 | 91 |
| Maps/plans | 86 | 94 | 84 | 86 | 94 | 92 | 90 |
| Models | - | 77 | - | - | 94 | - | 85 |
| Display items | 85 | 70 | - | 75 | 90 | - | 79 |
| Audio-visual | - | - | - | 85 | 87 | - | 86 |
| Exhibitions | 85 | 93 | - | - | 96 | 89 | 90 |

Percentages are of numbers of visitors expressing an opinion.

Where less than 20 visitors responded to the question, the percentage is not recorded.

Source: Seren, 1986.

Table 6.7.
Numbers of visitors regarding the display as essential

| Feature: | South Wales: | | | | North Wales: | | |
| | Tintern Abbey | Caerphilly Castle | Chepstow Castle | Caerleon Roman Baths and Fort | Caernarfon Castle | Conwy Castle | ALL sites |
| | % | % | % | % | % | % | % |
| Sound commentary | 28 | 22 | - | 24 | 50 | 0 | 32 |
| Directional signs | 58 | 70 | 57 | 62 | 66 | 79 | 69 |
| Plaques/wall panels | 66 | 64 | 67 | 44 | 72 | 83 | 71 |
| Guide book | 74 | 78 | 52 | - | 71 | 76 | 71 |
| Prints/photos | 51 | 68 | - | 71 | 50 | 68 | 60 |
| Maps/plans | 66 | 63 | 62 | 73 | 67 | 71 | 67 |
| Models | - | 56 | - | - | 23 | - | 43 |
| Display items | 40 | 36 | - | 64 | 36 | - | 43 |
| Audio-visual | - | - | - | 24 | 42 | - | 32 |
| Exhibitions | 56 | 77 | - | - | 72 | 46 | 63 |

Percentages are of numbers of visitors expressing an opinion.

Where less than 20 visitors responded to the question, the percentage is not recorded.

Source: Seren, 1986.

208

Tables 6.4 to 6.7 summarise, on a site by site basis, a number of visitor reactions to the various forms of interpretation. Visitors were asked if they had seen a specific form of interpretation, if they had then examined it carefully, whether they had formed the opinion that it contained the right amount of information and whether they regarded the particular display item as essential to their enjoyment of their visit. Using Figure 6.1 once again as a structure around which to develop the discussion, each of these main forms of interpretation will be considered, mainly using the Cadw evidence but also results from other research where appropriate. In addition to site-by-site variation, there were also differences by social class of visitors, age, etc, which can be considered. The focus in this section is on the extent to which forms of interpretation had caught the attention of visitors.

## Spoken word

Tilden argued that other things being equal no device is as desirable as interpretation by direct contact with the person. Ward (1980) stressed the importance of the two-way flow between visitors and staff and noted Michael Dower's observation that 'people stop most at people'. Of interest is Ward's own suggestion for the kind of interpreters needed at the restored 'plotland shanty' in Essex where Londoners were given a foothold in a rural area, now the site of Basildon New Town in the 1920s. Far better than a new college graduate, he argues, would be some-one who remembers, an old-age pensioner who could tell the story of life there in the early days. At Big Pit in Gwent, former coal-miners are used as guides. The passage of time of course hinders this ideal and interpretation must resort to media to convey such messages. Industrial sites frequently use tape-recorded reminiscences of old miners, tin-workers and craftsmen to give the flavour of conditions of life and work (several regions have established sound archives as for example at Manchester and Swansea) for more historic sites actors must intervene as with the Norse recordings at the Jorvik Centre. Guided tours were only available as occasional activities on Cadw sites and there was little visitor experience of them. Guides are more commonly used in museums, art galleries, historic houses and major public buildings. The ranger service in National Parks has an established pedigree in interpretation. Such guides are normally well versed and trained and their measure of success then depends upon their personal qualities as teachers in the full sense of the word. At Cadw sites, guided tours are occasional activities and could not be assessed in the survey period. At Tintern Abbey there are frequent guided tours with titles such as 'The Monk's Way' and 'Reflection of Monastic Life', and at Caernarfon more regular guided tours have been available. As already indicated, the direct surrogate for the presence of a guide is a device which contains a spoken message or commentary and these are increasingly used at heritage sites. Sound commentary devices fall into several types. Firstly, there

Table 6.8.
Use of sound and audio facilities at Cadw's sites

| Used | | Quality* | | Why not used? | |
|------|-----|----------|-----|---------------|-----|
| N = | 481 | | 183 | | 333 |
| | % | | % | | % |
| | | | | | |
| Yes | 31 | Easy to follow | 80 | Not interested | 28 |
| No | 69 | Can follow | 11 | Too costly | 2 |
| | | Difficult | 9 | Awkward | 25 |
| | | | | Other | 7 |
| | | | | Don't know | 38 |

* Those expressing an opinion

Source: Seren, 1986.


are static commentary positions with broadcast messages.
These can be placed at points of general access to give
overviews or at specific features to which the message
relates; usually they are activated by the visitor. Such
messages should be short, have controlled noise levels so as
not to be intrusive, have shelter and should ensure that all
features referred to can be seen. Secondly, the static
commentary positions with individual receivers have similar
features though the noise intrusion problem is removed.
Thirdly, there are portable commentary devices, usually
tape-recordings with sequenced messages appropriate to
different parts of the site. At Tretower Court and Castle,
for example, Cadw has used tapes which have sound effects
and commentary. A variation on this is at the Jorvik Centre
where each 'time car' in which the visitor travels is
fitted with a synchronised low level sound commentary which
can be heard above the general sound collage. The sound
commentary devices are very common and were available at
four of the Cadw sites. 31% of visitors to sites at which
sound commentaries were available had made use of them and
80% of those who did so found them easy to follow (Table
6.8). Of those questioned on reasons for non-use, 28% said
they were not interested but 25% were put off by
'awkwardness' in using them. Although only 31% had actually
used the sound commentary facilities, 45% said that they had
seen them; these figures still suggest a moderate level
of visitor interest and the devices did not seem to be
sufficiently well displayed. Of those who had used
listening devices, 86% thought they contained about the
right amount of information but only one-third of users
regarded them as essential parts of their visit. Evidence
from site variation suggested that the form of the device,
the way in which it was made available and, to a small
extent, the cost, affects usage. Visitors are deterred by
the smallest suggestion of technical difficulty in usage or
by a cumbersome or awkward appearance to the device. If
sound commentaries are to play a significant role in
interpretation, obvious ease of use is an important quality
which the devices must possess. Advantages of sound

commentaries which sites should deploy, include their
ability to create 'sound pictures' by, for example, using
voices from the past, their ability to create special sound
effects and their potential for commentary in a variety of
languages and thus serve overseas visitors.

Written word

As Figure 6.1 indicates, the written word can be conveyed in
many forms of interpretation from simple signs or labels to
detailed guide-books and specialist publications. It is
clear that for the interpreter, the emphasis must be on the
'simpler' end of the range. Most guide-books for example
are designed as souvenirs rather than as instant information
givers, it is not easy to look and read (Beazley, 1971).
Detailed guide books and special publications have anyway
only a limited appeal to the small minority of 'researchers'
into historic sites or those with strong conservationist
interests. Some evidence on the effectiveness of the
written word in interpretation can be assessed under the
four headings of signs, panels, posters and texts.

Signs

Sign-posting to sites is critical and involves collaboration
with other agencies such as the highway authorities. Such
signs have to be completely uncluttered and designed to
fulfil a dominantly directional role. The use of pictograms
has proved effective and good practice on siting,
distancing, etc. are now emerging. Within sites,
directional signs can be used to help visitors to follow the
most logical sequence of stops, to enable them to find
points of special interest and can help management to
regulate the flows of visitors. This type of sign-posting
within sites can learn a great deal from the longer
experience of national parks, nature reserves, etc., in
forming 'trails' which visitors can follow. These can help
visitors see and appreciate things of interest, persuade
them to visit neglected areas and not to tour sensitive
areas and to provide, through sequenced stops, a total
experience which leaves them with a good image of place.
The 'trail' principle has now been extended into urban areas
with town trails such as that which retraces the Swansea of
Dylan Thomas. The Dartington Trust's report on self-guided
trails published by the Countryside Commission analysed 46
trails out of the 400 nature trails, 300 town trails, 50
ancient monuments trails and 25 farm trails estimated to
exist in Britain in 1978.
    At Cadw sites there always were some forms of directional
signs though in some cases they only occurred on outside
roads and there were no signs to guide visitors within the
site. Just over half the sample, rather less than might
have been expected, said that they had come across
directional signs; of those who had seen the signs, 36% had
examined them carefully and 61% had only glanced at them.
14% wanted rather more information on the signs and

virtually all visitors thought they were either essential or useful.

## Labels, wall plaques, panels

This set of interpretative devices provide written text which goes beyond sign-posting aimed to guide visitors to or around the site. Experience suggests that this is amongst the most important of all forms of interpretation, it is generally the main medium through which the story of the site can be told. Labels do no more than identify components of a site or objects within it. There is always a balance to be struck in labelling of this kind. Beazley (1971) contrasts Basingwerk Abbey where labels/signs are so scanty that the monastic buildings could be mistaken for the abbey itself to the Crusader Castle of Belvoir on the River Jordan which is so thoroughly labelled that its own character is all but extinguished. Wall plaques and panels are examples of written interpretation which attempt more than signing or naming, they contain text which convey a message about the site.

One example of script development for interpretation is the scheme for New Lanark (Pierssene, 1981), a site developed between 1784 and 1817 as an industrial settlement with 2,000 people closely tied to the textile mills as its livelihood. The 'prologue' to the visit, for example, is based on the theme of the time, the people and the place and uses text along with pictures or cartoons to develop the story. A few of these are described for illustrative purposes:

Cartoon 1           Text 1
Poor peasant        In the late 1700s the population of
leaving the land    Britain was growing fast: there were more
                    people than the land could employ, so
                    labour was cheap.

Cartoon 4           Text 4
Obsolete spinning   Among these factories were the cotton
wheel               mills equipped with machines that could
                    spin thread: the old-fashioned spinning
                    wheel was obsolete.

The texts are clear, brief and build up to a whole picture of the settlement which allows visitors to derive more from the buildings and artefacts which they actually see.

The Cadw sites had wall plaques containing information placed outdoors in a weather-protected form. There was some variation in detail of content from one site to another but they typically contained notes on the monument or its component parts, giving dates, functions, individuals involved and also some information so the relationship of the site with the surrounding region. Three-quarters of the visitors interviewed said that they had seen informational plaques and of these two-thirds had examined them carefully. Put another way, of the total visitors in the sample 50% had both seen the informational plaques and had examined them

carefully.    If   one  adds  the  further 24% who had   seen   the
plaques and glanced at them,   this suggests a very effective
medium   of   interpretation.    Of  those  who  had  seen  the
informational plaques, 73% thought that they contained about
the  right  amount  of  information  but  26%  thought  they
contained  too  little.    Given the wide use made of plaques,
this minority view should be taken seriously,   especially as
virtually   no-one   thought   they   contained   too   much
information.    The  people who had seen the plaques regarded
them as either essential (79%) or useful (21%).    Of all the
interpretative   devices   used   at   Cadw   sites,    these
informational  plaques,   'notices  which  give  facts   and
details'  were  regarded  as  the most  important  and  must
clearly  form  essential components  of  any  interpretation
strategy.
    Posters  and wall charts are very similar to informational
plaques  in style and content.   They can be more artistic and
graphical  in  form and can usually be purchased  and  taken
away as souvenirs.

Guidebooks, pamphlets, guide-cards

This set of written material is designed to be given or sold
to visitors to historic sites.   As suggested earlier, guide-
books  are often too detailed and elaborate to be  used  on-
site and many visitors, probably the most dedicated interest
groups  tend  to keep them as references to browse  over  at
home.    Probably in reaction to this knowledge, the National
Park  Service  (U.S.A.)  now  produces  two  guides  for  old
properties as a matter of course;  a brief free guide to  be
read  on the spot and a guide book which can be bought.    At
Cadw  sites about one-third of all visitors said  that  they
had  seen  a  guide-book and 41% of those  claimed  to  have
examined it carefully.   This confirms the earlier discussion
in  that  only about 120 of 913 visitors in the Cadw  sample
had  actually used a guide book during the course  of  their
visit.    Most  of  those who had looked at  the  guide-books
thought  that  they  contained about the  right  amount  of
information and one in five of all visitors regarded them as
essential.
    In recognition of the limited value of guide-books for on-
site  interpretation,  most  organisations  now ·follow  the
policy  of  the  United  States National  Park  Service  and
produce  guide-cards  and  pamphlets  with  more  condensed
accounts  of  individual  sites.    The  Pembrokeshire  Coast
National  Park,  for  example,  has a set of  pamphlets  and
guide-cards  for  its historic sites.    A pamphlet titled  'A
Walk around Carew' offers basic information on six locations
which include the medieval castle,   the Flemish 17th century
chimney,   the  11th  century Carew Cross and the French mill.
Another pamphlet 'Castles of Pembrokeshire' has notes on the
sixteen  main castles (there are 51 all told) in the  county
whilst  laminated  guide-cards  are  available  for  historic
towns  such as Tenby and Haverfordwest.    Guide-cards  and
pamphlets were not generally available at Cadw sites in 1986
and  reactions to them could not be tested,  it  does  seem
clear however,   from research elsewhere,   that most visitors

are more likely to absorb the more limited amounts of information which cards contain and that guide books will remain minority interests. Doubtless for the normal 'casual' visitor, practicalities also have weight in that cards and pamphlets can be more easily handled, carried and stored. During 1988, Cadw has introduced a cartoon series of guide books, initially on the travels of Gerald in Wales in the 12th century. This uses cartoons, texts and maps to depict the journey and the types of landscapes and communities it traversed.

## Visual display

For visitors with a limited inclination to concentrate on 'words', the various forms of visual display have considerable potential. It has to be remembered that the expectation of a visit is anyway essentially visual. People come to see the remains of a castle or an abbey, they may expect to enjoy spectacular views from elevated positions and anything which adds to this visual panorama has a high potential for impact. Again there is a number of groupings under which the forms of visual display can be discussed.

## Graphical arts: maps, prints, photographs

Graphical components are almost constant elements of interpretation. Maps may show regional positions or serve as plans of the site, print may reproduce early maps or drawings of the monument, photographs can be used to good effect to show, for example, stages of restoration, and graphical techniques often accompany textual messages as in the cartoons at New Lanark. Particularly with maps and plans there are problems in presentation. It is dangerous to assume 'geographical literacy' and many people will make little sense of concepts such as scale, orientation and standard forms of representation. Maps are particularly useful in extensive historic sites such as Glendalough in Ireland where both the general area in which the monastic settlement developed and its internal morphology can be shown. In his case history of Clontuskert Priory in Ireland, Johnson (1975) uses maps, plans and photographs extensively to show how a process of restoration led to the present historic site.

Maps and plans indicating the location and detailed site features were available at all the Cadw sites included in the survey. A high proportion of visitors (72%) had seen them and of these nearly three-quarters had examined them carefully, with a further 23% having glanced at them. The large majority (90%) of those who had seen the maps or plans considered that they included the right amount of information, 67% thought them essential to their visit and a further 31% regarded them as useful. The evidence at Cadw sites (though very little was on view at the Chepstow site in 1986) and three-quarters of visitors to five sites had seen them with 77% of these having examined them carefully, 91% judging them to have the right amount of information and

Models, replicas, reconstructions, artefacts

The range within this heading is considerable in both
quantity and quality. At one end of the range are
exhibitions and centres such as the Jorvik Centre in which
all these elements are used to re-create a total experience
of life in tenth century York, at the other are the
occasional use of some form of three-dimensional model or
available object to lend authenticity to a little-developed
site. It is worth returning to the example of the Jorvik
Centre (Addyman and Gaynor, 1984). One element is a
complete reconstruction of an alley with rows of 10th
century timber buildings. In Coppergate alley there are
some twenty Viking figures, sculpted in clay and moulded in
fibre glass; buildings, figures and activities are detailed
and authentic reconstructions. Artefacts, implements and
tools found in the archaeological excavation are displayed
in the exhibition. On a smaller scale, the National Trust
for Scotland has represented the Battle of Killiecrankie
with artefacts of the period, a model of the battle and
paintings of soldiers. In Leicester, the Battle of Bosworth
can be followed on a large battle model with commentary
which traces the manoeuvres. At Bunratty in County Clare,
Ireland, dwelling houses, outhouses and workshops have been
reconstructed to form a folk museum and similar
reconstructions can be found at the Welsh Folk Museum at St.
Fagan's near Cardiff. Where these forms of interpretative
displays reach the scale of Jorvik, Bunratty and St. Fagan's
there is no doubt that they become major tourist
attractions. The range of visitors broadens considerably
and the entertainment/enjoyment function assumes a much more
significant role.
This kind of interpretation takes various forms at Cadw
sites but is generally not well developed. Of the sites
surveyed, only Chepstow had no introductory exhibition and
Caernarfon Castle was the only elaborate presentation.
Model reconstructions of sites were available at Caerphilly
and Caernarfon and models elsewhere were used to exhibit
clothes and to relate monument to region. Display items of
artefacts such as pottery were available at few of the
sites. 56% of visitors to sites with exhibitions had seen
them, of these 77% had examined them carefully, 63% thought
them essential and 90% thought they contained the right
amounts of information. Models were seen by two-thirds of
visitors to Caerphilly and just over half those at
Caernarfon. Display items were only seen by 38% of visitors
to the sites at which they were located (Table 6.4 for more
detail).

Audio-visual

Audio-visual interpretation can take various forms with
tape-slide presentation and video films amongst the most
common. At Bosworth, a half-hour extract from the film
'Richard 111' is shown to provide some historical context.
Caerleon and Caernarfon were the only two surveyed Cadw
sites with audio-visual aids. At Caerleon, visitors needed

to use a form of headphone but at Caernarfon a slide
sequence with spoken commentary was offered in a studio
setting. At Caerleon the monitors are in a prominent
setting and 84% had seen them but only one-third at
Caernarfon had done so. Thereafter the roles were reversed.
Only 31% of those at Caerleon who had seen them examined
them carefully, 51% ignored them. Although small numbers
noticed them at Caernarfon, 78% of these examined them
carefully. People will not seek out audio-visual displays
and they seem to appeal to a minority of visitors.

Introductory exhibitions

Five of the Cadw sites had introductory exhibitions which
combined various forms of interpretation but were generally
dominated by visual display. At these five sites, 56% of
visitors had seen the exhibitions, 77% of these had examined
them carefully, 63% of those visiting the exhibitions
thought them to be essential and the remainder judged them
as useful. The location of the exhibition within the site
is clearly important and the success of Tintern and
Caerphilly in drawing in visitors to exhibitions largely
relates to this factor. Introductory exhibitions can have
key roles in orientating the visitor, showing a sequence in
the site's history and presenting the whole picture.

Live performances

The idea of using actors and volunteers to re-enact events
at historic sites has increasing popularity. As with more
elaborate reconstructions these attract large numbers of
visitors. Each summer at Kentwell Hall in Suffolk some 200
local volunteers play the parts, in appropriate costume, of
the wide range of roles and activities in Tudor England.
Entitled 'Kentwell 1610' the event runs for three weeks.
Shorter events of one or more days are common. In 1986
'Behind the Battlements' was a theatre interpretation at
four historic sites in Pembrokeshire in which professional
actors and local helpers provide guided walks of the sites
and followed this with medieval entertainment. New forms of
heritage centre such as Wigan Pier and Beamish use full-time
professional actors. Several societies exist to re-create
specific historical events such as the Sealed Knot society
with its interest in battles of the Civil War. Although
Cadw has frequent events at some of its sites, such as the
Medieval Fayre at Beaumaris and re-enactments by actors of
the military drills of Roman soldiers at Caerleon, these
were not included in the 1986 survey.
Information was collected in the Cadw surveys on variables
such as social class, age and type of visitor and some of
the relationships these bore to people's reactions to
interpretation can be recorded. In general, greater
proportions of the higher status visitors were aware of the
displays, for example, 79% of category A visitors had seen
the introductory visits compared with 54% of D. Lower
status visitors have more casual attitudes and seem less
interested in more demanding forms of interpretation; there

was on the other hand little social class variation in attitudes towards basic things such as signs and wall panels. There is some evidence from the Cadw surveys that more tangible and novel forms of interpretation, such as models and audio-visual displays, have more appeal to lower-status visitors and this may have implications for any policy to broaden the range of visitors. Washburne and Wager (1972) noted a marked preference among visitors for dynamic, animated and changing stimuli and events of the type described above have succeeding in attracting large and diverse audiences.

The large majority of people interviewed during the Cadw interpretation survey (77%) were on holiday away from home and this group did reveal more interest in interpretation than did home-based visitors. Older people were more likely to have examined displays carefully, they relied more on directional signs and showed more interest in artefacts such as pottery and display items. As might be expected, the longer that visitors stayed at sites, the more likely they were to have seen and used various forms of interpretation. For example, over 80% of those spending over two hours at a site `had seen and examined prints and photographs compared to 60% of thsoe staying less than 30 minutes. People on short visits were often attracted by display items of pottery or implements.

The classification of forms of interpretation used in Figure 6.1 has allowed a structured discussion of the media widely used at historic sites. Other approaches to classification could have been used and it is worth noting Light's (1987) suggested four-fold typology of static, dynamic, animated and re-enactment forms of interpretation. These can be readily matched to Figure 6.1 but the 'dynamic' category is worth additional comment as it does bring out media, not evident at Cadw sites, which are designed to involve visitors and increase participation. Such approaches may involve worksheets to be completed whilst moving around the site, they may ask visitors to consider a number of issues during the visit, they may include recall tests or have points for 'hands-on' experience of some kind. Visitors can try their hand at some medieval craft, aid a restoration project or 'play' some historic role. If the aim is to increase understanding, especially for children, these dynamic approaches are of proven value.

Discussion so far has centred on basic reactions to interpretative displays such as whether they had been seen and whether they were judged to contain about the right amount of information. This type of enquiry was extended in the Cadw surveys with questions seeking general reactions to the interpretative experience and Tables 6.9 and 6.10 summarises these. Virtually all of those questioned would agree that interpretation had increased their understanding of historic sites and most people thought that it had increased a great deal. Similarly high proportions stated that interpretation had to some extent made them want to know more about the site, about abbeys and castles in general and about the Welsh cultural heritage.

Table 6.9.
Impact of interpretative displays

|  | Increased under- standing | Want to know more about: | | |
|---|---|---|---|---|
|  |  | this site? | castles and abbeys? | Welsh culture? |
|  | % | % | % | % |
| A great deal | 59 | 42 | 32 | 27 |
| A little | 37 | 42 | 42 | 41 |
| Not at all | 4 | 16 | 24 | 31 |
| Don't know | * | 1 | 1 | 1 |

* indicates greater than zero but less than one per cent.

Source: Seren, 1986.


Table 6.10.
Levels of sympathy

| Previous sympathy: | % | Increased sympathy: | % |
|---|---|---|---|
| Very sympathetic | 79 | A great deal | 43 |
| Fairly sympathetic | 18 | A little | 32 |
| Not sympathetic | 3 | Not at all | 25 |

| More resources: | % | All sites need displays: | % |
|---|---|---|---|
| Yes | 90 | Yes | 94 |
| No | 2 | No | 5 |
| Don't know | 8 | Don't know | 2 |

Source: Seren, 1986.


Visitors who responded in the category 'want to know a great
deal more' were probably more diagnostic in the sense  that
they  are likely to be genuinely motivated.   Here the range
was from 42% who wanted to know a great deal more about  the
site  to  28%  who had similar aspirations regarding Welsh
culture.   Interpretation has reached this set of people  in
very  positive  ways,  it  has  caught  their  interest  and
stimulated  them to seek greater understanding.   There were
visitors  with  totally  negative  reactions.    4%    said
interpretation  had not increased their understanding at all
and  31% still had no interest in learning about  the  Welsh
cultural heritage.   Against this,  over 90% of all visitors
thought  that  historic  sites  should  have  some  forms of
interpretation.

Table 6.11.
Attitudes to display developments

|  | Strongly in favour % | In favour % | Not in favour % |
|---|---|---|---|
| Special exhibitions of crafts, costumes, armour | 40 | 51 | 10 |
| Partial reconstruction of the site | 33 | 44 | 22 |
| Outdoor events which recreate historical happenings | 25 | 50 | 25 |
| Roofing of some rooms or areas | 25 | 44 | 31 |
| Historical tableaux | 17 | 55 | 27 |
| People in historical costume | 16 | 39 | 45 |

Source: Seren, 1986.

One aim of interpretation has been to gain support for the need to preserve. Almost 80% of visitors to Cadw sites said that they were already very sympathetic towards preservation and less than 5% said that they had no sympathy at all. Over three-quarters of those questioned said that they had more sympathy as a result of their visit and 90% wanted more resources devoted to historic site preservation. These findings from the Cadw survey suggest that there is already widespread support for protection of historic sites and that interpretation has a significant role in strengthening that support and in demonstrating the need for more resources. It should also be noted that the experience of the site in itself acts to generate sympathy.

The final section of the Cadw survey examined visitor reactions to possible developments which would increase levels of interpretation. As Table 6.11 shows, these were proposed as more significant innovations such as partial re-building, re-roofing, special events and live performances. In some ways these questions tested the strength of the preservationist 'lobby' as a 'purist' would keep sites much as they are arguing, for example, that disrepair brought about by the ravages of time adds to authenticity. For each proposal made, there was a majority view for change. Both partial reconstruction and re-roofing gained majority support with about two-thirds in favour. There was little resistance to the suggestion of special exhibitions of crafts, costumes and armour but less enthusiasm for 'actors' in historical costume, almost half were against this latter idea. Organized events and tableaux had good measures of support but significant minorities were against the idea. In summary, all of these proposals gained support but the conservatism of visitors showed up in the modest levels of

Figure 6.5.
Subjective evaluation of interpretative provision (after Aldridge, 1975)

TOPIC    COMPONENTS                        CHECKLIST

Introduction:

arrival    directions, signs, staff        were visitors at ease?
briefing   introductory exhibition         were visitors prepared?
rapport                                    did exhibition fulfil purposes?
                                           were staff helpful?

Facilities:

area       attractive comfortable environments    is there good upkeep?
buildings  weather proof                          are design standards high?
           good safety standards                  is there shelter in inclement weather?
                                                   are hazards avoided?

Media:

           range of interpretative media    were staff or media audible,
                                             visible, legible?
                                             did media aid presentation?
                                             did media create right mood?
                                             were media in good working order?
                                             did guide communicate?
                                             what skills did guide use?

Cont ....

Figure 6.5 continued ...

Structure:

evolutionary sequence
data linked to themes
inter-relationships

was a theme discernible?
did the interpretation have continuity?
did the parts relate to the whole?

Presentation:

teaching skills
content of messages

was pace and level right for the group?
was vocabulary clear?
was story accurate and balanced?

Management:

visitor control
concept of conservation
site protection

was a conservation message clear?
were sensitive areas protected?
was congestion/crowding avoided?

Visitor enrichment:

experience of visit

could visitors find their way
around the site at ease?
did visitors enjoy their visit?
did visitors learn something new?
were their opportunities to participate?
was interest in historic sites aroused
or extended?
did sympathy for conservation increase?

Source: Aldridge, 1975.

strong support, between 16% and 40%, and the significant groups against such developments.

There were some site variations on this topic. Visitors to Tintern Abbey consistently recorded less favourable responses to the proposed developments although there was still a general body of support. This less enthusiastic response may in part relate to the religious significance of the site and also to the visitor profile at Tintern which tends to be of older people with more focussed interests. Caerphilly Castle is at the opposite end of the range with well above average numbers of visitors strongly in favour of the developments. Caerphilly is a 'generalist' site with a strong local recreational role (and perhaps a limited sense of 'history' for many) at which a number of events had recently occurred. Social class was a significant source of variation. For four out of the six proposed developments, there was a steady and significant increase in support associated with decline in social status. This was most evident in terms of exhibitions, events, tableaux and costumes which could be grouped as having to some extent the role of entertainment. Although the lower social status groups may be well disposed towards the many roles of interpretation, they primarily wish to relax and to enjoy a leisure visit. Structural changes to sites drew a more even response across social class groups. The longer the time spent at a site, the more likely is the visitor to be in favour of interpretative developments. This applies particularly to the four 'entertainment' functions and suggests scope for enhancing visitor experience. There was, however, no increase in support for structural changes with increased length of stay.


## Evaluating the effectiveness of interpretation

Most observers now recognize and stress the importance of evaluating interpretative programmes; interpretation should have built-in means of evaluation. Thom (1980) argued that more attention should be given to measuring the effectiveness of individual provision; Roggenbuck and Propst (1981) offered an assessment of thirteen evaluative techniques which included peer judgements, panel reviews and surveys of visitor reaction; Aldridge (1975) developed a detailed checklist for the subjective evaluation of interpretative provision and although this is designed for countryside interpretation, much of it has general applicability (Figure 6.5). Evaluation and monitoring of effectiveness is accepted and these should be related to the objectives of any specific interpretative scheme; objectives and evaluation should go hand-in-hand. Tests can relate to technical effectiveness such as clarity of signs or legibility of wall panels or to whether equipment being used is in working order. It can also be tested in management terms such as levels of pressure on sensitive areas or number counts at specific points. More difficult areas for evaluation relate to success rates of interpretation in educational terms. How much information can be recalled? To

what extent are issues understood? Are there links between
levels of understanding and enjoyment gained from the visit?
Work by cognitive psychologists (Prince, 1982; Hammitt,
1984) have shown that learning does take place from
interpretation but, as Light (1988) shows, this is variable
and difficult to measure. Interpretation often lacks
specific aims at historic sites, it seeks to inform and
familiarise in generalist ways; it is mainly with children
in organized groups that interpretation assumes more formal
pedagogic roles (see Chapter 5). Methods of evaluation
which allow comparative analysis are evasive. One standard
procedure, followed in the Cadw survey, is to ask whether
visitors had seen an interpretative facility and then limit
questions about it to those who had done so. As an
alternative method Prince (1982) asked respondents to select
the display which they found most interesting. This ensures
that a visitor had seen an item, gave some rating of items
on levels of interest and elicited responses on a theme
where the visitor was well motivated to make judgements.
Disadvantages include the fact that 'most interesting' is a
relative measure and visitors may have found the entire set
of items of low interest, again, the approach may produce no
responses at all on a large number of interpretative items.
Another problem for evaluation of the educational
effectiveness of interpretation is that of accounting for
prior knowledge. Many schemes opt for before and after
testing to control for this source of variation, this in
turn calls for a good quality of control in sampling
procedure and sample numbers. Ideally, the same visitors
should be used for both tests so that individual increases
in knowledge can be assessed. A caveat here (Screven, 1976)
is that the 'before' test experience effectively sensitises
the visitor and can actually improve visitor learning.
Another method, that of asking respondents whether their
knowledge has improved (also used in the Cadw survey) relies
upon the honesty and good judgement of visitors. In
summarising this debate on the problems of evaluation, Light
(1988, p. 86) argued that: 'The most important of these are
a means of question selection which allow direct comparison
between different visitors and a valid method of taking some
consideration of prior knowledge'.
There are several reported studies in the research
literature which offer examples of empirical tests of the
effectiveness of interpretation. Olson, Bowman and Poth
(1984) followed a stratified random sampling procedure,
including before and after tests, to study 1409 visitors to
four Ohio nature reserves. In each reserve, three
interpretative strategies were developed, a brochure
disseminated on site, a set of signs and personal services
such as oral presentations and guided tours. The brochure
was a single sheet with text on both sides, there were two
types of sign, one offering directions and reminders of
rules, the other interpreting natural and historic features
of the reserve. Analysis of results concluded that visitors
were generally well educated, cared about conservation
issues and were receptive to messages about conservation
concepts. Interpretation did increase visitors' knowledge

and appreciation and in this context brochures and face-to-face presentations were much more effective than signs. In another reported study, Prince (1982) examined visitor learning at two visitor centres in the North Yorks Moors National Park. A sample of 550 visitors was asked three recall questions and 70% were able to answer at least one correctly. Visitor preferences were for interpretative displays which combined text with visual elements such as models, photographs and artefacts and the most effective interpretation followed a strategy of linking individual parts to a whole.

Moscardo and Pearce (1986) undertook a secondary analysis of data collected by the Countryside Commission in their 1978 survey of 17 visitor centres and 3,000 visitors. Three forms of reaction were tested - information recall, improved subjective knowledge and greater 'mindfulness' or a condition where the individual is mentally active and attentive. Tests showed that these were most evident at centres with historic or focused environmental themes. An example of a test of interpretative site is found in Mahaffey's (1970) study of the Fort Parker Historic Site in Texas. A self-guided tour was set up with nine stopping points, three of which conveyed messages with leaflets, three with signs and three with audio-recordings. Mahaffey found that differences were not great but slightly more correct information was retained from recorders (36%) and rather less from leaflets (33%). Asked to state a preference, over 70% chose recorders, 18% signs and 10% leaflets. Specific tests of visitor recall are rare but Griggs and Alt (1983) reported results of such exercises in the Natural History Museum suggesting that 36% of visitors had studied written text and about one quarter showed evidence of recall of design and layout features.

Although tests of recall are not common, some historic sites do practise these as part of a strategy of increasing visitor participation in the interpretation exercise. At Killiecrankie in Scotland where an exhibition uses a variety of media to tell the story of the battle at that site, visitors are asked a number of questions to test their recall. They are asked for example: 'Between which two sides was the battle fought?' 'The leader of one side was killed. What was his name?' 'What does this picture (of a fleeing soldier) show?' A scoring system is used which rewards greater detail and accuracy. Similarly at Bosworth near Leicester, the questions which follow the interpretative display include: 'What was the date of the battle?' 'What rose did Henry IV adopt?' 'Over what distance is the longbow accurate?' These are quite searching questions of recall and can provide measures of the effectiveness of interpretation in its educational/information giving roles. There are dangers in this type of exercise and the United States National Park Service does not interview visitors on the grounds that it affects their enjoyment and also that interviews or tests which irritate visitors may produce distorted and unreliable results.

Table 6.12.
The importance of different kinds of display

|  | Very important % | Quite important % | Not important % |
|---|---|---|---|
| Notices which give facts and details | 77 | 22 | 1 |
| Diagrams showing things as they were | 74 | 25 | 1 |
| Guide cards for a self conducted tour | 55 | 36 | 9 |
| Maps to show the site in its region | 53 | 41 | 7 |
| Exhibitions | 39 | 54 | 7 |
| Historical tableaux | 30 | 46 | 24 |
| Guided tours | 27 | 40 | 32 |
| Audio - visual presentations | 18 | 44 | 39 |
| Sound commentaries | 16 | 38 | 47 |

Source: Seren, 1986.

Item-specific recall questions were not asked during the 1986 Cadw survey, though subsequent research will examine this and other approaches. 1986 visitors were asked to rate the various forms of interpretation in terms of importance/effectiveness and Table 6.12 records the results obtained. Taking the proportions rating an item as 'very important' as a discriminator, notices, diagrams, guide cards and maps, in that order, appear at the top of the list. These are the most basic tools of interpretation and their role as parts of interpretative policy is confirmed. Guided tours, often favoured in traditional texts, were well down the list however, and it may be that visitors value their independence and privacy and the control over time spent at a site and attention required of them which these allow. Audio-visual presentations and sound commentaries have limited importance in the eyes of visitors and many people thought that they were not important at all. Almost half of respondents regarded sound commentaries as unimportant. These findings are valuable but must be taken in context. People relate views to their own experience (Mahaffey's report above where given experience of these media, sound recorders were preferred) and it might well be that a visit to the Jorvik Centre, with its sophisticated package of interpretative aids, would change assessments of what is effective. In line with earlier comment, the written word had more appeal to higher social class visitors whereas more visual displays, exhibitions and tableaux appealed to the lower social class groups.

## Conclusion

This chapter began by discussing the ideals and principles of interpretation which were identified in their most eloquent manner by Freeman Tilden several decades ago. In this conclusion we can remind ourselves of those ideals but also focus on practicalities and the policy implications of the evidence which has become available from research into historic sites in Wales. Figure 6.1 offers a schema which pulls together the various facets of an interpretative strategy. The principles are derived from Tilden, the aims are those which attract most support from the available literature. There are many forms of media or ways of conveying the message, the schema identifies broad categories and highlights some of the most common techniques used. Tilden and others have always emphasised the role of the guide, the teacher who tells the story and reveals the wonder of a place. For many sites now this is increasingly a minority feature of interpretation and the 'telling' or the 'revealing' must rest on intermediary devices of which the written word probably remains the most significant. Interpretation has outcomes. Many of these are aimed for by the interpreter and are attained by visitors. The hidden agenda usually comes through in the sense that interpretation enables better 'management' of visitors and ways in which they use a site and also imbues more and more people with a sense of sympathy for the needs of preservation. The gloss on this point is a reminder that much of the literature (including Tilden) focuses on natural environments in which the conservation aim is central. For historic sites, preservation remains important but is already widely accepted and the emphasis can be upon interpreting the site in a wider sense with some attention to the social environment as well as the natural and built environments (Goodey, 1979). Do people want interpretation? All the evidence suggests that although a minority actually seek it out, most do not resist it. The studious seeker after facts is in the minority but a large majority will take a passing interest and many will be more substantially affected by the messages which they receive. Empirical evidence suggests that interpretation does add to enjoyment and that it does inform. Interpretative displays do much to increase understanding of sites and stimulate interest in historical monuments in more general ways. Although visitors have sympathy for ideas of preservation and protection before coming to sites, interpretation increases that sympathy and enlists support for policies which seek to protect our cultural heritage. The evidence from the Cadw surveys suggest very little resistance to the further development of interpretative displays; there was in general a positive disposition towards these though the minority with doubts need to be respected.

Tilden's belief that interpretation should relate to the experience of the visitor has a strong grain of truth. Different sections of society, rich and poor, young and old, bring varying experiences and view sites through different kinds of filters. All visitors are using leisure time and are usually in an informal frame of mind. Within the visitor group there is the whole range from the dedicated 'student' of monuments to the completely disinterested, but between these is the majority of visitors, perhaps around 60%, who are receptive to interpretation in some forms, who gain from the experience and who tend to move towards greater support for preservation as a result of that experience. For this 'middle-ground' of visitor types, formal interpretation principles may be unsuitable, they are receptive but remain uncommitted and casual in their attitudes. There are some visitor characteristics which help understand varying attitudes towards interpretation. Higher social class groups who usually are better educated are often more interested in the learning aspects and have more supportive views on preservation, at the other end of the social class scale are groups who want to be entertained and to whom a different type of interpretation is more attractive. There are differences between young and old and families with children have distinctive needs. These variations affect the media used. For the more interested the detail which can be provided in texts or commentaries has more appeal, for those less so the 'gadgets' such as video displays and costumes, attain more importance. Given the episodic and often brief nature of visits, the guidelines of 'nothing in excess', brevity, succinctness, clarity and 'wholeness' remain crucial. In many ways the best bases upon which to introduce and develop interpretation have not changed over several decades. Better technology increases the possibilities but the guidelines of quality and good practice are constants.

This last part of the discussion has moved towards policy implications and it is useful to summarise these, with particular reference to the Cadw experience. Firstly, interpretation is a widely accepted practice at historic sites and should continue to be developed and enhanced in systematic ways. Secondly, increased interpretation can be justified on the several grounds that it informs a public which wishes to be informed, it enhances the enjoyment of a leisure activity and it nurtures sympathy for the broad aims of preservation. Thirdly, there is very limited resistance to interpretation and even more radical proposals may gain widespread support. In the Cadw survey over three-quarters of those interviewed were in favour of partial reconstruction of castles and over two-thirds of partial re-roofing. Projects of this scale, which would rank as major interpretative exercises, would have to be considered in site-specific terms but might well have significant effects upon levels of visiting. Fourthly, policies of organized events, re-enactments of historical happenings and use of attendants in historical costume had support but also showed stronger levels of resistance. It is likely that developments of this type would attract a different kind of visitor and this implication has to be held in mind. Fifthly, more basic forms of interpretation, such as wall plaques, signs, prints, photographs, plans and maps should be part of all sites. They are widely appreciated and much can be learned from sites which offer successful models of good practice. Many recent writers have emphasised the need to evaluate the effectiveness of interpretation and work along these lines is now well in hand. Whereas, however, it is relatively easy to measure effectiveness in more general terms - increased enjoyment, more awareness, more sympathy etc. - more detailed probes have yet to be attempted. Is there merit for example in attempting to measure how much visitors have learned and retained, whether increased sympathy for preservation is translated into positive action, whether return visits to sites or greater use of historic sites occurs.

Interpretation has become an integral part of the development and 'marketing' of historic sites. The interpreter has the role of 'broker' between the place and the visitor and has to relate his efforts to convey messages against the diversity of tastes and preferences which the clientele represents. Good practice is established though it will grow and change over time. For the policy-makers the issue is that of maintaining the balance between the 'sacred and the profane'. The value of the site is its heritage, purely in that form it appeals to a lesser number of people, the potential of a site may be as a leisure facility catering for the every needs of a larger public. The danger of achieving that potential is that the essential quality of heritage may become submerged. Lessons are simple. Some sites are more suitable for development than others, at all times interpretation which threatens the value or quality of a site should be avoided. Interpretation is here to stay but it is a strategy to be used in selective and sensitive ways.


References

Addyman, P. and Gaynor, A. (1984). An experiment in archaeological site interpretation. Heritage Interpretation, 26, pp. 3-5.

Aldridge, D. (1975). Guide to countryside interpretation, part one: Principles of countryside interpretation and interpretive planning. Edinburgh: Her Majesty's Stationery Office.

Beazley, E. (1971). The countryside on view. London: Constables.

Goodey, B. (1979). 'The interpretation boom'. Area, 11, 4, pp. 285-288.

Griggs, S. A. and Alt, M. B. (1982-83). 'Visitors to the British Museum of Natural History in 1980 and 1981'. Museums Journal, pp. 149-155.

Hammitt, W. E. (1981). 'A theoretical foundation for Tilden's interpretive principles'. Journal of Environmental Education, 12, pp.13-16.

Hammitt, W. E. (1984). 'Cognitive processes involved in environmental interpretation'. Journal of Environmental Education, 15, pp.11-15.

Harrison, J. M. (1985) (ed.). Interpreting Ireland's Heritage. Proceedings of a conference held at Bunratty Folk Park, Co. Clare. Shannon: Shannon Free Airport Development, Operations Division.

Iso-Ahola, S. E. (1983). 'Towards a social psychology of recreational travel'. Leisure Studies, 21, pp. 45-56.

Johnson, D. (1975). Case history. In Architectural Conservation. pp. 37-53. Dublin: Architectural Association of Ireland.

Light, D. (1987). 'Interpretation at historic buildings'. Swansea Geographer, 24, pp. 34-43.

Light, D. (1988). 'Problems encountered with evaluating the educational effectiveness of interpretation'. Swansea Geographer, 25, pp.79-87.

Mahaffey, B. D. (1970). 'Effectiveness and preferences for selected interpretive media'. Environmental Education, 14, pp. 125-128.

Moscardo, G. and Pearce, P. L. (1986). 'Visitor centres and environmental interpretation: an exploration of the relationships among visitor enjoyment, understanding and mindfulness'. Journal of Environmental Psychology, 6, pp. 89-108.

Olson, E. C., Bowman, M. L. and Roth, R. E. (1984). 'Interpretation of non-formal environmental education in natural resource management'. Journal of Environmental Education, 15, pp. 6-10.

Pierssene, A. (1981). New Lanark: a scheme for its interpretation to the public. Interpretive Planning and Design.

Prince, D. R. (1982). 'Countryside interpretation: a cognitive investigation'. Museum Studies, 82, pp. 165-170.

Prince, D. R. (1983). 'Behavioural consistency and visitor attraction'. International Journal of Museum Managers and Curators, 2, pp. 235-247.

Roggenbuck, J. W. and Propst, D. B. (1981). 'Evaluation of interpretation'. Journal of Interpretation, 6, 1, pp. 13-23.

Screven, C. G. (1976). 'Exhibit education: a goal-referenced approach'. Curator, 19, pp. 271-290.

Seren (1986). Herbert, D. T., Thomas, C. J., Prentice, R. C. and Prentice, M. M. Interpretation at Cadw's sites. Swansea: Social Economic Research and Environment, Department of Geography, University College of Swansea.

Thom, V. M. (1980). 'Evaluating countryside interpretation: a critical look at the current situation'. Museum Journal, 80, pp. 179-185.

Tilden, F. (1977). Interpreting our heritage. (3rd edition, first published 1957). North Carolina: University of North Carolina Press, Chapel Hill.

Uzzell, D. L. (1985). 'Management issues in the provision of countryside interpretation'. Leisure Studies, 4, pp. 159-174.

Ward, C. (1980). 'Goals for interpreters in the next five years'. Heritage Interpretation, 16, pp. 7-11.
Washburne, R. F. and Wagar, J. A. (1972). 'Evaluating visitor response to exhibit content'. Curator, 15, pp. 48-54.

# 7 Pricing policy at heritage sites: how much should visitors pay?

RICHARD C PRENTICE

## Introduction

In the sense that admission charges are often not made, access to many 'minor' historic sites is free. Clearly, the full costs of access generally involve the costs of private transport and walking to remote sites. The affect of this large reservoir of historic sites at which admission charges are not made on admission numbers at sites where charges are made is unknown. Much depends on whether or not visits are complementary, substitutes, or simply independent by site type. The basic absence of research into visiting patterns is a fundamental weakness in defining appropriate marketing mixes of product, place, promotion and price for historic sites.

The extent of sites with no admission charges which are promoted by public agencies should not be underestimated. Of the 110 sites in Wales promoted by Cadw on the map given to Heritage in Wales members in 1986, 76 had no admission charge. Similarly, in 1987 English Heritage promoted 372 sites in their guidebook, of which 231 had no advertised admission charge. The two British National Trusts own land as well as property, and these open sites are usually without admission charges or have 'honesty' boxes where visitors can place their donations. Alternatively, charges are made for entrance not to the whole site but to visitor centres which interpret the site, such as at Bannockburn and Culloden battlefields in Scotland. Both the official guardians of monuments and the National Trusts have developed membership schemes, to raise funds by giving members free access to sites where charges are made. Membership schemes can be seen as an alternative form of charging. For example, Cadw has developed the Heritage in Wales scheme and the Scottish Office, the Friends of the Scottish Monuments. These schemes are useful to promote the sites, and so it cannot be assumed that all members would have made as many trips to the sites if they had not become members. In contrast, some members do not visit sites, at least frequently, regarding their membership more as a subscription to a good cause than as a season ticket. Nor should it be assumed that the characteristics of members are the same as visitors in general.

## Objectives of a pricing system

As many historic sites are publicly administered or managed by private sector organisations for reasons other than profit maximisation, pricing objectives at historic sites usually involve other considerations than revenue generation to achieve profit maximisation. This is not of course to deny that charges may be levied at historic sites for the simple purpose of raising revenue, either for general purposes or for purposes specific to the site at which the charge is being levied. Government bodies may be influenced by Treasury policies concerning revenue raising, particularly in the 1980s era of public policies to contain public expenditure. Public policies are based also on attempts to influence the allocation of demand between recreation and non-recreation expenditure, and may also involve attempts to influence the allocation of demand between alternative recreation facilities (McCallum and Adams, 1980).

As well as revenue raising, at the site level, pricing systems may be used to achieve at least three further objectives. Firstly, they may be used to derive information on visitors' preferences and their valuation of the facilities provided; the 'revealed preferences' of visitors. Secondly, pricing systems may be used to regulate or to encourage demand. Pricing as part of the marketing mix may be underpinned by a desire to achieve a desired market share. Alternatively, pricing policy may be designed to deter some potential visitors at certain times, days of the week or in certain seasons. By so doing, costs may be decreased, the amenity of the site may be protected, and the satisfaction of visitors may be retained by avoiding over-crowding. With the traditionally low number of days per annum, if at all, on which most monuments reach their capacity in terms of visitors (B.T.A., 1976), pricing to divert demand is not a general objective in monument pricing, but may be more important at certain historic houses. Finally, pricing systems are used frequently to assist 'deserving' groups to enjoy publicly owned recreational resources; groups such as the elderly, or children.

Several options are available in pricing. Firstly, there is the question of where to charge, at the entrance, in the car park, or for separate facilities? As people may not like to pay twice it may be necessary to increase the admission price to include the cost of facilities the organiser would wish the visitor to enjoy; for example, it may be desirable to include, in the admission fee, the cost of a 'listening tube' to plug into a 'talking post' so that visitors who would not otherwise buy a tube may also enjoy the interpretative commentary available, and, hopefully, be more impressed with their visit than otherwise.

A second option is when to charge; all the year around, or with charges varied by season, by day of the week or by time of day? For example, for trips on its one remaining narrow gauge heritage railway, the Vale of Rheidol, British Rail charged a higher fare on midday services in the high summer season of 1988. A third option is whom to charge, and whether, or not, to grant concessions? Family tickets can set the maximum that a 'family' need to pay, usually constrained in terms of a maximum number of adults. Alternatively, if the attraction is mainly for children, additional children to a set number may be charged. For example, for trips on the Vale of Rheidol Railway in 1988 British Rail allowed one child a free trip for each adult fare paid, but charged for each additional child in the party. A fourth option is how to charge, for example, by membership or by season ticket? A final option, of particular relevance to monuments and museums where pricing has not been universal, is whether to charge at all? All of these options should be selected with the objectives in mind sought via pricing.

At least four types of objection can be raised against pricing at historic sites to indicate or to allocate demand. These include the 'merit good', 'distributional', 'intergenerational' and the 'cost of administration' objections. It is often argued that certain services cannot adequately be rationed by pricing because the beneficial aspects of the services are under-estimated by individual consumers. Education is a frequently quoted example, of a so-called merit good of this kind. If historic sites are considered to be educational rather then leisure resources, a merit good objection could be raised against high pricing, or against pricing at all. Indeed, as McCallum and Adams (1980) indicated, in Britain some forms of recreation are at least implicitly seen as merit goods, such as access to walking in the countryside. Both as an educational and as an often countryside located resource, historic sites may be regarded as merit goods by policy makers.

Distributional objections to pricing centre around the inequality of the distribution of income. People with low incomes can least afford to pay for non-essential services, and the pricing of such services may prevent consumption by the poor. Whereas the merit objection is based on the general benefit of historic sites, the distributional objection relates to unfairness. It is common to seek to redress distributional inequality by giving poorer people services free, which to some extent implies a public value judgement about what is good for these groups of persons.

Intergenerational objections to pricing are based upon what has been termed a 'national heritage' type of argument (McCallum and Adams, 1980). Some things, such as historic sites, may be considered so intrinsically valuable that their appreciation must be handed on to future generations, who are not alive now to protect their interests. It follows from this argument that the willingness of the present generation to pay for such heritage through admission fees is not an adequate indicator of their likely value to future generations.

The final objections to pricing are centred around the difficulty or impracticality of controlling access. If it is not easy to exclude people from visiting an historic site, charging is not easy. This circumstance usually results from low numbers of visitors making even part-time staffing to collect admission fees uneconomic. It may also result implicitly where a site can be viewed adequately from neighbouring and publicly accessible land. Townscape is a frequent example of this latter case, where frontages can often be readily viewed from public streets. However, the same can occur with sites located next to, or within, churchyards or beside public footpaths.

Decisions on pricing irrespective of the objectives explicit in their making may have distributional implications. The known income distribution and apparent consumption preferences of the British population mean that subsidies to the provision of historic sites, rather than charges levied on visitors, probably would represent a subsidy to higher income persons as these tend disproportionately to be the users. Provision of reduced cost or no cost admission fees may not benefit the poor for they may not wish to visit historic sites or may be unable to reach them without public transport. If the main reason for the low levels of visits to historic sites by low income persons is the high cost of access, often requiring a car, the provision or advertising of public transport may be a more appropriate response than low admission charges. Several National Parks are well known for initiatives of this kind. Likewise, in 1988 the Sports Council for Wales sponsored Sunday bus services from Mid Glamorgan to the Brecon Beacons heritage landscape, the 'Brecon Beacons Rambler Bus'. Similarly, in 1988 the Countryside Commission supported Badgerline Ltd., the major rural bus operator in Avon, in developing and promoting twelve country walks based upon existing bus routes, to encourage access to the countryside around Bristol. Public transport may not however encourage low income visitors to historic sites or heritage countryside: if low income people are disproportionately unaware of historic sites, targeted promotion may be the more appropriate response. Or if the lack of visits by low income persons reflects their preferences for other leisure activities, distributional arguments for low or no charges are clearly inappropriate, and users should pay the full costs, subject to the other objectives to pricing. Clearly, decisions on pricing need to be taken in an informed manner unless undesirable consequences are to follow. As the bulk of the present discussion considers the relationship of visitor numbers to price in the explicit context of revenue maximisation, the wider distributive consequences of pricing decisions should not be forgotten.


## Is there a relationship between price and the number of visitors?

In the previous section we noted that one management objective of a pricing system can be to exclude visitors or, conversely, to attract them by respectively either increasing or decreasing admission prices. These objectives depend in large part for their effectiveness of the sensitivity of visitor numbers to the prices charged. This relationship depends on several factors, including the incomes of potential visitors, their tastes, the prices of related commodities and the total number of consumers in the market. In particular, this sensitivity will be greatest where the number of close substitutes is largest; potential visitors may substitute one historic site for another of a similar kind if it is nearby and the price difference is known prior to their journey. In general, as for most commodities (Salvatore, 1986), if we consider an individual historic site rather than a group of sites, the greater the number of historic sites become potential substitutes, unless the site is unique in its class. In this way the sensitivity of visitor numbers to price facing any single seller tends to be greater than the overall effect for all competitors (Hirshleifer, 1984). For example, visitors seeking to include a castle visit as part of their holiday in Wales will likely do so, within reason, whatever the price charged for admission; as such, the admission prices at castles may be thought to have little effect on the numbers of visitors gained. But if we differentiate between castles the conclusion may differ; the potential visitor may substitute a cheaper visit for a more expensive one, assuming that the product offered by each site is thought to be similar by the potential visitor and the prices are known in advance for neighbouring sites. The most close substitute are likely to be those which have similar perceived attributes. As most historic sites involve the expenditure of time and money to reach them, being at a distance from where their potential visitors are residing, costs of access need to be included alongside price in any assessment of prices charged. The price of admission to a historic site may effectively include the costs of getting to the site, and thus the relationship between the admission charge actually paid and visitor numbers may depend only in part on the admission charge actually levied. The consequences of this effect has been much debated in the economics literature on tourism (e.g. McCallum and Adams, 1980). The extent of the change in visitor numbers resultant of a change in admission price will also depend on the period of time taken to measure the effect. Potential visitors have to learn of the change in price and adjust their visiting pattern; the effect is likely to be larger, therefore, the longer the period of time allowed in measuring the effect. Properly, the effect should be measured immediately after the price change (the short run) and after time has been allowed for adjustments (the long run).

The relationship between admission prices and visitor numbers may also depend critically on income levels, for some goods are substituted for others as incomes rise. Normal goods are those which a consumer purchases more of as income increases; inferior goods are those which a consumer purchases less of as income rises. For example, potential visitors may substitute more expensive visits for cheaper visits as their incomes rise, or visit more distant places. Foreign holidays may be substituted for holidays in Britain. It is unknown whether historic houses and like heritage sites should be regarded as normal or inferior goods, for the evidence is contradictory. For example, in the 1970s the two British National Trusts expanded their visitor numbers at a time when visitors to the State's monuments declined. The evidence is also contradictory by market segment: demand may be normal for 'second' holidays and day trips, but inferior for main holidays.

The relationship between price and visitor numbers is termed elasticity. Much of the present discussion considers the concepts of price elasticity and cross elasticity of demand. Price elasticity of demand is the relationship of the quantity of a product consumed (in this case, admission numbers) to the price charged (in this case, admission prices). For the range of prices charged at comparable leisure facilities this realtionship is often such that as the price increases the quantity consumed does not fall in proportion: technically, the prices charged are in the inelastic range of the demand function. Colloquially, we may say that demand is inelastic to price at the prices frequently charged. The second concept is that of cross elasticity of demand; this is the relationship of the quantity of a product consumed not just to its own price but to the quantity of another product and its price. Cross elasticity considers the importance or unimportance of competing facilities and the substitution of one facility for another by consumers. To emphasise that price elasticity does not consider competing facilities it is sometimes termed own price elasticity.

Price elasticity of demand is calculated from a market demand schedule, the quantity of a commodity (in our case, visits to historic sites) which consumers are willing and able to purchase over a given period of time at each price of the commodity, while holding constant all other relevant economic variables on which demand depends. Price elasticity of demand could be measured as:

$$\frac{\triangle Q}{\triangle P} \quad (1).$$

That is, price elasticity of demand equals the change in quantity of visits divided by the change in price charged.

Defined as such, this would be the inverse of the slope of the demand curve which is conventionally plotted with price on the vertical axis and quantity on the horizontal axis. The disadvantage of this definition is that it is expressed in the units of measurement used and is not comparable between goods, in our case, types of heritage sites. A more useful measure is one which is independent of the units of measurement: as such, price elasticity of demand measures **relative** or **percentage** changes in the quantity demanded and price. Strictly, price elasticity of demand is given by the percentage change in the quantity demanded divided by the percentage change in its price:

$$\frac{\triangle Q/Q}{\triangle P/P} = \frac{\triangle Q}{\triangle P} \cdot \frac{P}{Q} \qquad (2).$$

The negative sign is sometimes used by convention, and formula (2) is multiplied by -1. This is because quantity and price move in opposite directions, and the negative sign is sometimes used in the formula to make the value positive. In heritage studies the negative convention has not been followed consistently (e.g. Bovaird et al, 1984) and is not used here. Note that formula (1) is only part of (2), and (1) can be estimated by the B value of a regression equation, the coefficient of price in the regression equation. Formula (2) defines what is strictly known as the point elasticity of demand, the elasticity at a particular point on the demand curve. This has the disadvantage that different results are possible if we measure a price rise or price fall. To avoid this the average of the two possible calculations is used: this is the arc elasticity of demand, and is the elasticity between two points on the demand curve. Arc elasticity of demand is defined as:

$$\frac{\triangle Q}{\triangle P} \cdot \frac{(P_1 + P_2)/2}{(Q_1 + Q_2)/2}$$

$$= \frac{\triangle Q}{\triangle P} \cdot \frac{(P_1 + P_2)}{(Q_1 + Q_2)} \qquad (3).$$

Where $P_1$ is the higher of the two prices;
$P_2$ is the lower of the two prices;
$Q_1$ is the number of visitors at $P_1$; and
$Q_2$ is the number of visitors at $P_2$.

As price elasticity of demand, even when defined as arc elasticity, varies between prices elasticies are price specific. Because of this, conventionally, elasticity estimates are given as the average values of prices and demand, in the present case, the average numbers of visitors and admission prices. This has the problem that the elasticity values for all other price levels need to be calculated individually. This is possible only if the regression equations are given in the published papers by their authors.

Cross elasticity of demand is defined as the responsiveness or sensitivity in the number of visits made at site A as a result of a change in the price charged for admission at site B. Sites A and B are substitutes if more trips to A are made when the admission price at B is increased. Sites A and B are complements if fewer visits are made to A when the price at B is increased. Cross elasticity is defined as:

$$\frac{\triangle Q_A / Q_A}{\triangle P_B / P_B}$$

$$= \frac{\triangle Q_A}{\triangle P_B} \cdot \frac{P_B}{Q_A} \qquad (4).$$

Both price elasticity of demand and cross elasticity of demand each have critical ranges over which the relationship between price and visits is in the same direction, although not necessarily invariant. For any price level the relationship of the quantity of a product consumed to the price charged may be threefold. Firstly, a unitary price elasticity of demand is where the reduction in the quantity consumed as a result of a price increase is in the same proportion as the price increase. This relationship is where the price elasticity of demand is equal to -1 and should be regarded as a special case. Another case is where demand is price elastic; that is, where demand falls in greater proportion than the price rises. In this case revenue will fall as prices increase. In the case of elastic demand the price elasticity of demand lies in the range -1 to minus infinity. The final case is that of inelastic demand. This is where demand decreases less than proportionately when price rises. In the case of inelastic demand the price elasticity of demand lies in the range from 0 to -1. With inelastic demand as prices rise an operator's revenue increases. As it is usual that if admissions are fewer costs will be lower (such as the costs of wear and tear) a private operator will seek to move towards an elasticity position of -1, or above, up to the point at which marginal costs equate with marginal revenue. In this way profitability is likely to be maximised. This may not be an appropriate objective for an agency wishing to retain the number of visitors to its sites, for, if demand is inelastic, increased revenue will lead to reduced visitor numbers. Cross elasticity of demand demonstrates two cases. Any value of greater than zero indicates that sites A and B are substitutes because an increase in the price charged at site B leads to an increase in visitor numbers at site A. Conversely, a value of less than zero indicates that sites A and B are complements, because an increase in the price charged at site B leads to a reduction in visitor numbers at site A.

238

Figure 7.1.
Effects of changed demand curves on apparent
price elasticity of demand

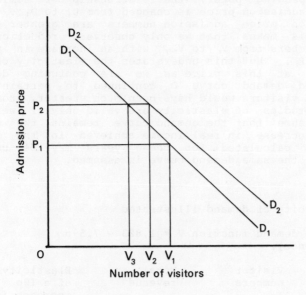

Figure 7.2

Figure 7.2.
Unknown demand curve and the site-operator's need
for guidance on changes in visitor numbers likely to
result from price changes

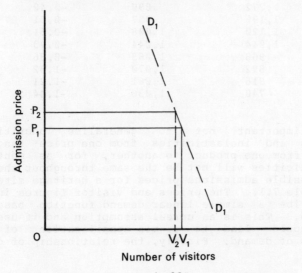

Much of the work on elasticities has used data of the 1960s and 1970s. This was an era of increases in real incomes. If historic sites are normal goods, apparent elasticities of demand to price rises may be understated by increases in the real income of those in work, and, hence, in their spending power. Figure 7.1 shows the effect of increased spending power; the relationship of admission numbers to admission price is changed from $D_1$ to $D_2$. For any admission price admission numbers are greater than before. This means that we only observe a reduction in admission numbers from $V_1$ to $V_2$, with an increase in price from $P_1$ to $P_2$. But this understates the elasticity of the relationship at this price as we are confusing demand curves. Had demand curve $D_1$ continued to pertain the decrease in visitors would have been much greater, from $V_1$ to $V_3$. Studies of elasticity are valid only if we can sensibly assume that the demand curve remains the same. With the increase in real income achieved in the 1970s elasticities calculated for these years may be under-estimated if the same demand curve is assumed.


Table 7.1
Price elasticity of demand illustrated

Hypothetical demand function V = 1,803 - 7.59p
(price in pence).

| Admission price | Visitor numbers | Total revenue | Elasticity of a 10p increase in admission price |
|---|---|---|---|
| P | V | | |
| £-.--p | | £ | |
| 50p | 1,424 | 712 | -0.27 |
| 60p | 1,348 | 809 | -0.34 |
| 70p | 1,272 | 890 | -0.42 |
| 80p | 1,196 | 957 | -0.51 |
| 90p | 1,120 | 1,008 | -0.61 |
| 1.00p | 1,044 | 1.044 | -0.73 |
| 1.10p | 968 | 1,065 | -0.86 |
| 1.20 | 892 | 1,070 | -1.02 |
| 1.30 | 816 | 1,061 | -1.21 |
| 1.40 | 740 | 1,036 | -1.44 |

It is important not to generalise uncritically elasticities and inelasticities from one price range to another or from one product to another, for as mentioned above, elasticities will not be the same throughout the full range of possible admissions prices for a heritage site, as shown in Table 7.1. The prices and visitor figures in this Table describe a simple linear demand function based on price alone. This is an unreal assumption and if used in analysis would lead to a mis-specification of the determinants of demand. Firstly, the relationship of demand

to price is unlikely to be linear.   Secondly, other factors
affecting demand are excluded.  For example, overall holiday
taking  in the locality is likely to have an affect  on  the
extent of demand.  This assumption is made for simplicity of
illustration,  as  is  the  failure to  distinguish  between
admissions  of  adults and of children.   As  can  be  seen,
successive increments of ten pence to the admission fee lead
to  decreasing  values of inelasticity.   In  this  example,
revenue peaks at about a charge of £1.20p.   From this point
higher charges mean lower overall revenue;  the relationship
of  price and demand is now elastic (the values have changed
from less than 1.0 to greater than 1.0).  This change occurs
even  when  we do not alter the realtionship of  demand  and
price.
Snaith   (1975)   produced  a   pioneering   analysis   of
elasticities for historic sites,  using data on 150 National
Trust  properties,  for  the  years 1965 to  1970.    Snaith
calculated arc elasticities,  derived from simple regression
models  for properties grouped by regional location  and  by
property type.  Snaith's general model may be defined as:

$\triangle V = f(\triangle P, T, R)$        (5)

Where     $\triangle V$ = proportionate changes in visitor numbers;

          $\triangle P$ = proportionate changes in admission prices;

          T   = property type; and

          R   = region.

A  separate  analysis  was  undertaken  for  1969-1970,   as
admission  prices were generally raised in the latter  year.
Property  types  were  included in this second  analysis  as
'dummy'  variables.  This  separate  analysis  produced  an
overall  estimate  of  short term elasticities.   Snaith's
findings  are summarised in Table 7.2.   It  is  likely  that
these elasticities were computed from the average prices and
average  numbers of visitors then pertaining.   Snaith found
negative elasticities ranging from -0.27 to -1.25,  as shown
in Table 7.2.   Overall,  Snaith concluded, '... The results
are  such that one could accept as a good working assumption
an  overall  price elasticity of c.0.4 for National  Trust
properties  as  a  whole' (Snaith,  1975,  pp.  145-146).
Reference  to  the  Table  shows that this  is  a  dangerous
generalisation;  some categories of properties, for example,
houses and gardens in the Midlands of England, were found to
have  elastic  relationships (coefficients  in  excess  of
-1.00).
The  summary  measure of -0.4 appears to derive both  from
Snaith's pooled data for 1969-70, summarising all sites, and
from  the national analyses of property types for  1965-70.
The  estimate  is  clearly  invalid at a  regional  level.
Further reference to Table 7.2 implies further caution,  for
the coefficients of determination are generally low,  except
for  the regional analyses.  This coefficient measures  the
amount  of variation in visitor numbers attributable to  the

Table 7.2
**Snaith's elasticity estimates for National Trust properties**

|  | Price elasticity | Coefficient of determination % (rounded) |
|---|---|---|
| National analysis 1965-1970: | | |
| Gardens | -0.34 | 2 |
| Houses | -0.35 | 1 |
| Houses and gardens | -0.51 | 4 |
| Regional analyses (where valid) 1965-1970: | | |
| Houses and gardens (Midlands) | -1.25 | 45 |
| Houses and gardens (South West) | -0.30 | 35 |
| Gardens (South West) | -0.27 | 34 |
| Gardens (South East) | -0.60 | 57 |
| Houses (Northern Ireland) | -1.18 | 45 |
| Pooled data (1969-1970): | | |
| All sites | -0.36 | 13 |

Source: Snaith (1975, p.145).


price changes: for those elasticity coefficients upon which the overall estimate made by Snaith of -0.4 appears to depend, the coefficients of determination are trivial. Despite these gross limitations inherent in this generalisation, -0.4 has become part of the folklore of price elasticity of demand at historic sites. For example, Stoakes (1979) used this figure in his discussion of the effects of oil price increases on countryside recreational travel. He suggested that as pertrol costs are only part of a family's day trip expenditure, a possible ten per cent reduction in visitor numbers to the countryside would follow a sixty per cent increase in petrol prices. His suggestion was unsubstantiated by evidence other than the general relationship of changes in the real price of petrol and visitor numbers to National Trust properties. No algebraically specified model was presented by Stoakes in the paper.

A further study of elasticities at historic houses in Britain was undertaken by Hendon (1982) who argued that up to an income of £100,000 per annum from visitors demand is relatively inelastic; at higher levels of income higher prices were associated with higher visitor numbers, the opposite to what would be expected. The analysis as reported is not replicable and is an unusual application of significance testing: the analysis represents a progressive division of the data and the testing of means for significant differences statistically. Hendon argued that a market segmentation existed, in which inelasticities pertained. 'Within the limits of demand segments, houses are free to charge somewhat higher prices, without any apparent negative impact on their visitor generated total revenues' (Hendon, 1982, p.xi). Coopers Lybrand (1979) made a similar comment about leisure facilities in the East Midlands of England.

The major recent study of price elasticity is that of Bovaird, Tricker and Stoakes (1984), using data from 82 National Trust sites and 115 Department of the Environment sites for the 1970s. Bovaird et al used three measures of elasticity; percentage change, absolute change and logged change, Percentage change is the least easily interpreted as a measure of elasticity: percentage changes in the number of visitors between pairs of years were regressed against percentage changes in admission prices in the corresponding period. Bovaird et al used the b coefficient of the regression equation as this measure of elasticity, a measure they acknowledge implicitly not to be a strict measure of elasticity. 'The resulting coefficient ... can be interpreted as a crude elasticity value' (Bovaird et al., 1984, p.45). This measure was noted as giving undue weight to extreme fluctuations, especially in the case of sites with low prices.

Bovaird et al.'s second measure of elasticity was conventionally derived from a linear demand function defined by regression. Bovaird et al defined a point elasticity of demand as in equation (2). As with all linear demand functions of this kind it is to be expected that at each site the price elasticity would be low at low prices and high at high prices, Bovaird et al presented elasticities based on average prices and average numbers of visitors.

The third measure used by Bovaird et al was logged change, The log of an index of changes in the number of visitors was regressed against the log of an index of changes in admission prices and other relevant variables. The resultant equations yield a direct estimation of the price elasticity of demand in the b coefficients of price. A function of this kind assumes a constant elasticity at all prices, and gives low weight to extreme values.

Bovaird et al undertook both cross-sectional and longitudinal analyses of inelasticity. Cross-sectional analysis is that undertaken for specific years, using many sites as data points. Longitudinal analysis uses data from single sites for a period of years. In the cross-sectional analysis only sites where price rises occurred were included; this analysis considers, therefore, not whether all sites lost or gained visitors, but the extent to which those sites with the largest price increases over a year had the most unfavourable changes in visitor numbers. Time series analysis has a number of advantages over cross-sectional analysis. Firstly, trends can be explored over time. Secondly time series analysis allows the inclusion of the effects of variables having similar values in any year for all sites, such as petrol prices. Longitudinal analysis also allows an analysis by property type, and for individual properties. The effects of weather on demand can also be disaggregated. The major theoretical weakness of the Bovaird et al study is that no account is taken of competing facilities (cross elasticities) or of the overall demand for countryside recreation. This has been recognised by the authors,

> ... Our approach is likely to underestimate the price elasticities of individual sites. The greater is the elasticity of demand for countryside trips and the higher the substitutability of one site for another in the eyes of visitors, then the greater liklihood of such underestimation. It was therefore concluded that a fruitful area for future study would be the inclusion in a time-series analysis of comparative variables for competing facilities, especially average changes in admission prices, facilities and promotional activities (Bovaird and Tricker, 1985, p.12).

The extent of this under-estimation is unknown. It may be of particular importance in Britain with the extensive growth of tourist and recreational facilities in the 1970s. Bovaird et al. confirmed the essential of the Snaith analysis: that is, that demand appeared to be inelastic to price increases at the average price then charged. For Department of the Environment sites the cross-sectional analysis suggested elasticities of between $-0.15$ and $-0.40$, compared to elasticities of between $-0.20$ and $-0.30$ by longitudinal analysis. The longitudinal analysis showed that these elasticities varied by type of site and by period. Similarly, the cross-sectional analysis showed elasticities of between $-0.30$ and $-0.60$ for the higher priced National Trust sites. Critically, Bovaird et al. found exceptions to these general elasticities. Hidcote Manor and Packwood were both in a range bordering on unitary elasticities; both Sheffield Park and Osborne were in the range $-0.6$ to $-0.7$.

Bovaird et al.'s expansion of the demand function from price alone, and Bovaird and Tricker's subsequent comments, remind us that demand is caused by many other variables than price alone. For example, the limited importance of price in affecting visitor numbers to museums has been shown for Boston; other, institutional, factors were found to be more important (O'Hare, 1975). Such factors included hours of opening and special exhibitions. Demand, in terms of visitor numbers, was shown to be highly inelastic, and to have a one third probability of being positively associated with price (the opposite to what would be expected). Most of the British literature on price elasticity of demand for historic sites ignores cross-elasticities, even between sites owned by the same organisations. However, the literature reviewed here clearly indicates the inelasticity of demand to price increases at the prices generally charged for admission to sites.

However, as so little is known about the demand functions for visits to historic sites, the more general question of what kinds of sites may be regarded as normal goods and

which as inferior, if any, remains unanswered. This more
general question has immediate implications for justifying,
or otherwise, expenditure on product improvement by
interpretation and the development of ancilliary facilities.
The concept of 'value for money' was advanced by Brown
(1983) to explain the decline in visitor numbers at State
monuments in Wales. Brown noted that National Trust charges
were greater than those at State monuments, but that the
Trust's properties were improving their market share of
visitors. Brown argued that the Trust's properties had more
to offer potential visitors who were becoming more
discriminating: the value for money offered by Welsh
monuments was less, and further amenities and facilities
would need to be provided if future price rises were not to
further reduce visitor numbers. Comparative prices at
properties clearly show that average prices charged relate
to the provision of facilities (English Tourist Board,
1982). In 1982 of the 1,481 properties regularly open to
the public and where charges were made the average summer
adult charge was 72 pence, but more at properties with
additional attractions; at those with contents this was 79
pence, at those with gardens, 95 pence, and at those with a
park £1.05p. This differentiation suggests that the
provision of additional facilities allows higher prices to
be charged for admission, but not substantially higher
prices.


## Attitudes towards pricing

In the absence of generally defined demand curves for
historic sites, a site operator may still need to know where
his prices are on the curve, if it were to be defined.
Otherwise, as price elasticity of demand can be expected to
vary by price, the prediction of the effects of price
changes is impracticable. A substitute for seeking to fully
define demand curves is to measure the attitudes of visitors
and deterred visitors towards the admission prices currently
charged at sites. Figure 7.2 details the site operator's
knowledge and lack of knowledge. The operator is unaware of
the demand curve $D_1$, but is aware of the price he charges $P_1$
and the number of visitors gained, $V_1$. The operator wishes
to increase his prices to $P_2$ and seeks an estimate of
visitor numbers at this new price, $V_2$, the latter which he
does not know. By surveying visitors arriving at the site
under admission price $P_1$ the operator may gain some guidance
as to future visitors' reactions to the price $P_2$. This
analysis can most usefully be undertaken at like sites
charging prices $P_1$ and $P_2$, and should include both visitors
paying the price and those apparently deterred from entering
the part of the site where admission charges are levied.
The literature on visitors' views on admissions prices at
historic sites is specific to sites, particular price levels
and structures. Three surveys apply particularly to Wales,
undertaken in 1973, 1985 and 1986. Only the latter survey
included interviews with deterred visitors. The Wales
Tourist Board's visitor surveys of 1973, which included

Table 7.3
Visitors' reactions to admission prices at certain Welsh tourist attractions

Adult entrance fees:

| | Fee | Too high | About right | Too low | Do not know | N |
|---|---|---|---|---|---|---|
| | pence | % | % | % | % | |
| Caernarfon Castle | 25p | 13 | 80 | 1 | 6 | 1,010 |
| Chepstow Castle | ? | 3 | 90 | 6 | 2 | 999 |
| St. Fagans Folk Museum | 10p | 1 | 82 | 16 | 1 | 828 |
| Talyllyn Railway | 40p (return) | 3 | 96 | 1 | – | 693 |
| Welshpool and Llanfair Light Railway | ? | 10 | 89 | – | 1 | 558 |
| Day yr Ogof Caves | ? | 17 | 79 | 1 | 3 | 1,000 |
| Penscynor Bird Gardens | ? | 13 | 84 | 1 | 2 | 1,023 |

Sources: Owen and Mears (1974a); Owen and Mears (1974b);
Owen and Mears (1974c); Mears (1976a);
Mears (1976b); Mears (1976c); Mears (1976d).

questions on visitors' views of prices charged, can not be used to present a systematic, if dated, analysis, for neither are all prices given, nor are all the facilities available listed. The surveys covered a wide range of attractions, using standard formats, but were not presented as a comparative study; rather they were reported as a series of separate surveys. The range of tourist attractions considered is presented in Table 7.3. As is to be expected from asking visitors, rather than non-visitors, most respondents by far thought that the admission prices charged were 'about right'. There was a notable difference between Caernarfon and Chepstow Castles in the proportion of visitors thinking that the admission price was 'too high'; thirteen per cent compared to three per cent, a difference which is significant statistically. However, the greater proportion of visitors to Caernarfon Castle, visiting because of their interest in castles, who thought that the price was 'too high', may have resulted from sampling error (Table 7.4) and so it would be unsafe to conclude that frequent castle goers may have disproportionately thought that the price was too high at Caernarfon Castle compared to the prices charged at other castles. The extent to which frequent castle visitors may expect to pay different prices

Table 7.4
Visitors' reactions to prices at two castles in Wales

Adult entrance fees:

Caernarfon Castle:

Reasons for visit:

|  | Welsh history | Interested in castles | Investiture took place | Take the children |
|---|---|---|---|---|
| N = | 90 | 304 | 102 | 94 |
|  | % | % | % | % |
| Too high | 7 | 14 | 11 | 6 |
| About right | 87 | 81 | 84 | 93 |
| Too low | – | 1 | 2 | 1 |
| Do not know | 7 | 4 | 3 | – |

Adult entrance fees:

Chepstow Castle:

Reasons for visit:

|  | Interested in Welsh history | Interested in castles | Somewhere to go |
|---|---|---|---|
| N = | 63 | 470 | 154 |
|  | % | % | % |
| Too high | – | 1 | 1 |
| About right | 81 | 91 | 92 |
| Too low | 11 | 6 | 4 |
| Do not know | 8 | 2 | 4 |

Sources: Owen and Mears (1974a); Mears (1976a).

than the holiday visitor intent on visiting one castle as part of his or her holiday would be worthy of investigation as part of a study of market segmentation. The holiday visitor may set his or her price expectations by comparison with other leisure attractions, whereas the castle enthusiast may not. Perceptions of this kind are important to the success or failure of the 'heritage club' memberships, such as 'Heritage in Wales' and 'Friends of the Scottish Monuments'.

The second study of visitor reaction to admission prices at Welsh monuments was undertaken for the Wales Tourist Board in 1985. This gives an indication of visitor satisfaction with pricing at six monuments (Public Attitude Surveys Research, 1985). Six monuments are insufficient to assess the effect of prices charged independently of other causes of satisfaction and dissatisfaction. Notably, the higher price charged at Caernarfon Castle, as in 1973, was

Table 7.5
Views of admission prices by visitors to Cadw's monuments

Sample survey undertaken in 1985

| | Opinion of admission charge paid | | | | | | | | Adult admission charge |
|---|---|---|---|---|---|---|---|---|---|
| | Too high | | About right | | Too low | | Other | | |
| | Day % | Stay -ing % | Day % | Stay -ing % | Day % | Stay -ing % | Day % | Stay -ing % | |
| **Castles:** | | | | | | | | | |
| Caernarfon | 28 | 25 | 67 | 72 | 0 | 1 | 5 | 3 | £1.60p |
| Conwy | 17 | 13 | 80 | 84 | 1 | 1 | 2 | 3 | 90p |
| Chepstow | 10 | 8 | 84 | 86 | 3 | 3 | 4 | 3 | 80p |
| Kidwelly | 11 | 16 | 79 | 80 | 0 | 1 | 9 | 3 | 70p |
| **Religious monuments:** | | | | | | | | | |
| Valle Crucis | 0 | 1 | 91 | 95 | 3 | 1 | 5 | 3 | 50p |
| Bishop's Palace | 8 | 8 | 83 | 91 | 0 | 1 | 9 | 1 | 60p |
| **Industrial monument:** | | | | | | | | | |
| Welsh Slate Museum | 4 | 3 | 72 | 91 | 12 | 2 | 12 | 4 | 80p |

Sample sizes:

| | Day visitors | Staying visitors |
|---|---|---|
| Caernarfon | 39 | 314 |
| Conwy | 95 | 479 |
| Chepstow | 61 | 172 |
| Kidwelly | 63 | 177 |
| Valle Crucis Abbey | 58 | 99 |
| Bishop's Palace | 12 | 139 |
| Slate Museum | 25 | 195 |

Source: Public Attitude Surveys Research (1985).

associated with a greater proportion of visitors thinking the price to be too high (Table 7.5). Generally, however, most visitors felt the prices charged at the sites to be about right; this was as is to be expected as people who have been deterred are by definition not visitors. The length of stay, whether a visitor had children with him or her, or type of weather at the time of visit had no affect on the visitors' views of the prices charged (Table 7.6).

Table 7.6
Visitors' views of admission prices at Cadw's sites by visitor characteristics

1985 sample survey of 2,163 visitors to seven of Cadw's sites

|  | Price: | | |
|---|---|---|---|
|  | Too high % | About right % | Too low % |
| Age of visitors: | | | |
| 16-34 | 17 | 78 | 1 |
| 35-54 | 12 | 85 | 1 |
| 55 and over | 4 | 88 | 2 |
| Weather: | | | |
| Sunny | 12 | 83 | 2 |
| Cloudy | 14 | 81 | 1 |
| Raining | 14 | 81 | 1 |
| Visit to site: | | | |
| First visit | 12 | 83 | 1 |
| Visited previously | 16 | 79 | 2 |
| Visitor type: | | | |
| Day visitor | 12 | 80 | 2 |
| Staying visitor | 12 | 83 | 1 |
| Region of residence: | | | |
| Wales | 8 | 84 | 1 |
| London/ S.E. England | 13 | 84 | 1 |
| English Midlands | 14 | 82 | 1 |
| S.W. England | 12 | 82 | 2 |
| N.W. England | 16 | 81 | 1 |
| Overseas | 11 | 81 | 1 |

N = 2,163

Source: Public Attitude Surveys Research (1985).

Table 7.7.
Visitors' opinions on pricing at Cadw's sites in 1986

| | Strongly agree % | Agree % | No strong feelings % | Dis- agree % | Strongly disagree % | N |
|---|---|---|---|---|---|---|
| The adult admission fee of ___ p at this site is value for money. | | | | | | |
| IN | 10 | 77 | 7 | 6 | * | 946 |
| OUT | 4 | 51 | 17 | 21 | 7 | 309 |
| ALL | 8 | 70 | 10 | 10 | 2 | 1255 |
| Admission to castles and historic sites owned by the state should be free. | | | | | | |
| IN | 2 | 23 | 11 | 62 | 2 | 949 |
| OUT | 9 | 28 | 7 | 51 | 5 | 452 |
| ALL | 4 | 25 | 10 | 58 | 3 | 1401 |
| The admission fee of ___ p is more than I would generally pay for admission to this kind of attraction. | | | | | | |
| IN | * | 16 | 7 | 72 | 4 | 946 |
| OUT | 13 | 35 | 7 | 43 | 2 | 440 |
| ALL | 5 | 22 | 7 | 63 | 3 | 1386 |
| Local people should be able to purchase a season ticket for this site for three pounds for the year. | | | | | | |
| IN | 4 | 51 | 31 | 13 | * | 919 |
| OUT | 9 | 58 | 18 | 13 | 2 | 432 |
| ALL | 6 | 53 | 27 | 13 | 1 | 1351 |
| Children should be able to buy an educational activity folder. | | | | | | |
| IN | 12 | 72 | 13 | 4 | * | 924 |
| OUT | 15 | 73 | 9 | 3 | * | 444 |
| ALL | 13 | 72 | 11 | 4 | * | 1368 |
| The entrance fee of ___ p was more than I would expect to pay. | | | | | | |
| IN | 1 | 15 | 4 | 75 | 5 | 936 |
| OUT | 21 | 27 | 6 | 44 | 3 | 446 |
| ALL | 7 | 19 | 4 | 65 | 4 | 1382 |

cont ....

Table 7.7 cont ....

| | Strongly agree % | Agree % | No strong feelings % | Dis-agree % | Strongly disagree % | N |
|---|---|---|---|---|---|---|
| **Admission fees should be charged in order to pay for the upkeep of sites.** | | | | | | |
| IN | 11 | 74 | 6 | 8 | 1 | 942 |
| OUT | 11 | 76 | 4 | 7 | 3 | 456 |
| ALL | 11 | 75 | 5 | 8 | 2 | 1398 |
| **Parents should be charged at most for two of their children when visiting as a family.** | | | | | | |
| IN | 7 | 63 | 17 | 12 | 1 | 927 |
| OUT | 19 | 60 | 8 | 12 | 2 | 449 |
| ALL | 11 | 62 | 14 | 12 | 1 | 1376 |
| **All in all, I enjoyed my visit here/ have enjoyed it so far.** | | | | | | |
| IN | 26 | 73 | 1 | * | * | 956 |
| OUT | 18 | 70 | 8 | 2 | 2 | 438 |
| ALL | 24 | 72 | 3 | * | * | 1394 |

N.B.: IN = Inside site;
      OUT = Outside site;
      ALL = All persons interviewed.

*   Indicates a percentage greater than 0 but less than 1.

Source: Seren (1986a).

251

Table 7.8.
Visitors' opinions on pricing at Caernarfon Castle in 1986

| | | Strongly agree % | Agree % | No strong feelings % | Dis- agree % | Strongly disagree % | N |
|---|---|---|---|---|---|---|---|
| The adult admission fee of ____ p at this site is value for money. | IN | * | 77 | 13 | 10 | 0 | 207 |
| | OUT | 2 | 32 | 6 | 43 | 17 | 90 |
| | ALL | 1 | 63 | 10 | 20 | 5 | 297 |
| Admission to castles and historic sites owned by the state should be free. | IN | 1 | 21 | 4 | 73 | * | 208 |
| | OUT | 14 | 15 | 2 | 59 | 10 | 123 |
| | ALL | 6 | 19 | 4 | 68 | 4 | 331 |
| The admission fee of ____ p is more than I would generally pay for admission to this kind of attraction. | IN | * | 31 | 10 | 59 | 0 | 209 |
| | OUT | 39 | 40 | 3 | 17 | 2 | 120 |
| | ALL | 15 | 34 | 7 | 44 | * | 329 |
| Local people should be able to purchase a season ticket for this site for three pounds for the year. | IN | 2 | 69 | 12 | 16 | * | 205 |
| | OUT | 14 | 46 | 20 | 16 | 3 | 119 |
| | ALL | 7 | 61 | 15 | 16 | 1 | 324 |
| Children should be able to buy an educational activity folder. | IN | 7 | 84 | 5 | 4 | 0 | 207 |
| | OUT | 20 | 64 | 9 | 6 | 0 | 118 |
| | ALL | 12 | 77 | 7 | 5 | * | 325 |
| The entrance fee of ____ p was more than I would expect to pay. | IN | 2 | 32 | 3 | 62 | * | 205 |
| | OUT | 55 | 25 | 0 | 19 | * | 124 |
| | ALL | 22 | 30 | 2 | 46 | * | 329 |

cont ...

Table 7.8 cont ....

|  | Strongly agree % | Agree % | No strong feelings % | Dis-agree % | Strongly disagree % | N |
|---|---|---|---|---|---|---|
| **Admission fees should be charged in order to pay for the upkeep of sites.** | | | | | | |
| IN | 5 | 81 | 4 | 10 | 0 | 209 |
| OUT | 18 | 69 | 2 | 6 | 5 | 125 |
| ALL | 10 | 77 | 3 | 8 | 2 | 334 |
| **Parents should be charged at most for two of their children when visiting as a family.** | | | | | | |
| IN | 2 | 74 | 10 | 14 | * | 206 |
| OUT | 40 | 50 | 6 | 3 | * | 120 |
| ALL | 16 | 65 | 9 | 10 | * | 326 |
| **All in all, I enjoyed my visit here/ have enjoyed it so far.** | | | | | | |
| IN | 10 | 89 | 1 | * | 0 | 208 |
| OUT | 17 | 66 | 10 | 4 | 3 | 119 |
| ALL | 12 | 81 | 4 | 2 | 1 | 327 |

N.B.: IN = Inside site;
OUT = Outside site;
ALL = All persons interviewed.

* Indicates a percentage greater than 0 but less than 1.

Source: Seren (1986a).

A greater proportion of younger adults, and possibly of
return visitors, thought the prices at Cadw's sites to be
too high; these represented a minority of visitors, however.
The tendency for older visitors to be more satisfied with
the prices charged was highly significant statistically.

The third Welsh study was undertaken in 1986 and in detail
covered six of Cadw's sites. Visitors who had paid to enter
the sites and persons appearing to turn away at the entrance
to the sites were interviewed. The survey focused
explicitly on the reactions of visitors to policies of price
banding and specifically to the prices charged. Most
respondents thought that admission charges should be levied.
Fewer than a third of respondents thought that admission to
castles and historic sites owned by the State ought to be
free. Three quarters of those sampled agreed that fees were
necessary for the upkeep of sites (Table 7.7). Explicit
discrimination in pricing in favour of lower prices for
local people and for families were generally seen as
desirable. Six out of ten persons responding thought that a
local season ticket would be desirable; likewise, nearly
three quarters thought that at most, two children should be
charged for. Comparative prices were also investigated.
Over the six sites, generally, a majority of respondents
considered that the admission fee charged was not more than
they would generally pay. Likewise, two thirds of
respondents disagreed that the fee was more than they had
expected to pay. Of those making a judgement, nearly eight
out of ten thought the admission charge to be value for
money. Even more striking, more than nine out of ten
visitors, including those not entering the site, had enjoyed
their visit.

Overall frequencies such as those for the six Cadw sites
surveyed in 1986 are usefully analysed by price charged.
The sites included two where 75p was charged for admission,
three at which one pound was charged, and a sixth at which a
price of two pounds was charged for adult admission. There
was little difference in the reaction of visitors to the two
lower prices. In contrast is the more expensive charge,
that levied at Caernarfon Castle. A comparison of Tables
7.7 and 7.8 indicates the main differences which attached to
the specific price charged. At Caernarfon Castle the fee
was clearly perceived less strongly as value for money, and
more strongly as comparatively expensive and more expensive
than expected. Adverse reaction was double that generally
found by the survey. For example, just over a quarter of
respondents generally thought that the entrance fees were
more than they had expected; but at Caernarfon Castle half
thought this. Likewise, whereas in total about one in eight
of the sample disagreed that the fee was value for money, at
Caernarfon a quarter disagreed. It is interesting that
these adverse comments are in proportion to the difference
in admission price between Caernarfon and the other sites,
and that at Caernarfon the price of admission had been
substantially increased, 1986 compared to 1985.

The summer pricing survey was also supplemented by general
surveys at Easter and in the summer which included a pricing
question, namely, 'The entrance fee was more than I expected

254

Table 7.9.
Visitors' to Cadw's sites views that the entrance fees paid were more than they had expected to pay, Easter 1986

| | Tintern Abbey | Castell Coch | Caerphilly Castle | Kidwelly Castle | Caerleon sites | Valle Crucis Abbey | Conwy Castle | Harlech Castle | Criccieth Castle | Caernarfon Castle | ALL SITES |
|---|---|---|---|---|---|---|---|---|---|---|---|
| N = | 273 | 290 | 349 | 120 | 181 | 111 | 357 | 205 | 166 | 211 | 2263 |
| | % | % | % | % | % | % | % | % | % | % | % |
| Strongly agree/agree | 34 | 22 | 21 | 19 | 23 | 37 | 17 | 30 | 41 | 41 | 27 |

Source: Seren (1986b).

Table 7.10.
Visitors' to Cadw's sites views that the entrance fees paid were more than expected, summer 1986

| | Tintern Abbey | Castell Coch | Caerphilly Castle | Raglan Castle | Caernarfon Castle | Conwy Castle | Harlech Castle | Beaumaris Castle | ALL SITES |
|---|---|---|---|---|---|---|---|---|---|
| N = | 237 | 259 | 202 | 243 | 236 | 186 | 227 | 221 | 1811 |
| | % | % | % | % | % | % | % | % | % |
| Strongly agree | 3 | 5 | 2 | 0 | 3 | 0 | 3 | 2 | 2 |
| Agree | 24 | 21 | 12 | 5 | 41 | 9 | 11 | 19 | 18 |
| No strong feelings/ don't know | 38 | 11 | 22 | 22 | 19 | 4 | 18 | 21 | 20 |
| Disagree | 34 | 55 | 62 | 69 | 37 | 87 | 64 | 55 | 57 |
| Strongly disagree | 1 | 8 | 2 | 2 | * | 0 | 4 | 3 | 3 |

Note: * indicates a percentage less than 1 but greater than zero.

Source: Seren (1986c).

to pay' and 'The entrance fee was more than I expected'
respectively (Seren, 1986b and 1986c). These surveys allow
some seasonal comparisons to be made. Reference to Tables
7.9 and 7.10 confirms the general pattern of acceptable
pricing at Cadw sites. However, clear variation between
sites is apparent. At Easter, Criccieth and Caernarfon
Castles and Valle Crucis Abbey all stand out as exceptions
with sizeable minorities finding the prices more than they
had expected. In the summer, Caernarfon Castle is again
exceptional. In contrast, in both seasons large majorities
of visitors at Conwy Castle found the admission charge
acceptable. The different mix of sites at Easter and in the
summer makes summary comparison of the acceptance of the
prices charged invalid. When the six sites present in both
surveys are abstracted no consistent seasonal effect is
apparent. However, if the exceptional site, Caernarfon
Castle is removed from the comparison, at four of the five
remaining sites a disproportionate number of Easter visitors
found the fees more than expected; notably so at Harlech
Castle. This effect needs further and systematic
investigation before firm conclusions can be made.
    It is important to see if apparently deterred visitors
are in fact deterred, and if so how far admission prices are
the deterrent. The 1986 detailed pricing survey of Cadw
sites showed that as the entrance fee increased, so did the
extent to which respondents interviewed outside the site
(those not entering) thought the price to be less value for
money than did those interviewed inside the site (and who
had paid the admission fee). At Caernarfon Castle six out
of ten persons interviewed outside the site thought the fee
to be poor value for money, compared to one in ten
interviewed inside the site. In contrast, at the sites
where one pound was charged for admission, two out of every
eleven persons not entering the sites thought the fee to be
poor value for money, compared to one in twenty persons
inside the site. This is a marked difference between
Caernarfon Castle and the other sites. This may in part
result from ignorance of the range of facilities available
inside Caernarfon Castle. However, the likely behavioural
affect of high prices seems clear. That the admission price
has both a general and specific deterrent effect can be
surmised from visitors expectations about prices. Non-
entrants frequently thought the fees more than expected or
more than generally paid compared to visitors inside (Table
7.7). These differences existed for each price charged, but
were marked for the two pounds fee charged at Caernarfon
Castle. At this site just under eight out of ten non-
entrants considered the fee more than they generally paid.
A similar proportion of non-entrants interviewed at the site
also said that the fee was more than they had expected.
Clearly, admission fees are not inelastic continuously, as
would be expected from theory, but somewhat contrary to the
general impression given by the literature on the subject.
    The 1986 pricing survey of Cadw sites can also be used to
see if certain groups are disproportionately deterred from
entering sites by the fees charged. A comparison of the
social class, ages and distances travelled·by entrants and

Table 7.11
Breakdown of selected characteristics of persons interviewed
inside Cadw's sites and of those interviewed outside who did
not intend to enter the site

Note: the percentages summate downwards by    section.

| | Inside site | Outside site not entering |
|---|---|---|
| All persons interviewed: | | |
| N = | 961 | 369 |
| | % | % |
| Social class of household head: | | |
| Professional | 16 | 13 |
| Intermediate | 34 | 36 |
| Skilled non-manual | 13 | 15 |
| Skilled manual | 25 | 22 |
| Partly skilled/ unskilled | 7 | 6 |
| Economically inactive: unspecified retired/unemployed /full time student | 5 | 8 |
| Holiday status: | | |
| On holiday, away from home | 79 | 75 |
| On holiday, at home | 9 | 7 |
| Not on holiday | 12 | 18 |
| Age: | | |
| 15-19 | 3 | 5 |
| 20-29 | 19 | 22 |
| 30-39 | 34 | 31 |
| 40-49 | 23 | 21 |
| 50-59 | 11 | 12 |
| 60 and over | 10 | 9 |
| Distance travelled: | | |
| 5 or less miles | 20 | 21 |
| 6-20 miles | 37 | 32 |
| 21-30 miles | 18 | 21 |
| 31-40 miles | 10 | 9 |
| 41-50 miles | 4 | 9 |
| 51-75 miles | 4 | 3 |
| 76-100 miles | 3 | 2 |
| Over 100 miles | 4 | 3 |
| Previous visits: | | |
| None | 73 | 57 |
| One | 17 | 16 |
| More than one | 10 | 27 |

Source: Seren (1986a).

non-entrants showed no significant differences (Table 7.11). It would seem that manual workers are not, immediately at least, deterred by the admission charges; it is more the case that they do not arrive at the sites in the first place. However, persons not on holiday are found disproportionately amongst non-entrants, although this effect was small. More sizeable was the effect of repeat visiting; over a quarter of non entrants had visited the site previously on more than one occasion, compared to one in ten entrants. It may be that in some part that visitors are deterred by admission fees because they have already paid to experience the historic sites, and do not consider that paying a second time will bring them sufficiently extra benefit to warrant payment.

Further evidence on visitors' attitudes to pricing can be gained from studies of sites outside of Wales. One such study is the 'Schlackman' report for the Department of the Environment (Jones, 1984). This report considered pricing at Hampton Court and the Tower of London; clearly, these are exceptional monuments in terms of international importance. At Hampton Court visitors do not pay on entry, but only to visit the State Apartments, for which a fee of two pounds was charged at the date of survey. At the Tower of London an entry fee of three pounds was charged at the date of survey, with a further charge for visitors to the Jewel House. As Table 7.12 shows most of those who had paid to visit these monuments thought that the fee represented 'good value' or 'very good value'. This is to be expected as these are exceptional monuments, with widely known reputations. The views of the visitors to Hampton Court who did not visit the Apartments may be regarded as a comparison on pricing with those who did visit the Apartments. Clearly, from Table 7.12, the non-visitors contained a greater proportion who thought that the entrance fee was 'not such good value'; a difference which is highly significant statistically. Likewise, a smaller proportion of visitors to the Tower than to Hampton Court thought that the fee was 'very good value'; this difference is highly significant statistically and may derive from the higher fee charged at the Tower. Visitors who turned away from the Tower were not interviewed. Of the minority of visitors to the Tower of London who thought that the admission price was 'not such good value' or was 'poor value', fewer than a third thought that the fee was 'too expensive' (Jones, 1984). Fewer than one in ten found the Tower uninteresting. The most common reason given was that an all inclusive price would have been preferred; these visitors disliked being asked to pay again if they wished to visit the Jewel House. However, the majority of visitors who did not visit the Jewel House did so, they reported, not because it was too expensive, but because the queues were too long. In contrast, the minority finding the admission fee 'not such good value' or 'poor value' at Hampton Court mostly thought that the admission fee was too expensive.

Surveys of visitors to National Trust properties confirm a view of price inelasticity. The views of visitors on value for money and their overall satisfaction with their visit

Table 7.12.
Visitors' reactions to admission prices at two major London properties

| | HAMPTON COURT: | | TOWER OF LONDON | |
|---|---|---|---|---|
| | Visited apartments | Not visited apartments | All visitors | Visitors from North America |
| N = | 145 % | 117 % | 340 % | 115 % |
| Visitors thinking price is: | | | | |
| Very good value | 29 | 8 | 9 | 18 |
| Good value | 43 | 35 | 64 | 63 |
| Fairly good value | 17 | 23 | 13 | 11 |
| Not such good value | 10 | 28 | 10 | 5 |
| Poor value | 1 | 2 | 1 | 0 |
| Could not say | 0 | 4 | 0 | 0 |

Source: Jones (1984).

have been shown to be independent of the admission price charged, and possibly (in terms of satisfaction) related positively to the admission charge (Table 7.13), and not, as would be expected, to be inversely related. In interpreting these findings the relationship of quality of property and admission charge should not be ignored. Higher charges may well be associated with more to see. Similarly, it should not be assumed that members of the two British National Trusts necessarily object to commercial policies (Table 7.14).

Two surveys in Ireland confirm the British experience that pricing at sites has not necessarily been the most important deterrent to visitors of the 1980s. At Powerscourt upwards of seven out of ten visitors, both day trippers and tourists, found the entrance charges 'reasonable', and only one in five found these charges high. In terms of the hypothetical maximum adult charge they would pay, day trippers differed from tourists, but not consistently. Whereas tourists were prepared to pay more to visit the gardens at Powerscourt this was not the case for visits to the waterfall at the site (Bord Failte, 1981). Similarly,

Table 7.13.
National Trust visitors' perceptions of value of admission
charges paid

(Data from 1977 and 1978 visitor surveys combined)

|  |  | Admission prices seen as: | | | |
|  | N | Very good value % | Reasonable value % | Poor value % | Did not pay % |
| --- | --- | --- | --- | --- | --- |
| Level of price: | | | | | |
| Low price | 2,032 | 34 | 59 | 4 | 3 |
| Medium price | 1,342 | 34 | 59 | 4 | 3 |
| High price | 1,158 | 30 | 59 | 7 | 4 |

|  | N | Very satisfied % | Satisfied % | Dissatis-fied/ Very dissatis-fied % | No opinion % |
| --- | --- | --- | --- | --- | --- |
| Level of price: | | | | | |
| Low price | 1,555 | 65 | 33 | 1 | 1 |
| Medium price | 1,125 | 67 | 29 | 1 | 1 |
| Higher price | 748 | 76 | 23 | 1 | 1 |

Source: Mass Observation (U.K.) Ltd. (1978).


Table 7.14.
Views of the National Trust for Scotland's membership on
commercial policies

|  | Strongly object to commercial policies % | Dislike commercial policies % | Accept commercial policies in moderation % | Approve of commercial policies on practical grounds % |
| --- | --- | --- | --- | --- |
| New members | 1 | 5 | 43 | 51 |
| All members | 1 | 6 | 48 | 45 |

Source: McGrath (1982).

at Fota Island only a quarter of visitors found the entrance
charges high; and the main reason for not visiting the house
was not that the admission charge was too expensive but, for
nearly half of the non-visitors, that they had insufficient
time to make this visit (Research Surveys of Ireland Ltd,
1983).

Survey evidence suggests that visitors to museums and
galleries in England would generally be prepared to pay for
admission, and, where charges are already levied, to pay
more (Table 7.15). This applies particularly at national

Table 7.15.
**Museum and gallery visitors' opinions of admissions prices**

At free museums:

|  | All visitors | Visitors at local authority museums | Visitors at national museums |
|---|---|---|---|
| N = | 1,021 | 282 | 739 |
|  | % | % | % |
| Would not have come if charged | 12 | 18 | 12 |
| Depends how much | 16 | 29 | 15 |
| Would still have come | 70 | 51 | 72 |
| Do not know | 2 | 2 | 2 |

Where admission charges made:

|  | Norwich Castle | York Castle | Bath Roman Baths and Pump Room |
|---|---|---|---|
| N = | 114 | 105 | 107 |
|  | % | % | % |
| Charges: |  |  |  |
| Less than expected | 54 | 7 | 4 |
| About as expected | 43 | 61 | 42 |
| More than expected | 4 | 30 | 47 |
| Do not know | 0 | 2 | 7 |
| Adult charge: | 25p | £1.00 | £1.20 |
|  | % | % | % |
| Worth the charge | 99 | 100 | 93 |
| Not worth the charge | 1 | 0 | 7 |
| Would pay more | 84 | 65 | 48 |

Source: English Tourist Board Market Research Department
(1982).

261

Table 7.16.
Museum and gallery visitors' preparedness to pay admission charges to museums

|  | All visitors | Visitors to local authority museums | Visitors to national museums |
|---|---|---|---|
| N = | 1,347 | 608 | 739 |
|  | % | % | % |
| Levels of adult charges: |  |  |  |
| Prepared to pay £1.00 | 65 | 52 | 68 |
| Prepared to pay £1.50 | 34 | 30 | 36 |
| Prepared to pay £2.00 | 15 | 10 | 17 |
| Prepared to pay £2.50 | 10 | 3 | 11 |

Source: English Tourist Board Market Research Department (1982).

museums, which, in terms of the museums surveyed, had the largest collections. But Table 7.15 shows clearly that even local museums may be able to charge, although the size of their charge is likely to need to be less than that for entry to the national museums if a significant decline in visitor numbers is not to be induced (Table 7.16). As at the Cadw sites, a majority of museum visitors thought that the public should be charged for admission to museums and galleries (Table 7.17). At the same time, aged persons, school children and students were seen as varying exceptions to this general view.

Evidence from the Isle of Man, however, suggests some caution is apposite in assuming that entry to all heritage sites can be charged for. Whereas support was found amongst Island residents for charging for admission to the Island's Wildlife Park, both residents and tourists to the Island objected in large proportion to charging for admission to the Island's National Glens (Table 7.18). Whereas entry is presently free at the latter natural heritage sites, but not at the former, in the past charges were also levied at some of the former sites too. The difference in opinions on pricing between the two types of natural heritage sites is irrespective of public awareness of the need to conserve and manage both the Glens and the Wildlife Park (Prentice, 1986, 1988a, 1988b; Prentice and Prentice, 1987).

Reactions to pricing have not been systematically investigated in terms of the benefits to be gained from visits, nor by the purpose of visits. Few studies of this kind exist. Schools visits have been locally surveyed to find out how much teachers would be prepared for each child to pay for their visit to a stately home (Cooper and Latham, 1985). The distribution was bimodal, but most teachers thought that a charge of 30p to 50p (pence) per child to be appropriate (Table 7.19). Information of this kind for

Table 7.17.
Museum and gallery visitors' views on charging for admission
to museums and galleries

|  | All visitors | Visitors to local authority museums | Visitors to national museums |
|---|---|---|---|
| N = | 1,347 | 608 | 739 |
|  | % | % | % |
| Public: |  |  |  |
| Public should pay | 61 | 75 | 58 |
| Public should not pay for admission | 34 | 20 | 37 |
| Do not know | 5 | 5 | 5 |
| Senior citizens should: |  |  |  |
| Pay full rate | 5˙ | 5 | 5 |
| Half rate | 38 | 58 | 33 |
| No charge | 55 | 37 | 59 |
| Do not know | 2 | 0 | 2 |
| School children should: |  |  |  |
| Pay full rate | 1 | 1 | 1 |
| Half rate | 36 | 59 | 31 |
| No charge | 61 | 40 | 66 |
| Do not know | 2 | 0 | 2 |
| Students should: |  |  |  |
| Pay full rate | 8 | 10 | 8 |
| Pay half | 52 | 66 | 49 |
| No charge | 38 | 24 | 41 |
| Do not know | 2 | 0 | 4 |

Source: English Tourist Board Market Research Department
(1982).

other market segments is unknown, other than from the Irish
studies. This lack of knowledge is surprising, and needs
overcoming if our understanding of reactions to pricing at
heritage sites is to be developed.


Guidelines for a pricing policy

Private sector agencies responsible for heritage sites
clearly have to keep revenue generation as a central
objective of any pricing strategy. But much the same is
true for their public sector equivalents. Admissions income
will remain central to the public sector funding by central
government as long as the State monuments are not expected

Table 7.18.
Perceptions of charging for admission to 'natural' heritage sites on the Isle of Man

'Admission charges should be made at the (Wildlife) Park to help meet costs'

| | Strongly agree | Agree | No strong feelings | Disagree | Strongly disagree | N |
|---|---|---|---|---|---|---|
| | % | % | % | % | % | |
| Island residents (a) | 15 | 70 | 6 | 8 | 1 | 757 |

'People should pay an admission charge to the Glens'

| | Strongly agree | Agree | No strong feelings | Disagree | Strongly disagree | N |
|---|---|---|---|---|---|---|
| | % | % | % | % | % | |
| Rural residents (a) | 4 | 13 | 6 | 43 | 34 | 388 |
| Urban residents (a) | 2 | 13 | 7 | 42 | 36 | 912 |
| Summer visitors to Island (b) | 0 | 11 | 13 | 61 | 15 | 424 |

Note: (a) household survey; (b) visitor survey in the Glens.

Sources: Prentice, 1986, 1988a, 1988b;
         Prentice and Prentice, 1987.


Table 7.19.
School teachers' perceptions of acceptable charges per pupil for a half day visit to a stately home

| | Acceptable charges: | | | | | |
|---|---|---|---|---|---|---|
| | up to 25p | 30-50p | 60-90p | £1.00 | £1.20p to £2.00p | £5.00 |
| | % | % | % | % | % | % |
| Schools: | | | | | | |
| Junior/First | 5 | 54 | 15 | 22 | 3 | 0 |
| Middle | 16 | 53 | 2 | 27 | 2 | 0 |
| Secondary/Upper | 11 | 46 | 9 | 26 | 5 | 2 |
| Six Form College | 14 | 57 | 14 | 14 | 0 | 0 |
| All (N = 284) | 11 | 52 | 10 | 23 | 4 | * |

Note: Percentages summate across table;  * = less than 1%.

Source: Cooper and Latham (1985).

to be solely supported by the taxpayer. Despite the
opportunities taken by some museums to broaden their income
base beyond admissions income alone, the importance of
admissions income to museums remains substantial. If the
public sector were to develop interpretative and other
facilities comparable to these museums, admissions income
would still remain important. In their feasibility study
for the Scottish Mining Museum, PEIDA showed that the
proportion of total income represented by admissions income
for five existing industrial museums varied between 82 per
cent and 42 per cent (see Table 7.20). It should be
remembered that these are sites with interpretative and
other facilities generally far more developed than those of
the public sector monuments funded by central government.


Table 7.20.
Sources of income of selected museums

|  | Beamish | Tramway | Ironbridge | Avoncroft | Quarry Bank Mill |
|---|---|---|---|---|---|
|  | (1981) % | (1980) % | (1978) % | (1981) % | (1980) % |
| Admissions | 82 | 42 | 79 | 75 | 55 |
| Retail | 11 | 22 | - | 16 | 28 |
| Catering | 4 | 18 | - | 3 | 9 |
| Other | 3 | 18 | 21 | 6 | 8 |

Source: PEIDA (1983).


The importance of admissions income has, however, been
recently questioned in an English Heritage manual for the
presentation and interpretation of archaeological
excavations (Binks et al., 1988). In the manual the
following advise is given regarding charging for site
admission by general visitors,

> Providing visitors have enjoyed the presentation you
> give them, they are more likely to give you a donation,
> and spend on publications and souvenirs, if admission is
> free or the fee low (Binks et al., 1988, p. 76).

For visits by groups of school children similar advice is
given regarding souvenir purchase,

> If some return on staff and material costs is needed it
> could be made through shop sales - most children come
> with pocket money to spend on pens, pencils etc.
>                               (Binks et al., 1988, p. 73).

No evidence is given in support of these views in the manual
and in this context they may at best be regarded as specific
to archaeological digs and like sites.

Accounting criticism of another part of the leisure sector has, in the 1980s, focused further attention on leisure pricing generally. The Audit Inspectorate (1983) were concerned at, what they considered to be, inadequate managerial accounting and information in the management of leisure centres by local authoritites. The Inspectorate reported that decisions appeared to have been taken by local authority committees as to the range and mix of facilities without reference to the revenue consequences, especially in catering. Frequently, policies were found to be uncosted. The Inspectorate found that decisions on pricing were based on what comparable providers of facilities were charging, (that is, an intuitive realisation of cross elasticity) but were unrelated to a consideration of what specific users would pay, or to the cost of providing particular facilities. The Inspectorate observed that the relationship between marketing and pricing was often unappreciated by the decision-takers, the elected members. The management practices of authorities were found to be rarely compared, or their effectiveness measured. An implicit policy of nearly covering inflation every year was identified, with the inevitable consequence over a number of years of falling real charges.

Techniques for determining prices tend implicitly to ignore the distributive consequences of this decision. Our earlier discussion has noted the merit good, distributional and intergenerational objections to pricing at heritage sites, and these considerations should properly provide a critique for the techniques presented now. Similarly, pricing is properly seen as only one part of the marketing mix of product, place, promotion and price, each of which needs to be considered in an overall marketing strategy. The Wales Tourist Board's Welcome Approach, for example, demonstrates a strategic approach of this kind, focusing particularly on intuitive cross elasticities (Wardley, 1985). Certain questions pertain in particular. Does the visitor get value for money at the site? Does the pricing structure deter any visitors? Does the site meet with, or exceed, the visitor's expectations? Does the visitor find the site pleasant, enjoyable and relaxing? Does the site entertain, educate, stimulate, intrigue or provide some sort of lasting experience for the visitors? Does the site appeal to as wide a range of visitors as possible? Does the site have limited appeal in certain weather conditions or do other factors limit visitor numbers? Does the visitor find the site easy and convenient to visit? Does the site open at times and periods most suitable to visitors? Finally, but of great importance, does the visitor leave the site wanting to come back again, and wanting to tell others about it?

Questions of this kind can be operationalised for pricing in a manner suggested by Baker and Gordon (1975) in their Aonach Mor skiing centre evaluation. Central to Baker and Gordon's technique was the presentation and assessment of options. Each option was assessed in terms of the number of user tickets needed to be sold in order to recover the investment's capital cost: these were expressed as REWUDs,

Required Equivalent User Days. The numbers of REWUDs necessary to amortise the capital investment for twelve alternative installations were computed under different assumptions for ticket prices, winter and summer demand, weather conditions and rates of return. Baker and Gordon were then able to ask whether these REWUDs were feasible, particularly in view of experience at other sites. The decision takers were critical in this judgement, using their experience guided by what the options involved. As the consultants explained, 'The purpose of our model has been to compute the number of users required on a daily basis to amortise the original capital investment under a variety of assumptions - in other words the reader is asked to assess if it is reasonable to expect a given level of demand rather than having to forecast a level of demand and then computing its consequences' (Baker and Gordon, 1975, p.47) (emphasis added). Applications of this kind, defining a range of outcomes and their dependence on critical assumptions have been developed over the past two decades, and a range of models are available (e.g. Baum and Carlson, 1974; Clarke and Prentice, 1982).

Specific techniques to set prices include cost-plus, follow the leader, product analysis and contribution targets (Hill, 1985). Cost-plus is probably the most widely used technique in the private sector generally, but is unsatisfactory in several ways. The technique requires the identification of direct costs, adding overheads and then a profit percentage. It is unsatisfactory as the price in large part depends upon how overheads are apportioned and takes no account of whether a higher price would be acceptable. The technique also leads to price increases when demand falls and decreases when increases in demand occur. This is because the overheads are spread over the volume of sales, such as admission tickets sold. Follow the leader, as an alternative technique, is simple: if there is a market leader the supplier simply asks himself whether to price his product slightly more expensive or cheaper. Product analysis may be applicable as an alternative if the attribute 'purchased' by consumers visiting a site can be defined. This technique then prices these attributes if purchased elsewhere, and gives an idea of pricing for the particular bundle of attributes offered by a site. Contribution targets are an alternative approach; this technique requires an understanding of the way costs change and the impact of sales volumes on contributions to meeting these costs. Contribution is defined as the difference between sales value and the marginal cost of sales. Marginal cost is defined by the amount to which aggregate costs are changed if the volume of output, visits in our case, is increased or decreased by one unit. Typically the marginal cost is the unit variable cost, that cost which is affected by variations in volume. The contribution of total sales must in aggregate exceed fixed costs if a trading surplus is to be obtained. Both the contribution targets and product analysis techniques imply differentiation between consumers in terms of pricing: different types of consumers, or consumers at different places, may be charged differently. Critically, therefore, once again we return to questions of marketing mix and visitor segmentation as fundamentals of pricing policy. These alternatives apply equally to the public as to the private sector, although the former is not dependent directly on profitability for continued operation.

## Conclusions

It is difficult to generalise from the somewhat varied studies of visitor reaction to pricing. However, several comments can usefully be made. Firstly, there is a general expectation to pay for admission to at least major historic sites, despite the public ownership of many sites. Secondly, the attitudinal evidence concurs with the findings of demand curve analyses, namely, at the prices generally charged for admission to heritage sites in Britain that demand is generally inelastic to price. However, the more expensively priced sites in terms of admission may be an exception. Thirdly, most studies consider paying visitors only, and ignore the deterred visitor. Such studies are unable to offer a comparison with non-entrants to sites. Where deterred visitors have been surveyed, reasons other than price seem generally to be responsible for deterrence. These conclusions do however need to be considered within the general context of visitor characteristics at sites: visitors are often holiday-makers and disproportionately persons from higher socio-economic groups. In particular, any substantial broadening of visitor profiles in terms of purpose of visit or socio-economic status may alter this perspective of inelasticity to the prices generally charged for admission. At present we only have substantial evidence for current visitors and analysis frequently generalised across all visitors and across types of sites from limited numbers of case examples. Also lacking is any comprehensive analysis of the reasons why non-visitors or infrequent visitors do not visit heritage sites. Despite the substantial body of material discussed our understanding of the role of pricing at heritage sites remains elementary.

Conclusions about inelasticity and the unimportance of admission prices are not universally valid at sites with more expensive admission fees. Visitors to Hampton Court and, in particular, to Caernarfon Castle, demonstrate that at higher admission fees deterrence results in part from price, and at the latter site, in substantial part. The generality of this effect is unknown, as is the point at which demand ceases to be inelastic to price. However, the attitudinal evidence may suggest that this point is not far away from these higher prices. More studies are needed, in particular considering the attitudes of deterred visitors. A further point is that increases in admission charges could generally be made, if the pattern of demand remained much the same, without further undesirable distributive consequences in terms of disproportionately excluding the socially disadvantaged. Visitors of the latter kind are generally non-visitors rather than visitors deterred at the

site by price: lack of car ownership, lack of disposable
income and different leisure tastes may be the answer to the
under-representation of much households as visitors to
historic sites. The issue of their exclusion by price only
arises if more determined policies to get such groups to
sites are to be pursued. Finally, a further comment
concerns a deficiency in the literature on attitudes. We do
not know the effect of deterrence by price on the propensity
of people to visit other historic sites. It may be that an
affect of finding prices too high at a major monument is to
suggest to the 'lost' visitor that all heritage sites are
too highly priced. At present the importance of this
determinant on visitor numbers is unknown, and is worthy of
research.


## References

Audit Inspectorate (Department of the Environment) (1983).
Development and operation of leisure centres. Selected
case studies. London: Her Majesty's Stationery Office.
Baker, M. J. and Gordon, A. W. (1975). Aonach Mor. A
feasibility study. Baker, Gordon (Business Research) Ltd.
Baum, S. and Carlson, R. C. (1974). Multi-goal optimisation
as managerial science. Omega, 2, 607-623.
Binks, G., Dyke, J., and Dagnall, P. (1988). Visitors
welcome. London: Her Majesty's Stationery Office.
Bord Failte (1981). Powerscourt visitor survey, 1981. A
research and planning report. Dublin: Bord Failte.
Bovaird, A. G., Tricker, M. J. and Stoakes, R. (1984).
Recreation management and pricing. The effect of charging
policy on demand at countryside recreation sites.
Aldershot: Gower.
Bovaird, T. and Tricker, M. (1985). Demand elasticity and
pricing policy for major recreation facilities:
econometric approaches. Paper to the ESRC Urban and
Regional Economics Group, seminar at Gregynog Hall, Powys,
June 1985.
British Tourist Authority (1976). Historic properties in
Great Britain. A study of resources and their
utilisation. London: British Tourist Authority.
Brown, J. (1983). Henebion Cymru - Historic monuments of
Wales. Ways of making them more enjoyable, more
enlightening, more profitable. (The Brown Report).
Leigh, Worcester: John Brown Tourism Services.
Clarke, M. and Prentice, R. C. (1982). Exploring decisions
in public policy making: strategic allocation, individual
allocation and simulation. Environment and Planning, A,
14, 499-524.
Cooper, C. P. and Latham, J. (1985). The market for
educational visits to tourist attractions. Dorset:
Department of Tourism and Field Sciences, Dorset Institute
of Higher Education.
Coopers Lybrand Associates Ltd. (1979). Rufford Country
Park marketing study. (A report to the Countryside
Commission and Nottinghamshire County Council).
Cheltenham: Countryside Commission.

English Tourist Board, Market Research Department, and NOP Market Research Ltd. (1982). Visitors to museums survey of 1982. London: English Tourist Board.

English Tourist Board (1982). English heritage monitor. London: English Tourist Board.

Hendon, W. S. (1982). The economics of historic houses: the sources of admission income. The Historic Houses Project. Akron, Ohio: Centre for Urban Studies, University of Akron.

Hill, R. H. (1985). Pricing principles for a small buisiness, Administrator, December 1985, pp 2-4.

Hirshleifer, J. (1984). Price theory and applications. Third edition. Englewood Cliffs, N. J.: Prentice Hall.

Jones, S. (1984). Research on public reaction to pricing policy among visitors to Hampton Court Palace and H. M. Tower of London. Summary Report. (Prepared for the Department of the Environment). London: Schlackman Group Ltd.

Mass Observation (U.K.) Ltd. (1978). National Trust visitors survey 1978. Part 1. Report of principal findings. London: Mass Observation (U.K.) Ltd.

McCallum, J. D. and Adams, J. G. L. (1980). Charging for countryside recreation: a review with implications for Scotland. Transactions of the Institute of British Geographers, n.s., 5, 350-368.

McGrath, C. (1982). Survey of members' attitudes and interests. Edinburgh: The National Trust for Scotland.

Mears, W. (1976a). Survey of visitors to tourist attractions 1974. Report 6, Chepstow Castle. Cardiff: Wales Tourist Board.

Mears, W. (1976b). Survey of visitors to tourist attractions 1974. Report 7, Dan yr Ogof Caves. Cardiff: Wales Tourist Board.

Mears, W. (1976c). Surveys of visitors to tourist attractions 1974. Report 8, Penscynor Bird Gardens. Cardiff: Wales Tourist Board.

Mears, W. (1976d). Surveys of visitors to tourist attractions 1974. Report 9, Welshpool and Llanfair Light Railway. Cardiff: Wales Tourist Board.

O'Hare, M. (1975). Why do people go to museums? The effect of prices and hours on museum utilization. Museum, 27, 135-146.

Owen, E. and Mears, W. (1974a). Survey of visitors to tourist attractions 1973. Report 3, Caernarfon Castle. Cardiff: Wales Tourist Board.

Owen, E. and Mears, W. (1974b). Surveys of visitors to tourist attractions 1973. Report 5, Welsh Folk Museum, St. Fagans. Cardiff: Wales Tourist Board.

Owen, E. and Mears, W. (1974c). Surveys of visitors to tourist attractions 1973. Report 4, The Talyllyn Railway. Cardiff: Wales Tourist Board.

PEIDA, Planning and Economic Consultants with Thorburn Associates (1983). Scottish Mining Museum. Development and marketing study. Edinburgh: PEIDA.

Prentice, R. C. (1986). Rural residents' leisure use of Manx National Glens. St Johns: Isle of Man Forestry, Mines and Lands Board.

Prentice, R. C. (1988a). The domestic market for the Curraghs Wildlife Park. St Johns: Isle of Man Department of Agriculture, Fisheries and Forestry.

Prentice, R. C. (1988b). Amenity resources and tourism: the present role of the National Glens and the Wildlife Park as summer tourist attractions. St Johns: Isle of Man Department of Agriculture, Fisheries and Forestry.

Prentice, R. C., and Prentice, M. M. (1987). Urban residents' leisure use of Manx National Glens. St Johns: Isle of Man Department of Agriculture, Fisheries and Forestry.

Public Attitude Surveys Research Ltd. (1985). Attractions to Wales survey. All sites - day/staying visitors. (PAS 11435). (Prepared for Wales Tourist Board). High Wycombe, Bucks: Public Attitude Surveys Research Ltd.

Research Surveys of Ireland Ltd. (1983). Bord Failte - Fota Island study. Dublin: Research Surveys of Ireland Ltd.

Salvatore, D. (1986). Microeconomics. Theory and applications. New York: Macmillan.

Seren (1986a). Herbert, D. T., Prentice, R. C., Thomas, C. J., and Prentice, M. M. Pricing policy and visitors' satisfaction at Cadw's sites. Swansea: Social Economic Research and Environment, Department of Geography, University College of Swansea.

Seren (1986b). Herbert, D. T., Prentice, R. C., Thomas, C. J., Edwards, J. A., Humphrys, G., and Prentice, M. M. Easter 1986 visitor survey. Final report. Swansea: Social Economic Research and Environment, Department of Geography, University College of Swansea.

Seren (1985c). Herbert, D. T., Prentice, R. C., Thomas, C. J., and Prentice, M. M. General survey at Cadw sites. Summer 1986. Swansea: Social Economic Research and Environment, Department of Geography, University College of Swansea.

Snaith, R. (1975). What price heritage? Estimating the price elasticity of demand for National Trust properties (and some related issues), in Searle, G. A. C. (Ed). Recreational economics and analysis. pp. 141-159. Harlow: Longman.

Stoakes, R. (1979). Oil prices and countryside recreation travel. Countryside Commision working paper number 20. Cheltenham: Countryside Commission.

Wardley, J. R. (1983). The Welcome Approach. A tourism development report. Cardiff: Wales Tourist Board.

# 8 Historic sites and their local environments

J ARWEL EDWARDS

## Introduction

The environments of historic sites, whether natural or man-made and whether internal or external in location, provide the basic reasons for the attraction of visitors. The term environment has traditionally been concerned with the natural/physical elements of land, air, water, flora and fauna. More recently, however, Lerner(1977) has argued that the term should be extended to encompass 'people, their creations and the social, economic and cultural conditions that affect their lives'. This chapter will adopt this broader perspective and concern itself with the identification and analysis of three key environmental elements, namely physical, socio-cultural and economic impacts of visitors at historic sites and monuments.

Studies of the environments of historic sites are few in number (P.A.S., 1985) in comparison with more general tourism impact studies. This is because many sites are in public ownership where the traditional concern has been with preservation and conservation activities. The responsible organisations had limited marketing and publicity budgets, few marketing skills and were not required to adopt measures to enhance significantly higher visitor attendance. Historic sites, with few exceptions, occupied a low public and research profile. In contrast, the more general field of tourism has generated much interest which reflects the economic and social significance of tourism, especially mass tourist movements. Secondly, there are considerable contrasts in the balance of types of impact studies between tourist and historic site studies. In the former, Mathieson and Wall (1982) argue that 'a concentration upon economic questions has occurred at the expense of research on physical and social impacts of tourist developments'. In the specific study area of historic sites, the impact studies have concentrated more upon physical than social and economic dimensions. However, changes are occurring which are likely to reduce the above contrasts. The growing popularity of certain historic sites has imposed a range of pressures which require positive planning and management responses in order to conserve and preserve their attractions. This may be expensive and governments are concerned to increase income to meet higher costs. A second, more indirect, pressure has come from the example provided by the aggressive marketing methods of owners of many private historic sites which have helped to boost attendance figures and income. Private owners in the United Kingdom also showed a major organisational initiative· in banding together in 1973 to form the Historic Houses Association to act as a powerful lobby on their behalf. There is a determination by governments to extend such methods and success to publicly-owned sites. The educational, leisure and economic benefits of increased knowledge of and attendance at historic sites are seen by governments, whether national, regional or local in scale, as most worthwhile.

## Is there an environmental/physical cost?

The inherent conflict between preservation and access is an inescapable feature of the National Trust's work. The more the Trust succeeds in the proselytising side of its work, the more difficult its central obligation to preserve is likely to become. (National Trust, 1979).

At the heart of this conflict are the growing pressures imposed by visitors upon historic sites and monuments. The scale of these pressures is very considerable. For example, in 1987 the Tower of London attracted 2.3 million visitors, Edinburgh Castle 967,424 visitors and Caernarfon Castle 259,506 visitors (B.T.A./E.T.B., 1988).
A key concept in the relationship between preservation and visitor access referred to above is that of carrying capacity. This has been defined by Lime and Stanley (1971) as '... the character of use that can be supported over a specified time by an area developed at a certain level without causing excessive damage to either the physical environment or the experience of the visitor'. The concept is based on the idea that a site is suitable for use by only a strictly defined number of people. Early researchers sought to identify and measure the innate visitor capacity of recreation resources. This view was most prominent when the concern was more with resource protection than with the management of visitors (Clark, 1974). It was felt that attendance beyond a pre-set figure would diminish the attraction and experience of a site (Countryside Commission,

1977). However, it has become recognised that various
parameters may change and alter capacities. Gradually the
consensus of opinion that has emerged is that attempts to
identify a specific and precise carrying capacity of an
attraction are futile (Mercer,1979). As McKaskey (1975)
wrote of the experience of Colonial Williamsburg: 'New
limits are set and then surpassed. As they are succeeded,
old methods of interpretation and presentation have been
upgraded, and former procedures for controlling the flow
through the village altered'.

Visitor impact has been identified by OECD as one of four
key activities in generating environmental stress (Pearce,
1981). Such stresses can be subdivided between natural and
man-made environments (Lerner, 1977; Mathieson and Wall,
1982) and between external and internal environments. This
section will concern itself with the identification of
problems and management responses to these divisions.

Serious damage can and does occur to historic site
environments as a result of excessive visitor pressures.
Bates' pioneering study (1935) on the effects of trampling
on vegetation on and around footpaths subsequently
stimulated considerable research into this field (Mitchell,
1980). The Countryside Commission has been particularly
active in such research in the external environment. Its
study of Tarn Hows (1977) has played a crucial role in the
understanding of the impacts of wear and tear upon heavily
used areas of the countryside. Further work was undertaken
by Coppock (1980) who identified visitor impacts as
involving destruction or modification of habitat;
destruction or modification of landscape (natural and/or
man-made), including visual impact; destruction or
disturbance of flora and fauna, geology and soils; and
pollution of land, air and water.

Cohen (1978) has also identified four principal factors on
which the physical impact of tourism depends the intensity
of tourist site-use; the resilience of the eco-system; the
time perspective of the developers; and the transformational
character of touristic developments.

Examples of visitor impacts on the physical environment
are numerous. The damage that could be caused to
archaeological sites was noted by the Cornwall Committee
(1983). The consequences of ploughing, animal damage, hedge
or stone wall removal, quarrying or mining, the erection of
buildings, and the impacts of visitors were identified as
specific elements which could cause problems. These have
occurred at many sites including Silbury Hill, Long Man
prehistoric earthwork in Sussex, the Chalk Horse at
Uffington and, in particular, at two of Europe's major prehistoric sites, the Lascaux caves in Perigord, France and at
Stonehenge. The Lascaux caves were discovered in 1940 and
quickly became a major tourist attraction. However, the
large number of visitors so changed the atmosphere within
the caves that deterioration of the wall paintings began to
occur. As a result, the caves were closed to the public in

1963. In England, an English Heritage report (1985) identified the problems at Stonehenge:

> In the early 1960's when visitor numbers were between 300,000 and 400,000 a year, the turf within the circle had become so worn that it was necessary to replace it and gravel was laid to provide a more durable surface. By the mid 1970's it was clear that the gravel itself was causing damage as it adhered to visitors shoes as they climbed over the recumbent stones. In 1978, therefore, visitors were denied access to the stone circle to avoid further damage and the gravel was replaced with turf ... Visitor numbers reached ... 800,000 in 1977 ....
> (English Heritage, 1985, para. 2.2).

Conservation and preservation of the interiors of historic sites and monuments provides another field of concern. Jane Fawcett reviewed visitor erosion in the internal environment of cathedrals in a study for the English Tourist Board (1978). She commented:

> ... it is during the past decade that the drastic increase of visitors to cathedrals has set up a visible process of deterioration ... It would be ironical if these visitors in their search for history should be found to have destroyed history, but in my view this is what is happening.

Evidence of concern into environmental impacts at historic sites (as opposed to tourism in general or specific ecological impacts) emerged strongly during the 1970s as mass tourism and extended opening hours increased visitor numbers, In the United States McKaskey has highlighted the problems of the growing popularity of Colonial Williamsburg (1975). In the United Kingdom the problems of visitor pressure upon Stonehenge led the Department of the Environment to set up a Working Party whose Report, and a Memorandum of Dissent by some members of Salisbury District Council, was completed in 1979. The Government decided not to act upon the recommendations of that report, which has not been published . In addition to the work of Fawcett noted above, The National Trust (1979) observed that at least two dozen of its houses (e.g. Hardwick, Saltram, Dunster, Pole) and around ten gardens were suffering in some noticeable way from over-visiting. Wingperson (1979) also highlighted some of the issues, problems and controversial policy alternatives facing such popular attractions as Westminster Abbey, Stonehenge, Hadrian's Wall and Silbury Hill.

Management responses to the range of problems noted above have been varied. Two examples of external environment responses may be noted, the one from France, the other from the United Kingdom. In Lascaux, the extreme measure of permanent closure of the caves to visitors (with few exceptions and by prior permission) has been adopted. Instead, a new complex, Lascaux II, was opened in 1983 in

# Figure 8.1.
# Plan of Stonehenge

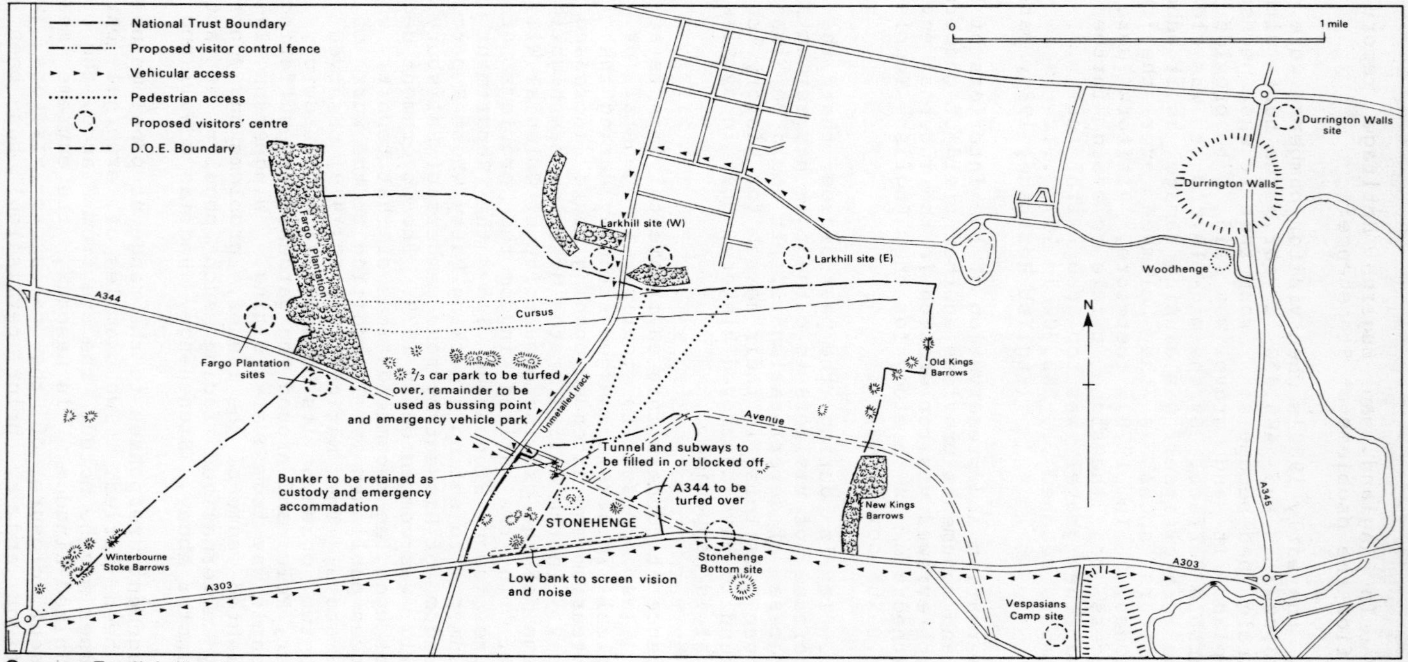

Legend:

- ——— National Trust Boundary
- ·········· Proposed visitor control fence
- ▲▲▲ Vehicular access
- ·········· Pedestrian access
- ◌◌◌ Proposed visitors' centre
- —·—· D.O.E. Boundary

Source: English Heritage

276

the caves of an adjacent quarry complex. This contains faithful reproductions of the paintings from two of the major galleries of the original Lascaux caves. It attracts large numbers of visitors.

In the United Kingdom, English Heritage re-examined (1985) the problems posed by the consequent wear and tear of the popularity of Stonehenge. In 1983, annual attendance figures averaged 600,000. Its report noted that there was no immediately apparent best long-term solution to the problems of Stonehenge. Rather, it identified a series of possible solutions relating to the landscape, roads and visitor facilities (Figure 8.1). In order to open up the landscape around Stonehenge, it was proposed that a network of paths be developed to give access to as many of the sites and monuments in the neighbourhood of Stonehenge; the interpretation facilities be extended; and that more sympathetic methods of controlling visitors and protecting the monument be implemented. The presentation of Stonehenge could be greatly improved if changes were considered to the two adjoining major roads, the A 303 and A 344: firstly at the A 303, a bank could be constructed along its northern side to screen off vehicles and to reduce noise; secondly regarding the A 344, three alternatives are considered, to be left open, which would satisfy local opinion but provide no solution to severe problems caused by its proximity to Stonehenge, to provide limited access only, to be completely closed. As for visitor facilities, a new visitor centre should be initially capable of handling at least one million visitors per annum, and of being further expanded. Because access to the monument is always likely to be restricted, consideration should be given to a reconstruction of Stonehenge at the visitor centre, but only if sited away from the monument. Eight possible sites for new visitor facilities are identified, in three groupings: 'near' sites, at present car park and at Stonehenge bottom; 'middle distance sites', to the west or south of Fargo Plantation, Larkhill East and Larkhill West; 'distant' sites, at Vespasian's Camp and Durrington Walls. By mid 1988, no firm decision had been taken on site selection.

A good example of an internal site management response is provided by the improved circulation system for viewing the Crown Jewels in the Tower of London (Murphy, 1985). Popular demand and over-crowding led to the introduction of a dual-circulation system so that visitors next to the showcases had to move rapidly while those on a raised, more distant platform moved more slowly (Figure 8. 2). This example also shows the methods by which carrying capacities may be increased without diminishing the quality of visitor enjoyment. More specific conservation approaches for the interiors of historic properties have been well established by The National Trust. This is a charitable organisation founded in 1885 in England and Wales specifically to conserve heritage properties. It is the guardian of over 300 major houses and gardens and its experience over many decades has now resulted in the publication of a manual of conservation and housekeeping of historic properties (National Trust, 1984). The acquisition, conservation and

Figure 8.2.
Visitor circulation at the Tower of London

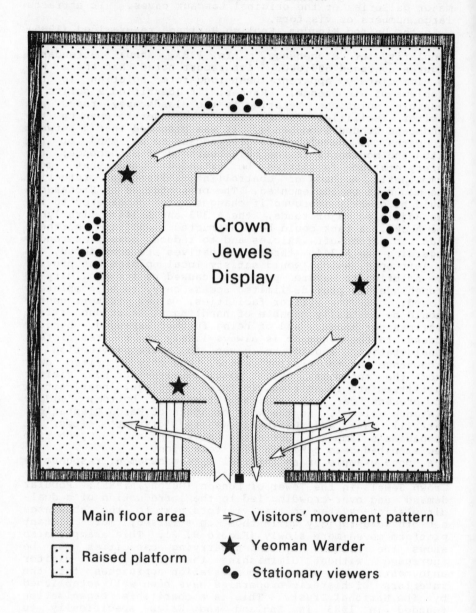

Main floor area    ⇨ Visitors' movement pattern

Raised platform    ★ Yeoman Warder

   •• Stationary viewers

Crown
Jewels
Display

restoration of many properties by The National Trust is not simply a task of physical restoration. There is also a concern for lifestyle and social structures. For example, one of the reasons for the acquisition by the Trust of the old country house of Erddig in the County of Clwyd, North Wales, was the detail of its social history.

Apart from specific measures such as those noted above, a broader range of management measures may be noted. For example, The National Trust (1979) has identified a range of methods of control which might need to be considered in the light of over-pressures from visitors, including: restricted advertising and publicity; differential pricing policies, e.g., (i) higher entrance charges at weekends, (ii) higher entrance charges at selected properties; restricted opening hours; timed entrance tickets; other methods, including (i) improved methods of routing visitors, (ii) reducing the size of visitor parties, (iii) increasing the number of room stewards; the development of complementary attractions; the development of information.

In the United States various management controls were identified by McKaskey (1975) in a paper highlighting the problems of visitor pressures at Williamsburg. These included the provision of Recreation Centres, Information Centres, free non-diesel circulating buses, more exhibitions, crafts shops and outdoor demonstrations, the strict control of group tour visits, extensive training programmes for escorts, hostesses and interpreters, and programmes of publicity, promotion and travel advertising.

In spite of the examples provided above, the knowledge of environmental/physical impacts at historic sites is but little developed. Indicative of this is that it was only in late 1987, under the aegis of ICOMOS (International Committee on Monuments and Sites), that English Heritage and The National Trust embarked upon a joint programme of investigation of the environmental impacts of visitors. English Heritage assumed responsibility for ruins and earthworks, The National Trust for the internal fabric of buildings and roofs, and both agreed to examine impacts upon selected gardens. The sites chosen by English Heritage include Stonehenge, Belsay, Dunstanburgh, Housesteads, Corfe and Tynemouth Castles.

Research into environmental impacts upon historic sites suffers from many of the weaknesses identified by Mathieson and Wall (1982) and Duffield and Walker (1984) in the field of more general tourist environmental impacts. These are that most studies have been partial, incorporating only a few elements of the environment and there has been a neglect of holistic studies; research has been topically uneven; there has been a failure to study and measure both cause and effect of impact, i.e. to measure the degree and intensity of use as well as the evaluation of change; studies have invariably been post hoc and few pre-impact patterns have been measured; and there has been a failure to develop a convincing theory/set of theories and/or models of environmental impact in spite of studies of individual sites.

There **is** encouragement, however, in that the specific studies of ICOMOS and of English Heritage in Stonehenge may, in time, provide the bases for the development of physical impact models. These have been developed in other fields. For example, Stankey's integrative model for carrying capacity in the wilderness (1972) or Kasperson's model for stress management (1969) are indicative of approaches which may be adopted in the light of the particular pressures imposed by visitors on the internal and external, natural and man-made environments of historic sites and buildings.

## Socio-cultural attitudes towards monuments

There is a virtual absence of literature both on the attitudes of residents to local monuments and of the impacts of sites upon the cultural life of the communities in which they are based. The relevant studies are those on tourism in general and the impact of particular expressions of tourism such as 'contrived' events (e.g. jousting tournaments) or second homes. Occasionally within this literature there are references to monuments which occur as elements of more general arguments for and against tourism. Most studies do not isolate cultural effects for special analysis but include them as part of a wider cost-benefit equation which is largely concerned with economic indicators.

Public attitudes towards tourism are invariably mixed. Some surveys (Getz, 1979; Market Opinion Research International, 1978; W.T.B., 1981) have found a strong set of favourable attitudes. Getz found that most people in the Badenoch/Strathspey area of Scotland were in favour of tourism though they were not wholly convinced that the truly local people derived much benefit from it. The Wales Tourist Board Survey (W.T.B., 1981) was of eight individual localities in Wales where 1077 in-depth interviews of residents were conducted. Amongst the main findings were that over two-fifths of the residents were very much in favour of tourists visiting their community, while only 3% stated categorically that they disliked the tourist presence. The support given by residents to tourism was based on rather generally defined economic factors (e.g. additional money for the community), whereas opposition related clearly to specific disadvantages (e.g. traffic congestion, crowded streets, difficulty in shopping, etc.). On balance, 63% of residents thought the benefits of tourism to the community outweighed the disadvantages, and only 7% thought to the contrary. The Economist Intelligence Unit (1984) concluded that most people wanted more tourists but would like to see them spread more evenly throughout the year and visiting a wider range of places and areas. Despite some personal and environmental drawbacks, British people generally agreed that tourism is financially necessary and conceptually desirable. Some of these studies contain comments of direct relevance to monuments. The Economic Intelligence Unit (1974) identified the view that without tourists many stately homes and monuments would not be as well preserved as they are and the English Tourist Board (1978b) found that when prompted people recognised the benefits of tourism to the preservation of buildings. More recently, the Chairman of English Heritage, Lord Montague of Beaulieu wrote:

> Elsewhere in the world, great houses have deteriorated. What a different scene there is in Britain. There are over 1700 historic buildings open to the public, attracting over 55 million visitors a year. As a result of welcoming visitors, our historic buildings are not only in better repair but have become Britain's top tourist attractions. (Alcock, 1986).

Not all local communities and residents welcome tourism. The concept of physical carrying capacity noted earlier may be complemented in the socio-cultural context by stress carrying capacity concepts. For example, Doxey (1975,1976) has developed an 'irridex' whose levels reflect progressive levels of changing attitudes to visitors, viz:

Level 1: EUPHORIA : Initial phase of development; visitors and investors welcome; little planning or control mechanism

Level 2: APATHY : Visitors taken for granted; contacts between residents and outsiders more formal (commercial); planning concerned mostly with marketing

Level 3: ANNOYANCE : Saturation points approached; residents have misgivings about tourist industry; policy makers attempt solutions via increasing infrastructure rather than limiting growth

Level 4: ANTAGONISM : Irritations overtly expressed; visitors seen as cause of all problems; planning now remedial but promotion increased to offset deteriorating reputation of destination

Level 5: FINAL : Recognition of loss of original environment in scramble to develop. If destination can cope, mass tourism will continue to thrive.

Antagonism may extend to the extreme of physical violence as is the case in, for example, Wales with the arson attacks upon the owners of second homes (Bollom, 1978). The direct relationships of such attacks with historic sites may appear to be tenuous, but it certainly exists within the context of culture concepts. Zelinsky (1973) has noted that cultural systems are three-dimensional, including first the three intrinsic components of artifacts, sociofacts and mentifacts; second, there are spatial components at different levels (regional, subregional); and, finally, there are subcultural components including occupation, social attitudes and values, ideologies. These complex dimensions of culture may and, in some cases do, inter-relate to provide a focus for the fears of some local residents that visitors, who may well be drawn to a local area to enjoy historic sites (amongst other attractions), can damage the historic but living local culture. Hence the occasional occurrence of violent reactions to visitors.

Not all cultural relationships are negative, however. One particular dimension of historic site development which may have a cultural impact is that consequent upon the growth of 'contrived attractions' (Cohen, 1978) or 'staged touristic situations' (Cohen, 1979). Cohen argued in (1972) that tourism, when achieving a large enough scale, tended to develop a recognisable ecological sub-system. He then proceeded (1978) to argue that the environmental dynamics of this sub-system consisted of 'a constant expansion at the margins and intensification at the mature core, leading to the creation of 'contrived' attractions both at the core (as 'natural' attractions decline) and the margins (to supplement meagre 'natural' attractions as tourism expands into less attractive regions)'.

Contrived and staged touristic attractions may be transitory or permanent. An example of the former would be the staging of events and performances by local organisations to depict, for example, medieval jousting tournaments, local folk dancing/singing traditions, or the re-creation in dramatic form of a local historical event and staged within the confines of a historic site to provide 'authenticity and atmosphere'. An example of the second would be more permanent creations, usually in the form of heritage museums and, in some cases, the permanent wearing of historic costumes within the confines of the museum. Their origins lie in the concern of Scandinavian social anthropologists during the inter-war years at the likely dilution and possible complete loss of their cultural heritage in the face of urbanisation and industrialisation. They conceived the idea of a folk museum,

A folk museum represents the life and culture of a nation, including the arts and crafts, and in particular the building crafts, of the complete community, and including in its illustration the activities of the mind and spirit - speech, drama, dance and music - as well as of the hand. Such museums are in two parts; galleries for the systematic display of the materials of life and culture, where the research student can study the details of folk life in exhibits emphasising the evolution and distribution of types, their chronology and many other problems. The environment of the national life is presented in the open-air section. As circumstances enjoin and funds permit, suitable houses of various dates and character, condemned to destruction for a variety of reasons, are rebuilt on the site: craft

workshops are brought together and illustrated, until
the complex of structures and their fittings presents a
picture of the evolution of society covering a period of
several hundred years. Furniture and furnishings occupy
their rightful place in houses; carts, ploughs and other
implements their place in sheds and barns. This is no
imaginary picture: it has been fully achieved on several
sites in the Scandinavian countries, where the influence
of the folk museum in improving the standard of taste
and maintaining the pride of the people in the best
traditions of their past has been remarkable. Such a
museum, indeed, comes to be a cultural centre for the
nation which it serves.

                    (National Museum of Wales, undated).

In the United Kingdom, the Welsh Folk Museum at St.
Fagans, near Cardiff, provides an excellent example of such
a contrived tourist space with a strong historic emphasis
(Figure 8.3). It attracted 247,000 visitors in 1987
(+25% on 1986). Among 22 buildings reconstructed at the
Museum is one from the 15th century, five from the 16th
(including the original St. Fagan's Castle), two from the
17th, seven from the 18th, seven from the 19th and one from
the 20th centuries. Bunratty Folk Park in Ireland,
strategically located to attract visitors entering or
leaving the country via Shannon Airport provides another
example. In 1987, the Jorvik Viking Centre in York
attracted 886,000 visitors to make it the seventh most
popular museum gallery in Britain. Industrial folk museums
have also been created - at Ironbridge in Shropshire
(293,000 visitors in 1987), and at Beamish in County Durham
(365,600 visitors in 1987), both in England. An urban
example is provided by the re-creation of Colonial
Williamsburg in Virginia, U.S.A.. Here, a largely abandoned
settlement has been rescued from continuing decline through
refurbishment, renovation and reconstruction. In addition,
an attempt has been made to recapture the lifestyle of
inhabitants during the 18th century.


## Economic impact of the historic site

The research literature in the more general field of tourism
is very extensive indeed and a recent appraisal by Mathieson
and Wall (1982) contains some thirty relevant sections.
They note a range of reasons for this interest: that
impacts are relatively easy to measure; that there are well-
established methodologies for their measurement; that much
relatively reliable and comparable data have been collected;
and that there is a belief that tourism can yield rapid and
considerable returns on investment. It can be a positive
force in remedying economic problems and in generating
economic development.
However, the literature which is specific to the economic
impacts of historic sites is negligible. It could be argued
that this is of limited consequence since Britain's historic
sites have become its top tourist attractions (Alcock, 1986)

283

Figure 8.3.
Diagrammatic layout of Welsh Folk Museum

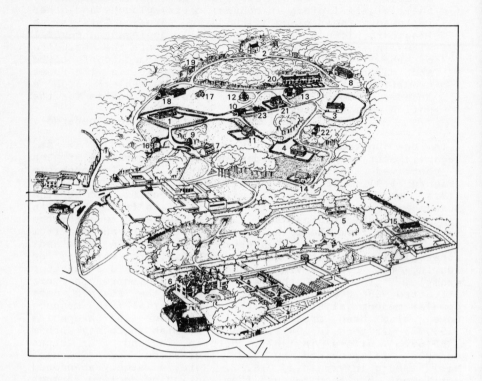

| 15th Century | 18th Century | 19th Century |
|---|---|---|
| 1 Hendre'r-ywydd Uchaf farmhouse | 9 Hendre Ifan Prosser Pigsty | 16 Melin Bompren |
| 16th Century | 10 Tollhouse | 17 Ewenny Pottery Kiln |
| 2 Y Garreg Fawr farmhouse | 11 Llainfadyn | 18 Tannery |
| 3 Cilewent | 12 Cockpit | 19 Gorse Mill |
| 4 Abernodwydd | 13 Smithy | 20 Rhyd-y-car Houses |
| 5 Stryt Lydan | 14 Capel Penrhiw | 21 Maestir School |
| 6 St. Fagan's Castle | 15 Esgair Moel | 22 Hayshed |
| 17th Century | | 20th Century |
| 7 Kennixton | | 23 Derwen Bakehouse |
| 8 Hendre Wen | | |

Source: National Museum of Wales, Welsh Folk Museum

and hence the literature pertaining to general economic
tourism impacts is automatically applicable to historic
sites. However, there are important areas of specific
research interest which need to be identified and evaluated,
and for which research is currently very limited and
variable. These include the cyclical nature of economic
impacts, the benefits and costs of visitors, and the
expenditure of visitors to historic sites.

The cyclic nature of tourism is of interest in the study
of the economics of historic sites. Such cycles may be
studied in three time-durations (Murphy, 1985): short-term,
medium-term and long-term. The benefits of tourism may be
studies under a wide range of headings but the most common
are those of expenditure analyses and economic multipliers.
Expenditure analyses are mostly concerned with actual

Table 8.1.
Tourist spending at historic sites, 1984

|  | Average amount spent by visitors spending anything on: | | Proportion of visitors spending anything on: | |
|---|---|---|---|---|
|  | Refreshments | Brochures etc. | Refreshments | Brochures etc. |
|  | £ | £ | % | % |
| Stonehenge | 0.40 | 0.48 | 38 | 40 |
| Dover | 0.57 | 0.30 | 35 | 73 |
| Abbeys: |  |  |  |  |
| Whitby | 0.78 | 0.40 | 10 | 37 |
| Battle | N/A | 0.25 | N/A | 43 |
| Rievaulx | N/A | 0.29 | N/A | 43 |
| Roman sites: |  |  |  |  |
| Chester's | 0.39 | 0.41 | 52 | 50 |
| Wroxeter | N/A | 0.50 | N/A | 53 |
| Castles: |  |  |  |  |
| Kenilworth | N/A | 0.42 | N/A | 54 |
| Carlisle | N/A | 0.53 | N/A | 34 |
| Dartmouth | N/A | 0.24 | N/A | 56 |
| Tynemouth | N/A | 0.17 | N/A | 28 |
| Houses: |  |  |  |  |
| Audley End | 0.42 | 0.23 | 36 | 72 |
| Chiswick | 0.56 | 0.32 | 5 | 42 |
| Other: |  |  |  |  |
| Grimes Graves | N/A | 0.30 | N/A | 65 |
| All sites combined | 0.44 | 0.39 | 36 | 46 |

Source: Public Attitude Surveys, 1985.

expenditure by type of visitor (social class, day tripper/longer term), by type of accommodation (serviced/unserviced), and by category of activity. Most studies inter-relate these elements so that individual analyses may be impossible. This is one area where surveys have been undertaken of visitors to historic sites. In 1985, fourteen English Heritage sites (Public Attitude Surveys, 1985) were surveyed (Table 8.1). It was established that only just over one-third of visitors spent any monies on refreshments (range 10 to 52 per cent) but almost one-half purchased brochures (range 28 to 73 per cent). An average of 0.44p was spent by each visitor on the seven sites that had refreshment facilities (it ranged from 0.39p to 0.78p) and an average of 0.39p spent on brochures for the 14 sites (range 0.17p to 0.53p per head). A 1986 survey for Cadw (Seren, 1986) of eight Welsh castles concentrated on distinguishing between those with no intention to make a purchase and the rest. An average of 49 per cent of visitors had no intention of making a purchase or intended doing so by the end of their visit. Variations in levels of purchasing behaviour by sites was significant, ranging from a high of 64 per cent of purchases made or intended at Caernarfon Castle to a low of 36 per cent at Conwy Castle, although most sites recorded near to average figures. There was no obvious explanation for the variation. The shops and items available for purchase at Caernarfon Castle elicited particularly favourable visitor reactions which appeared to be reflected in a higher level of purchasing. However, the same effect was not noted at Harlech Castle which achieved only an average level of purchases (51.5 per cent) despite visitor attitudes equally favourable to those at Caernarfon Castle. Similarly, the lower level of purchase at Conwy Castle was not related to particularly unfavourable visitor attitudes to the shop and items available.

The Welsh survey established, not unexpectedly, that purchasing behaviour varied by the holiday status of the respondents. Those on holiday away from home were rather more likely to purchase items (54 per cent) then either home based holiday makers (45 per cent) or those not on holiday (43 per cent). Obviously this reflected the greater tendency of the staying holiday makers to purchase souvenirs/brochures of their visit than the home based visitors, although the differential was not substantial. The implication follows that sales potential and expectations should be a little higher in sites in the holiday areas relative to the remainder. It was found that the age of visitors was not consistently related to purchasing behaviour. Those aged 20 to 29 recorded lower purchasing levels than the average (44 per cent) while the 40 to 49 group recorded the opposite tendency (59 per cent), but most groups recorded near to average levels. Finally, variations by social class of visitors were even less well marked. All social groups recorded purchasing levels near to the average, a finding which suggested that the character of shops and array of items for sale had a wide appeal across the social spectrum, albeit at a moderate level.

These findings need to be placed within the context of much more detailed and extensive research into the more general field of tourism including those by category of activity, type of accommodation, duration of visit and social class of visitor. In the studies by category of activity, e.g. Skye (Brownrigg and Greig, 1974), Gwynedd (Archer, 1974), that for northern Scotland (Research Bureau, 1981) contains much useful information. It examined six areas, viz. Inverness, Oban, Skye, Speyside, North West Sutherland and Lewis/Harris and found that visitor expenditure originating by organised coach transport was far in excess of that by personal or other/public transport. For example, coach tour based tourists spent an average of £4.65p on gifts/souvenirs while car based tourists spent only £1.51p each and other/public transport £1.40p each. Seasonal surveys showed that mid-season tourists averaged £1.50p expenditure on gifts/souvenirs while late season tourists averaged £2.68p. It also established that average expenditure for all tourists (£17.47p) ranged between £21.19p in Inverness and £10.44p in North West Sutherland. The principal difference lay in non-accommodation spending especially gifts, souvenirs, clothing and entertainment. Spending patterns were closely related to spending opportunities and choices and, in this respect, Inverness was better provided for than the other areas. These and other studies (e.g. Tourism and Recreation Research Unit, 1981) have also provided information on type of accommodation. It is evident that very considerable differential expenditure patterns occur between occupants of serviced and unserviced accommodations. Generally speaking, the studies of the early 1980s showed that for every £1.00p spent by a visitor in an unserviced caravan/tent, the visitor staying in an unserviced flat would spend about £1.40p. In the serviced sector expenditures were higher, about £2.00p per visitor in bed and breakfast and £4.00p in a hotel. The amount of information on spending patterns is becoming better known. For example a 1977 survey (Overseas Visitor Survey) established that the average amount spent in total per day in London by overseas visitors was £18.00p - but of this only 5p was spent on historic buildings. A study of day trippers in Rhyl and Llandudno (Peat Marwick, 1984) calculated that an average of 100,000 visitors went to the area on a typical day during the peak season and each spent an average of about £5.80p.

Finally, it is worth mentioning a historic site study which sought to establish the relationship between expenditure and 'levels of enjoyment' (Public Attitude Surveys, 1985). Wroxeter Roman City emerged uniquely as having 'high enjoyment and high expenditure' while Stonehenge had 'low enjoyment but high expenditure'. Battle and Tynemouth were seen as having 'high enjoyment but low expenditure'. The study concludes, 'The inference which emerges is that increased visitor expenditure to a site may not stem from improved sales facilities alone but also from enhancement of total visitor experience. Since this is already 'high' at Battle, Tynemouth and Wroxeter these three locations possible offer quicker returns from any extensions to sales space or range of goods'.

The multiplier measures 'the relationship between an autonomous injection of expenditure into an economy and the resultant change in income which occurs' (Archer, 1977). This injection results in direct and secondary (indirect and induced) impacts which have been identified by Archer as: firstly, direct expenditure which refers to the monies brought in from outside the area by tourists to be spent locally on, for example, admission charges, purchases of goods/ souvenirs/ refreshments, hotel charges etc.; and secondly, the secondary effects which are composed of the indirect and induced expenditures: indirect expenditure, is where a proportion of monies brought in by tourists remains within the area to be spent, for example, on payments of wages/salaries to local employees, the replenishment of stocks for which extra local employment may be needed; induced expenditure, is where the above two expenditures result in increased local income and disposable income. This results in an increase in consumption which, in turn, leads to increased economic activity.

In a more specific context the tourist multiplier can be defined as 'the number by which the initial tourist expenditures must be multiplied in order to obtain the total cumulative income effect for a specified time period' (Mathieson and Wall, 1982). Archer (1977) has identified four types of tourism multiplier which are in common use. The first of these is the sales or transaction multiplier, which measures the effect of an extra unit of tourist spending upon economic activity levels in the economy, i.e. it relates tourists' expenditure to the increase in business turnover which is created by the tourists' expenditure. The second multiplier is the output multiplier, which relates a unit of tourism expenditure to the resultant increase in the level of output in the economy. The third is the Income multiplier, which shows the relationship between a unit of extra tourist spending and the changes which result in the level of income in the area. This income may include household and governmental incomes. The fourth is the employment multiplier. This describes the ratio of direct and secondary employment generated by additional tourism expenditure to direct employment alone. A second form of multiplier relates the amount of employment created by tourism to a given unit of tourism expenditure.

Multipliers are not a constant but vary depending upon variations in an area's economy and especially its dependence upon imported goods and services used by tourists. Archer (1977, Table 4.4) identifies values for 21 countries and regions. Using the 'unorthodox' method of calculation, the multipliers ranged from a high of 1.906 in Ireland to 0.250 in the Isle of Skye but most multipliers (and this is supported by Vaughan, 1979) range between 0.2 and 0.4. It is evident that there is a relationship between size of settlement and size of multiplier. The Tayside study (Henderson and Cousins, 1975) established that major nodal towns had the largest multiplier because of their range of services and the fact that a higher proportion of the subsequent chain of transactions could be conducted internally.

The three types of income generated by tourism are paralleled in employment (Goffe, 1975). Firstly, there is **direct employment** which results from direct visitor expenditures e.g. guides, keepers, hoteliers. Secondly, there is indirect employment which is employment in sectors which service tourist expenditures e.g. the manufacture of souvenirs, the supply of food to hotels. The third type of income generated is induced employment, which is the additional employment resulting from local residents re-spending the additional money earned from tourists. It does not appear that economic impact studies of historic sites have been undertaken within the United Kingdom.

Finally, while the majority of studies have concentrated upon the positive benefits of tourism, there is a growing awareness of the negative economic costs. Studies have been undertaken at various scales including the Westmorland Lake District (Capstick, 1972), the South West Economic Planning Council (1976), and Norfolk (Heeley, 1980). Such studies seek to identify and quantify extra public authority expenditures attributable to tourism. Refuse collection and disposal, public conveniences, parks and open spaces, highways, car parks, fire services and hospital coasts are examined. In the Norfolk study Heeley calculates that 'against every £1.00p of tourist expenditure is a public authority cost of £0.09p'. In commenting upon the Heeley work Murphy (1985) comments 'This favourable situation in Norfolk should be tempered by the fact that the analysis is incomplete... the indirect and induced costs still remain to be calculated ... (and) another point Heeley could have raised is that local people can and do use many of the tourist facilities provided by both the public and private sectors'.


Conclusion

The publication of registered visitor attendance figures at all tourist attractions in Britain in 1987 (B.T.A.,1988), excluding religious buildings, indicates that six of the top twenty were historic sites and monuments. These were The Tower of London (2,289,000), Edinburgh Castle (967,000), Bath Pump Room and Roman Baths (837,000), Windsor Castle (709,446), Warwick Castle (642,249) and Stonehenge (617,295). The importance of this component of tourism is undeniable, yet studies of environmental impact are largely conspicuous by their absence.

In the light of evidence presented in this chapter, it is suggested that the scope for impact studies is particularly great in the field of physical/ site management. It is here that the conflict between ever-increasing numbers, who generate essential income for preservation, conservation and enhancement, and actual damage is at its most acute. Impact studies are also urgently needed in socio-cultural contexts where evaluations of inter-group relations are necessary to preserve equanimity between local residents, cultures and values and visitors. There is also a need for in-depth studies of visitor satisfaction at 'contrived' historic attractions which are playing an increasingly important role in tourism. Finally, it would appear that methodological studies of economic impact analysis may be best integrated into the more general field of the economic impact of tourism, with derivative studies being undertaken for specific historic sites.

With the exception of great State occasions, historic sites and monuments rarely make headline news. Yet, at the time of writing this conclusion (June 21st, 1988) Stonehenge has been the focus of extensive media coverage. The pitched battles between the police and many thousand 'travelling people' over open access to the dawn summer solstice ceremony provided an extreme illustration of the problems facing the custodians of one of the world's great monuments. It should not obscure the fact that many sites and monuments are constantly under extensive environmental pressures and that much needs to be done in research, conservation and management to ensure the continuance of this very precious heritage.

## References

Alcock, S. (1986). Historic houses, castles and gardens open to the public. East Grinstead: British Leisure Publications.

Archer, B.H. (1974). The anatomy of a multiplier. Tourist research paper TUR 5. Bangor: University College, Bangor, North Wales, Tourist Research Division.

Archer, B.H. (1977). Tourism multipliers: the state of the art. Bangor Occasional Papers in Economics, number 11. Cardiff: University of Wales Press.

Bates, G. H. (1935). 'The vegetation of footpaths, sidewalks, carttracks, and gateways'. Journal of Ecology 23, pp. 470-87.

Bollom, C. (1978). Attitudes and second homes in rural Wales. Aberystwyth: University of Wales Board of Celtic Studies.

Brownrigg, M. and Greig, M. A. (1974). Differential multipliers for tourism. Discussion Paper number 28 in Economics, Finance and Investment. Sterling: University of Sterling.

Capstick, M. (1972). Some aspects of the economic effects of tourism in the Westmorland Lake District. (A report to Westmorland County Council). Lancaster: University of Lancaster, Department of Economics.

Clark, R. N. (1974). Social science, social scientists and wildlife management. Transactions of the Thirty-eighth Provincial Wildlife Conference. Victoria, British Columbia, Canada, pp. 103-112.

Cohen, E. (1972). Towards a sociology of international tourism. Social Research, 39, pp.164-82.

Cohen, E. (1978). The impact of tourism on the physical environment. Annals of Tourism Research, 5, pp.215-37.

Cohen, E. (1979). Rethinking the sociology of tourism. Annals of Tourism Research, 6, pp.18-35.

Coppock, J. T. (1980). Nature conservation and tourism in Great Britain. Paper to Nature and Tourism Conference, held in Perth, Australia, in April.

Cornwall Committee for Rescue Archaeology (1983). Archaeological survey and conservation in West Penwith, Cornwall, September.

Countryside Commission (1977). Tarn Hows: an approach to the management of a popular beauty spot. CCP Report 106. Cheltenham: Countryside Commission.

Doxey, G.V. (1975). A causation theory of visitor-resident irritants, methodology and research inferences, The impact of tourism. Sixth Annual Conference Proceedings of the Travel Research Association, San Diego, pp.195-8.

Doxey, G. V. (1976). 'When enough's enough: the natives are restless in Old Niagara'. Heritage Canada, 2 (2), pp.26-7.

Duffield, B. S. and Walker, S. E. (1984). The assessment of tourism impacts. In Clark, B. D. and Gilad, A., Perspectives on environmental impact assessment. pp.479-516. Dordrecht: Rerdal Pub. Co.

Economist Intelligence Unit Ltd (1974). Attitudes held by British people towards foreign tourists. (Prepared for the British Tourist Authority). London: The Economist Intelligence Unit Ltd.

English Heritage (1985). Stonehenge Study Group Report. London: English Heritage.

English Tourist Board (1978a). English Cathedrals and Tourism. London: English Tourist Board (E.T.B.).

English Tourist Board Market Research Department and N.O.P. Market Research Ltd. (1978b). Report on a survey of London residents' opinions of tourism. Report number TGM/pm6/3. London: English Tourist Board Market Research Department and NOP Market Research Ltd..

Getz, D. (1979). Effects of tourism on the host population. A case study of tourism and regional development in the Badenoch-Strathspey district of the Scottish Highlands. Summary report. Edinburgh: Department of Geography, University of Edinburgh.

Goffe, P. (1975). 'Development potential of international tourism, how developing nations view tourism'. Cornell Hotel and Restaurant Administration Quarterly, 16, pp.24-31.

Heeley, J. (1980). Tourism and local government with special reference to the County of Norfolk. (2 vols.). Unpublished PhD. dissertation, University of East Anglia, Norwich.

Henderson, D. M. and Cousins, R. L. (1975). The economic impact of tourism. A case study of Greater Tayside. TRRU research report No 13. Edinburgh: University of Edinburgh, Tourism and Recreational Research Unit.

Kasperson, R. E. (1969). 'Environmental stress and the municipal political systems'. In Kasperson, R. E. and Minghi, J. V., Editors, The structure of political geography. pp. 481-96. Chicago: Aldine.

Lerner, S. C. (1977). Social impact assessment: some hard questions and basic techniques. (unpublished workshop paper). University of Waterloo, Ontario, Canada.

Lime, D. W. and Stanley, G. H. (1971). Carrying capacity: maintaining outdoor recreation quality. In Forest Service, North-eastern Forest Experiment Station, Upper Danby. Recreation Symposium Proceedings. U. S. Department of Agriculture. pp.174-184.

Mathieson, A. and Wall, G. (1982). Tourism - economic, physical and social impacts. Essex: Longman.

McKaskey, T. G. (1975). Conservation of historic areas - management techniques for tourism in the USA. In Burkhart, A.J. and Medlick, S., The management of tourism. Chapter 15. pp. 151-159. London: Heinemann.

Market Opinion International Research (1978). Attitudes of the general public towards tourists. (Research prepared for the Evening Standard). London: MORI.

Mercer, D. (1979). Outdoor recreation: contemporary research and policy issues. In O'Riordan, T. and D'Arge, R. C., editors. Progress in resource management and environmental planning, Volume 1. pp.87-142. New York: Wiley.

Mitchell, B. (1980). 'Models of resource management'. In Progress in Human Geography, 4 (1), pp.32-55.

Murphy, P. (1985). Tourism - a community approach. London: Methuen.

National Museum of Wales (n.d. but ca. 1987). Amgueddfa Werin Cymru - Welsh Folk Museum. Cardiff.

National Trust (1979). Internal memorandum.

National Trust (1984). National Trust manual of housekeeping. London: Allen Lane.

Pearce, D. (1981). Tourist development. London: Longman.

Peat Marwick Mitchell and Co. (1984). Rhyl resort area tourism study. Revised July 1984. Cardiff: Wales Tourist Board.

Public Attitude Surveys (1985). Historic buildings survey 1984. 3 vols. Prepared for English Heritage, London.

Research Bureau Ltd. (1981). Visitor expenditure survey, summer 1980. (Prepared for the Highlands and Islands Development Board, job RBL 11827). London: Research Bureau Ltd..

Seren (1986). Herbert, D. T., Prentice, R. C., Thomas, C. J. and Prentice, M. M. Pricing policy and visitors' satisfaction at Cadw's sites. Swansea: Social Economic Research and Environment, Department of Geography, University College of Swansea.

South West Economic Planning Council (1976). Economic survey of the tourist industry in the South West. London: H.M.S.O..

Stankey, G. H. (1972). A strategy for the definition and management of wilderness quality. In Krutilla, J. V., editor, Natural environments: studies in theoretical and applied analysis. pp.88-114. Baltimore: John Hopkins University Press.

Tourism and Recreation Research Unit of Edinburgh University (1981). The economy of rural communities in the national parks of England and Wales. Edinburgh: T.R.R.U..

Vaughan, D. R. (1979).  What have we learnt from tourism multiplier studies? Some lessons from studies in Scotland. Working paper 4.  Edinburgh: Tourism and Recreational Research  Unit, University of Edinburgh.

Wales Tourist Board (1981).  Survey of community attitudes towards tourism in Wales.  Cardiff: Wales Tourist Board, Strategic Planning and Research Unit.

Wingperson, L. (1979).  'Heritage under siege'.  New Scientist, 27 September.  pp.962-5.

Zelinsky, W. (1973).  The cultural geography of the United States.  New Jersey: Prentice-Hall.

# 9 Research and the heritage operator

E A JOHN CARR

## Introduction

The author of this chapter, John Carr, is the Director of Cadw. Cadw, is a division of the Welsh Office. Its activities are guided by a Steering Committee whose membership is: the Secretary of State for Wales, the Minister of State for Wales, the chairmen of the Historic Buildings Council and Ancient Monuments Board, the Wales Tourist Board and the Principal Establishment Officer of the Welsh Office.

## Research and the heritage operator

When Cadw - Welsh Historic Monuments - was created by the then Secretary of State for Wales in October 1984, the estate in care was already a prime but under-exploited resource for tourism in Wales. Within its estate of 127 monuments were (and are) some 60 fine upstanding castles and abbeys and Roman sites, many of which enjoy world renown. At that time, some 31 sites charged admission; previously, however, and before a rationalisation of civil service staffing levels in the early 1980s, more than 40 monuments were manned and charged entry.

In the 1970s more than 2 million visitors were recorded. By the 1984-5 financial year that figure had fallen to 1.28 million (Figure 9.1). Despite the reduction in manned sites (those de-manned accounted for a very small proportion of visitors) it was evident that this potentially powerful

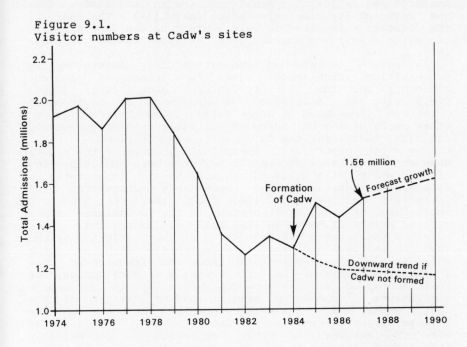

Figure 9.1.
Visitor numbers at Cadw's sites

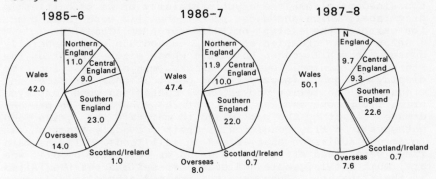

Figure 9.2.
Geographical origin of members of Heritage in Wales

**Geographical Origin of Members**

resource was suffering a steady decline in attendance. Even the Principality-wide celebration Cestyll'83 - The Year of the Castles - resulted in only a minor upturn in visits to the major sites; the smaller ones continued to fall in 1984-1985.

The estate in care had been meticulously maintained by conservation architects, the Inspectorate of Ancient Monuments and the Directly Employed Labour force (DEL). Every site had the benefit of a Department of Environment guidebook (the Blue or Green guides), which were (as in other parts of the UK) renowned for their scholarly accuracy but also, sadly, for the dullness in presentation.

Many of the major (and, inexplicably, some of the minor) monuments (in terms of visitor numbers) were beneficiaries of extremely high standard exhibitions and interpretative displays. Notable among these were Caernarfon and Caerphilly Castles and Castell Coch, the former not only reflecting international interest in the Investiture there of the Prince of Wales in 1969 but also containing, inter alia, a fascinating reconstruction of the Castle and walled town in the 14th century. The Caerphilly display, which still stands, is even more ambitious and effective in that it contains models of the various stages of development, of instruments of war and a comprehensive (within the space limitations imposed by panels) potted history of the Castle's past and of its conservation and restoration. The William Burges extravaganza at Castell Coch, reconstructed for the Marquess of Bute, contained an academically interesting display of Burges's preparatory drawings and a brief history of other buildings he had designed. Apart from the mini-museum operated by the National Museum for Wales at Segontium (the Roman camp near Caernarfon) and displays at Strata Florida Abbey near Pontrydfendigaid in Mid Wales and Criccieth Castle, no other sites in State care contained more than the cryptic Ministry of Works battleship grey labels which announced that the public were looking at, for example, the 'Solar' or 'Refectory' or 'Chapel'.

Before the creation of Cadw, custodians were generally housed in small wooden buildings whose size permitted the storage of minimal levels of stock, minimal areas for the display of goods (souvenirs and publications) for sale and frequently no toilet provision. Custodians were employed primarily to oversee the fabric of the monument, to prevent damage of it by the public and to maintain the grass and pathways in a tidy condition. Their secondary function was to accept admission charges and to sell goods. In the main they were (and still are) a group of dedicated people who are most knowledgeable and even possessive about the sites in their charge. They were not trained either in customer relations nor in sales techniques - not surprisingly because they were not originally employed for such purposes.

Although only one comparatively junior executive officer in the Welsh Office was engaged, part time, in identifying and purchasing souvenirs and publications, nearly 900 separate items were available for sale at sites. It is not in the least surprising that the range of items (and particularly the ordered quantities) were rather catholic.

Career civil servants in administrative grades are not usually born entrepreneurs or even small shopkeepers by nature!

Prior to the creation of Cadw, the people engaged on this specialist activity generally had career moves every 2-3 years. While they no doubt fulfilled their duties to the extent of their abilities, the fact that they had no training; that there was insufficient analysis of sales data due to other work pressures; and that there was no market research information available to them in assessing consumer preferences and market influences led to a less than precise commercial approach.

All these factors - the perceived potential of the monuments for increasing admissions and public enjoyment, for increasing sales, for enlivening presentation - led the Welsh Office to consider ways of improving matters. In 1983 John Brown Tourism Services was engaged to assess and report on the potential of each of the 127 monuments in care. The study was published in 1984 and it comprehensively examined every monument and proposed how each site (or, in the case of the field monuments of Anglesey, groups of sites) could be developed or enhanced to make it more attractive to the public. The report contained minimal assessment of market data and few concrete proposals or assessments of opportunities for commercial exploitation. It was nevertheless an invaluable document which reinforced the Welsh Office's decision to follow the lead given by the Department of the Environment in the formation of English Heritage (the Historic Buildings and Monuments Commission).

In Wales, however, it was decided to create not a 'quango' (an organisation outside the government) but to add a commercial arm of specialists (recruited via the Wales Tourist Board) to an existing division of the Welsh Office. Cadw is thus a sort of hybrid: it is responsible to the Secretary of State for all statutory matters in relation to historic buildings and ancient monuments in Wales; it is charged with conservation and preservation of the 127 sites in care; and now has the additional duty to him to excite the interest of the public and to maximise revenue - in other words, to be the operator of Wales' most widespread and popular group of tourist attractions.

At the time of writing (April 1988) of the total full-time staff complement of 223, 19 (or 8.5%) are engaged on 'commercial' activities. Their posts are permanently seconded via the Wales Tourist Board, and the specialisms include Marketing, Development (of site projects), Interpretation, Education, Publications, Sales and Information (i.e. Press and Public Relations) and Events. At Easter 1988 the Commercial Branch was restructured to reflect both the need for greater emphasis on manpower input into certain activities and reduction of activity in less productive or relevant areas of marketing.

The assessment of potential arising from the John Brown Report led to the identification of a Commercial Branch framework and the perceived need for a non-civil servant with commercial experience to be recruited from the private sector as Director of Cadw. During the recruitment process for that position other posts within the structure were filled progressively from August 1984 to February 1985. The Director assumed his responsibilities in January 1985 when the framework had already been established and the majority of staff with specialist skills had been recruited.

Expectations of performance, and morale, were high. Cadw had been launched in a flurry of public relations. Activity in marketing and development, sales and interpretation resulted in extensive programmes for new, colourful and informative guidebooks; installation of exhibitions in the, albeit limited, covered areas in monuments; installation of explanatory panels on sites in phases over 3-5 years; comprehensive, Wales-wide signposting to monuments; upgrading visitor reception and sales facilities; identification of a range of new souvenirs; production in English of seven colourful area marketing leaflets, show cards for display in hotels, tourist information centres, public places (leaflets since reduced to five but with addition of a leaflet entirely in Welsh); launch of an annual season ticket scheme - Heritage in Wales; joint marketing with consortia of tourism operators; reorganisation of custodians and changes in the emphasis of their duties; and, the launching of an aggressive campaign aimed at tour operators.

It is perhaps not surprising, therefore, that the downward trend in admissions was reversed in Cadw's first full year of operation (Figure 9.1). Admissions increased by 17.3% to 1.5 million and revenue by 25% to £1.3 million.

However, it was immediately apparent in early 1985 that all this activity was taking place on the basis of instinct and some experience rather than market analysis. While it was easy to guess that the socio-economic groupings A, B and C1 - being the more affluent and better educated market sector - made up the bulk of visitors, Cadw's executives had no firm data on such fundamentals as age, origin, resident or temporarily immigrant, nor of differences in, for example, visitor patterns or profiles as between monuments in North and South or West Wales etc.. Nor did they have information on visitor expectations, income levels, disposable income, preferences as between types of monument (i.e. castles versus abbeys), superficial or committed interest in contributing to the conservation ethic - and many, many other questions the answers to which would enable a more accurate targeting of markets and expenditure to be undertaken.

No research directly relevant to the historic estate in care had been carried out since the Wales Tourist Board surveys in the early 1970s. Much time had passed; visitor patterns to and within Wales had changed and were continuing to change; Cadw was expected not only to reverse the downward decline of 32.5% in visits to monuments between 1978 and 1981 (and continuing) but also to apply marketing and management techniques effectively in order to accrue greatly increased revenue with limited marketing expenditure.

From a management standpoint it was considered to be essential first and foremost to have an understanding and

knowledge of what data already existed. Of special
relevance would be the results of research applied to
similar collective bodies - such as English Heritage, the
National Trust and the Historic Houses Association. While
of some interest, research based on individual properties
would be unlikely to be usefully applicable to the heritage
estate in Wales, containing as it does such a variety of
sites with such a range of facilities spread over greatly
differing and distinctive geographical areas whose visitor
catchment zones could be assumed to be equally diffuse.

Of secondary, but nonetheless important, relevance would
be information gathered and collated by other bodies whose
attractions and philosophies might appeal to a similar
assumed socio-economic grouping but would otherwise be more
directly concerned with special interest aspects of
conservation and the environment - such as the Countryside
Commission, Nature Conservancy Council, Forestry Commission,
Royal Society for the Protection of Birds and so forth.

Accordingly, in April 1985 a research brief was prepared
for a Desk Study to evaluate existing data and facts.
Tenders were sought and the contract let to Seren
(Department of Geography, University College of Swansea) in
August of that year. During the pre-tender discussion
process it became more and more apparent that very little of
value or direct relevance existed. It was, therefore,
decided to extend the research beyond what might already
exist to original and up-to-date research into visitor
profiles (home and overseas), regions or places of origin
methods of transport, perceptions of (a) the heritage as a
concept, and (b) the estate in Cadw's care, target markets,
the leisure and educational role of the monuments, admission
price sensitivity, the impact of the monument or the estate
as a whole on environmental, cultural and economic aspects.
In addition, Cadw decided to carry out a survey of the
membership of Heritage in Wales as well as its own simple
review of visitors to unmanned sites in order to gauge their
popularity as leisure destinations.

The assumption was that Heritage in Wales members would
provide a more intimate and refined picture of the general
profile of visitors to monuments and the survey would,
therefore, provide valuable information on how better to
target the dominant socio-economic groupings. This analysis
was also undertaken by Seren. It was contemplated that an
increasing core of loyal Heritage in Wales members would
result in a readily reached audience for the sale of
souvenirs and publications by mail order.

It is of some interest to note the membership figures for
the three years since Cadw's formation and the areas of
origin (Table 9.1). The percentage rate of membership
renewal fluctuated between 50% and 58% respectively over the
past two years. This has led Cadw to consider whether
around 12,500 is the 'natural' level of membership and,
therefore, not to seek new members with any aggressive and
costly marketing which could have only short-term benefits
or whether the 'plateau' is higher (as some in Cadw suggest)
at a point between 18,000 and 25,000 members).

Table 9.1.
Membership figures for the three years since Cadw's
formation and the areas of origin: Heritage in Wales

| | 1985-6 | 1986-7 | 1987-8 |
|---|---|---|---|
| N (Total number of members) = | 9,457 | 12,308 | 12,806 |
| | N | N | N |

Total number of memberships
by category:

| | | | |
|---|---|---|---|
| Adult | 1,580 | 2,177 | 1,932 |
| Family | 1,843 | 2,354 | 2,761 |
| Senior Citizen | 527 | 707 | 837 |
| Child | 22 | 29 | 27 |
| Student | 395 | 530 | 448 |
| Life | 22 | 37 | 59 |
| Joint Life | - | - | 20 |
| Total number of memberships | 4,389 | 5,834 | 6,084 |

| | % | % | % |
|---|---|---|---|
| Renewal Rate | - | 50 | 58 |

Geographical origin of members:

| | % | % | % |
|---|---|---|---|
| Wales | 42 | 47 | 50 |
| Northern England | 11 | 12 | 10 |
| Central England | 9 | 10 | 9 |
| Southern England | 23 | 22 | 23 |
| Scotland/Ireland | 1 | 1 | 1 |
| Overseas | 14 | 8 | 8 |

Source: Cadw.


The value of the findings

Market research was undertaken because of its value in
assisting in management's decision-making. It is, of
course, a truism that there is no point in having the
information unless use is made of it. It is equally true
that however thorough the research and however expert the
coding and collation the application of the findings of
research rests with the organisation for which it was
discovered; and it is the quality of that organisation's
management thinking and determination which first identifies
the most beneficial markets and then pursues them with
imagination and vigour. It should also be recognised that
what was identified as the 'picture' in 1985 or 1988 may,
and probably will, change by 1988 or 1992. Management must,
therefore, be alive to the need to continue to obtain

information about its existing public and the greater majority of visitors to Wales who do not visit monuments. Expenditure on research is a prerequisite for aiming the rifle; the scattergun approach will consume more funds less efficiently and less effectively and produce poor results from a static level of money available for marketing. (It is Cadw's policy that marketing cash allocations will not advance at the same rate of inflation as other heads of expenditure unless it is clear beyond reasonable doubt that a new market is available through the judicious application of funds. Marketing allocations should be reduced to approximately 10-12.5% of revenue rather than the 18-20% allocation between 1985-87).

The research by Seren clearly identified that there are two distinct customer bases for monuments: one for the North Wales sites and another for those in the South. It is conceivable, though not yet substantiated, that there is a sub-section of the South Wales product and market in the West.

The first findings showed that the majority of visitors travelled less than 30 miles one way to visit a monument (75%) and that of all visitors, 88% had travelled no more than 50 miles. These facts applied equally to residents of Wales and to visitors. It was also revealing to learn that 91% travelled by car. As 1.8 million of the 2.8 million population live in the South in a band from Llanelli to Chepstow and bounded by the Heads of the Valleys road, it was plain that here lay a strong potential marketplace. The economic mix in this area suggested also that this population was better off and better educated - the match for the ABC1 image of the heritage estate. And so it has proven. In fiscal year 1986-87 admissions to all Cadw sites declined by 7% following the 17% rise the year before. But admissions in South and West Wales advanced by 5% in that bad year, though subsequently increased by a lower percentage level in the South in the 1987-88 year just finished (7%) than they did in the North (12%). In 1986-87 the North fell away badly, dropping 15%.

Management was, therefore, on the one hand able to capitalise on a resident market but on the other was faced with the problem of attempting to recapture the North Wales visitors. Different techniques are needed and needed urgently. The dominance of the North Wales sites - which captured more than 62% of all visits in 1985-86 - is unlikely to alter substantially (though in 1987-88 their performance dropped to 59% of an improved market overall). The North is home to the 'Big Four' World Heritage Castles of Edward 1 - Caernarfon, Conwy, Harlech and Beaumaris. Collectively they attract some 700,000 visitors or 80% of all visits in the North. When they sneeze Cadw gets the shivers!

Paradoxically, the North is the less controllable market. Its traditional catchment area is outside Wales (whether day trip, short or long stay) in the Wirral, Cheshire, West Midlands and south-east of England. The Seren research confirmed that. Whereas Cadw's marketing remit extends beyond Wales, the funds required to market effectively in the Central TV conurbations of Birmingham and Wolverhampton and in the Granada TV areas of Manchester and Liverpool (whether on TV or though printed media) are so great as to be beyond Cadw's resources. Cadw is, therefore, reliant upon others who have the remit to market Wales to draw the public into the North. Once visitors have arrived, locally targeted promotion (i.e. the 30 mile radius phenomenon) begins to bite.

Another factor which militates against Cadw making substantial progress in the North is the profile of the traditional holidaymakers and their accommodation. The majority of bed spaces in Wales are in the North. (Llandudno alone has 70% of all the serviced accommodation throughout Wales.) A very high proportion of accommodation is in self-catering caravans and chalets. Typically these are taken by the C2, D and E socio-economic sectors - precisely the opposite end of that market spectrum which forms Cadw's typical visitor profile.

Of considerable significance over the past three seasons has been the decline of visitors into Wales - from 12 million to just short of 10 million (or 17%). The fact that the largest decline has been in the North has to a degree been softened by growth in the South but the milch cow of Caernarfon fell from its new level of 320,000 in 1985-86 to 270,000 the following year - in percentage fall terms almost exactly matching the overall decline of Wales as a whole. Other sites such as Conwy, Beaumaris and Harlech fell less dramatically.

Again of significance is the evidence from research, in both 1985 and 1987, that of the visitors to Caernarfon in the peak season 27% were from overseas. The conclusion that the fear of both Chernobyl fall-out and of the Libyan crisis in 1986 had a marked effect on overseas visitors' journeys to north-west Wales is easily arrived at. But it does not even hint at a possible solution other than that Cadw should try to take a larger slice of the lower socio-economic cake in order to try to maintain a more constant level of visits. The overseas market is demonstrably very important, but is also more prone to influences beyond Cadw's control.

More directly accessible is the Education market - an area not formally researched but known to have potential. For example in 1985-86 some 108,000 individuals in school parties or 7% of total visits went to Cadw sites by prior arrangement. In the poor year of 1986-87 the percentage dropped to below 7%. In the year 1987-88 just concluded, that percentage has grown to 8% and amounts to some 125,000 attendances. It is a surprising fact that in Cadw's first two years of operation 75% of schools visitors originated from outside Wales. In 1987-88 more schools in Wales took advantage of the educational assets which often are within walking distance of the school gates.

Cadw believes that this market of more than 2,067 schools in Wales is not only valuable in terms of revenue (from sales only, as educational visits are free) but, more importantly, in terms of capturing the interest of young people who, when they emerge as adults with families, may be more inclined to visit the rich heritage of Wales. As schools span all socio-economic levels it is conceivable that a well planned and interesting programme for school children will result in growth in the C2, D and E sectors. It is a notion worth investigating further: comparatively non-productive investment of resources today may well repay dividends in the future.

Despite the absence of formal research results, it is evident from responses by schools to specially themed events at sites - such as the traditional Welsh Christmas celebrations held at Caernarfon and Caerphilly, and the Monastic Days at Neath Abbey and Valle Crucis- that both teachers and children find them enjoyable and rewarding. To capture this virtually permanently rolling audience will require skill and a clearly defined programme of activity which fits into the educational curriculum.

Such programmes are key to the 'living interpretation' of a site. It was interesting to note from research in 1986 that the more traditional approach to explanation - e.g. two-dimensional exhibitions and site explanatory panels ('books on walls') found less favour among the lower socio-economic groupings but were relatively well appreciated by the higher income groups. Similarly, special events - such as re-enactments of battles at Raglan Castle - where the 'blood and guts' of warfare can be more readily imagined - were seen as adding greater enjoyment even though the directly educational and lasting benefits are minimal. Cadw has refined its events policy and programme by (a) fixing certain large-scale events at specific weekends of the year, and (b) reducing the numbers and range of events. Manpower resource is not the only reason - though a programme of 600 events each year is plainly a daunting task; the most obvious influence on policy must be cost-effectiveness (i.e. return on cash invested).

It will be interesting to discover if Cadw's perception of the value and focussing of events over the next few years is substantiated. In the first flurry of enthusiasm, each of the three UK heritage bodies has been responsible for encouraging the growth - and earnings - of re-enactment organisations like The Sealed Knot, Ermine Street Guard etc. They are decidedly the flavour at least of the half decade. But the public is both fickle and hungry for new experience. It is also becoming more and more sophisticated in terms of what is required to produce a satisfying experience. By the early 1990s it will demand a freshness of approach and Cadw along with its sister organisations - and the re-enactment companies - must urgently review current policy. That will require further and very detailed research if events are to give the sort of return the investment demands.

Like any multi-branch business venture, Cadw has to recognize that its outlets - or sites - should perform sufficiently well commercially, to cover operating costs and to produce a surplus. Unlike a chain of supermarkets, however, Cadw's sites are not in prime High Street locations, nor can the sophisticated arts of packaging and frequent image changes be employed. These ancient sites were built for reasons which are not part of today's marketing philosophies. They are frequently ruinous, largely without modern facilities and often a long way off the beaten track. The consumer must be wooed in a way totally different to the hype of TV commercials pushing soap powder or coffee. But if the heritage is seen to be a product or commodity then, just as the marketeers of the soap companies do, Cadw must be aware of the fads and inclinations of its potential audience.

If the heritage product is to run and run - as certainly seems likely in this age of greatly enhanced awareness of the need for conservation - then its capacity to support its own costs (at least partly) must be exploited to the full. That suggests that the future for market researchers in the field of heritage presentation is indeed secure.

# Index

306